THIRD EDITION

Speaking Clearly

THIRD EDITION

Speaking Clearly
THE BASICS OF VOICE AND ARTICULATION

Noah F. Modisett
James G. Luter, Jr.

LOS ANGELES CITY COLLEGE

Burgess Publishing **bp**

A Division of Burgess International Group, Inc.

Publisher: Brete C. Harrison
Editor: Barbara Pickard
Production Manager: Larry Lazopoulos
Production Assistant: Carolyn Chandler
Cover and Interior Design: Rick Chafian
Art Illustrations: Tim Blakey
Proofreaders: Betty Alexander and Merry Bilgere
Composition: Jonathan Peck Typographers
Printing/Binding: Burgess Printing

Library of Congress Cataloging-in-Publication Data
Modisett, Noah F.
  Speaking clearly.
  Bibliography: p.
  Includes index.
  1. Voice culture.   2. Elocution.   3. Speech—
Physiological aspects. I. Luter, James Gray,
1932- . II. Title.
PN4162.M52 1988 808.5 87-38228
ISBN 0-8087-3295-1

Address editorial questions to:
Burgess Publishing
4415 Sonoma Highway
P.O. Box 4089
Santa Rosa, California 95402-4089

Address book orders to:
Burgess Publishing
7110 Ohms Lane
Edina, Minnesota 55435
(612) 831-1344

Burgess Publishing
A Division of The Burgess International Group, Inc.
7110 Ohms Lane
Edina, Minnesota 55435

CREDITS: *Figure 3.2, 3.3* from *The Speech Chain* by Peter B. Denes and Elliot N. Pinson. Copyright © 1963 by Bell Telephone Laboratories, Inc. Reprinted by permission of Doubleday & Company, Inc. *Figure 3.4* from *Basic Voice Training for Speech, 2nd Edition,* by Elise Hahn et al. Copyright © 1957 by McGraw-Hill Book Company, Inc. Reprinted by permission. Additional permissions are listed on page 234.

Contents

9 Pronunciation   173

Types of Mispronunciation   174
   Omission of Sounds   174
   Addition of Sounds   175
   Substitution of Sounds   176
   Reversal of Sounds   176
   Misplacement of Stress   177
Summary   178

10 Vocal Variety and Expression   179

Pitch Variety   179
   Inflection   179
   Step Shifts   181
Time Variety   185
   Rate Variety   185
   Duration Variety   187
   Pause Variety   188
Loudness Variety   190
Word Emphasis   190
   Materials for Practicing Unstressed Words   191
Vocal Integration   193
Summary   193

11 Reading Selections   194

Preface

*Speak the speech . . . as I pronounced
it to you, trippingly on the tongue.*

Shakespeare, *Hamlet*

How fortunate it would be if we were all able to follow easily Hamlet's advice to
the players. Unfortunately, instead of speaking "trippingly," we sometimes trip or
stumble and fall over our words. Listeners may say, "Speak up," "Repeat that,
please," or maybe even, "Huh?" Some of our voices are too soft, too loud, too
rough, or too breathy; articulation may be incomplete or indistinct. For many
reasons, some of us may need help to improve our speaking ability.

This text is designed for just that purpose: to help you to understand how
speech is produced and to guide you in the improvement of your speech production.
Specifically, it provides instruction in the processes of respiration, phonation, resonation, and articulation and their coordination in pronunciation and effective vocal
expression.

Based on professional users' reviews, the organization of this third edition
remains the same as the previous ones. The artwork and charts have been completely
redone and two new appendices have been added.

In the first chapter, the dialects of American speech are presented. This discussion is followed by basic information about speech production.

In Chapter 2, the process of respiration is described, with emphasis on breathing
for speech. Updated terminology is introduced in our discussions of phonation and
resonation in Chapters 3 and 4. Vocal production is explained behaviorally.

Chapters 5 through 8, on articulation, present both diacritic and phonetic
symbols for each of the sounds of Standard American English. The diacritic system
used is from the *American Heritage Dictionary*. In the articulation chapters, each
sound is defined and described on a single page. Its facing page contains practice
material (single words, contrasting word pairs, sentences, and a tongue twister).

New word pairs and word lists are introduced and arranged in consistent order. Word pairs for consonants emphasize the more troublesome contrasts and likely substitutions.

Chapter 9, on pronunciation, demonstrates common pronunciation faults and gives exercises to correct them. Chapter 10, on vocal variety and expression, illustrates different pitch, time, and loudness patterns. The use of "stair step" sentences is particularly effective for the visualization of pitch changes. Chapter 11, as before, contains a wide selection of readings.

Appendix A provides worksheets for voice and articulation analysis. Frequently mispronounced words are listed in Appendix B to provide pronunciation practice and vocabulary development in conjunction with Chapter 9. The new Appendix C provides instruction and practice for students wishing to learn different dialects and accents for acting. Appendix D, also new in this edition, is written for students coming to English from other languages, particularly Spanish, Korean, Chinese, Japanese, Tagalog, and Vietnamese. Appendix E describes consonant blends, and Appendix F presents the relationships between spelling and pronunciation.

The exercises throughout this text have been selected from those used successfully in a large college voice and articulation program (900 students per year). An Instructor's Manual is available with this edition. It contains diagnostic tests for vowels and selected consonants and sample test questions. Especially useful is the transparency master section which contains eighteen anatomical line drawings, as well as the complete pronunciation lists from Appendix B, prepared for easy duplication.

We are indebted to James E. Hansen, M.D. for his review of the respiration chapter and to our students and colleagues at LACC for their insightful suggestions. We would also like to give special thanks to the following reviewers: Dwight Freshly, University of Georgia; Douglas Harris, Illinois State University; and Elaine Klein, Westchester Community College.

Noah F. Modisett
James G. Luter, Jr.

February 1988

To the Student

You are unique.

Unlike the nonhuman inhabitants of our planet, you can speak. Like other humans, you do so in your own personal way. Your speech has been influenced by those around you—your family, friends, and teachers. Nevertheless, your voice, pronunciation, vocabulary, and manner of speaking are, like your fingerprints, original. This uniqueness makes you special.

At some point you have probably heard yourself talk on an audio recording or videotape. More than likely, you heard some characteristics in your speech that you did not like. Perhaps you mumbled or ran words together. You may have found that you kept your mouth nearly closed while speaking, hardly moving your lips. Or, you spoke in a controlled manner, allowing only short bursts of words to come to the surface. Perhaps your speech came out in a rush. Your thoughts may have come so fast that you interrupted yourself in the middle of one thought and jumped to another. Maybe your voice sounded too high, too low, too loud or too soft. You may have noticed errors in pronunciation and word choice. Of course, you also may have heard no problems in your speech.

In any case your speech now reveals you as you are at this moment. It is the product of your inheritance, environment, and learning experiences. Your speech abilities are closely related to your personality. If you have a good self-image and are generally an outgoing person, your speech will reflect these characteristics. If your self-image is poor and you tend to be fearful in speaking situations, this too will be expressed.

The close relationship between speech and personality provides an effective self-teaching tool. As you learn and practice ways of improving your manner of speaking, you will find your self-confidence has improved and your self-image has strengthened. Conversely, as you improve your self-image, your speech will show gains. These two human attributes are so interrelated that they mutually assist each other in the speech improvement process.

As a college student, you may be planning a career that will involve social and professional contact with others. Your speech therefore, should be as clear as possible. The better you can be understood, the more effective you will be in meeting and influencing others.

What Will a Course Like This One Do for You?

You are probably enrolled in this course because it is required, but we believe there are excellent reasons for you to be here, anyway. Taking this course will improve your chances of reaching your personal, social, and professional goals.

Your current friends probably speak the same way you do. Your future friends likely will, too. One way a person becomes accepted by a particular group of people is by possessing and using the speech of that group.

Your professional success and advancement may depend on your speaking skills. Many jobs require clear, understandable speech. You have probably seen help-wanted ads that say, "good communication skills required." This phrase can be translated as: "applicant must speak clearly and accurately and have an appropriate vocabulary." In fact, studies indicate a direct relationship between the size of an individual's vocabulary and probable lifetime earnings.

For these reasons you are smart to be enrolled in this course—even if it *may be* required.

What Will Happen in This Course?

First you will need to learn how speech is produced. You will analyze your own speaking habits and, more than likely, discover one or more that need improvement. When you have devoted enough time and effort to study and practice, you will accomplish the following:

1. Acquire the sounds and stress patterns of the Standard American English dialect, the most easily understood dialect in the United States. This does not necessarily mean that you must give up your present dialect; you can have both, if you wish.
2. Increase the strength of your voice; that is, you will be able to control its volume to suit any speaking situation. You will master breathing skills to reduce fatigue when talking for long periods.
3. Improve the resonance of your voice; that is, you will develop a richer, fuller tone quality.
4. Develop clear, articulate speech. As you learn to articulate each sound accurately and completely, you will develop the skill of pronouncing each word exactly. No more mumbling or garbling for you.

As you integrate these talents with vocal expression based on your thoughts and inner feelings, you will accomplish the purpose of this course. You will be *speaking clearly.*

What Will You Need to Do to
Make All These Changes?

A puzzled tourist standing on a street corner in Manhattan stopped a New York
pedestrian carrying a violin case and asked, "How do I get to Carnegie Hall?" The
musician replied, "Practice, man, practice!" A similar answer might be given to
the question, How do I improve my speaking skills? Practice, practice, and more
practice.

   This book and your professor will show you what you need to do, but you
are the one who needs to do it. To succeed, you should try to practice aloud each
day at least a page of exercises of sounds, words, and sentences. Practice in front
of a mirror and observe your movements. Tape record a minute of each practice
period. Listen to your recording, re-record and listen again. Learn to recognize
your errors and your correct production. Ask your professor for advice and instruction on any exercise you do not understand, but do not expect lectures and books
to improve your speech skills. Practice, they say, is what makes perfect.

1

Basics for
Speaking Clearly

The ability to speak distinguishes humans from all other inhabitants of this planet. Other creatures communicate with barks, whistles, movements, and howls, but only humans use the spoken word.

Imagine this scene: The telephone rings. You pick up the receiver and say, "Hello." Instantly the party on the other end recognizes your voice, and when you hear the response, you recognize the caller. This scene is reenacted thousands of times daily throughout the world: a person says one word and is immediately recognized by another. How is this possible? You might respond, "Because of the way we speak," but what is it that makes a person's speech unique and easily identifiable? Your unique speech behavior is, in part, the result of your experience with *language, accent,* and *dialect.*

LANGUAGE, ACCENT, AND DIALECT

We can easily understand our family and friends, and the people in our cultural group, our neighborhood, but we often have difficulty with the speech of people of other nationalities or from other cultures or regions. Such misunderstanding is often the result of differences in language, accent, and dialect. To help you understand and use these terms in this course, we offer the following definitions.

A *language* is the body of words and the methods of combining these words into meaningful patterns that is peculiar to a nation, people, or race or that is limited to a specific geographic area. Two main principles apply to the concept of language: all societies have a language, the rules of which are determined by the people who speak it; and all languages are constantly changing. A changing, spoken language is the primary tool with which we communicate.

An *accent* is the sound and sound structure of a speaker's first language carried over into a second language. It is the effect of the phonetic habits and the mode of utterance of a particular language on the speaker's new language. For example, if your first language were Japanese, since it contains no *l* sound, you would probably say *rate* for *late*. Likewise, if you originally spoke German, which has no *th* sound, you would probably say *dem* for *them*. For the past 400 years in what is now the United States, the accents of immigrants from various language areas have contributed to the formation of the numerous dialects of American English.

A *dialect* is a variation of a spoken language. Dialects may differ in articulation, pronunciation, stress, intonation, meaning, and structure. Simply, a dialect is a variation of the language of a particular speech community. Dialects can be classified into geographic, socioeconomic, and ethnocultural categories.

These can be further divided into many subcategories. The number of dialects of some languages is in the hundreds. In some countries dialects are so different that they seem to be different languages. In the United States, however, almost all dialects are understood by other speakers of English.

Dialects are similar to languages in many ways: they are structured, they are determined by the people who speak them, and they are constantly changing. One significant characteristic of both is that they differ in their *vocal expression*. *Pitch* (highness and lowness) and *stress* (loudness and softness) patterns differ considerably from language to language and dialect to dialect. Each is unique. As a result, these pitch and stress patterns are carried over to newly learned languages and dialects, just as articulation, pronunciation, and grammar patterns blend with the new speech.

In the following discussion we will be concerned with only the articulation and pronunciation differences among the various dialects of American English.

DIALECTS IN THE UNITED STATES

In the United States, the largest country in the world to have a single predominant language, numerous dialects are spoken. All speakers of American English use one dialect or another. We can categorize the dialects of American English in the following manner.

1. Geographic categories
   a. Standard American
   b. Eastern American
   c. Southern American
   d. Special American

2. Socioeconomic categories
   a. Formal educated
   b. Informal educated
   c. Formal uneducated
   d. Informal uneducated

3. Ethnocultural categories
   a. Black American
   b. Spanish American

    c. Asian American
    d. Euro-American
    e. Yiddish American

Most of the variations in sound and form of American English are intelligible to all of its speakers, but a few are so different, because of their isolation from the mainstream, that they are almost separate languages. We use an informal spelling system to represent pronunciations in the various dialects in this chapter.

Geographic Dialects

Several major dialects can be delineated along geographic boundaries.

Standard American (also called General American).   Unlike dialect regions in England, which have remained almost constant for centuries, dialect regions in the United States have shifted their boundaries as a result of people's mobility. The westward movement, the spread of education, and the influence of radio and television have combined to produce a Standard American dialect. It is heard most in the North Central, Plains, Northwest, Pacific, and Southwest regions of the country. Approximately half the population of the United States makes up this dialect region. The Standard American dialect is closest to the network standard speech of radio and television. It is a relatively homogeneous dialect, with a few interregional differences, and is easily understood throughout the country.

Eastern American.   The Eastern American dialect is heard in the New England states of Maine, Vermont, New Hampshire, Massachusetts, Rhode Island, and Connecticut and in some parts of upstate New York. The articulation of the *r* sound is one feature distinguishing this dialect from Standard American English. It is sometimes dropped at the end of a phrase or sentence, so that:

> *father* sounds like *fatha*
> *later* sounds like *lata*
> *teacher* sounds like *teacha*
> *water* sounds like *wata*

Also, the *r* sound is added to certain words within a phrase or sentence, so that:

> *the idea of it* sounds like *the idear of it*
> *sawing a board* sounds like *sawring a boad*
> *papa and mama* sounds like *paper and mamar*
> *America, the beautiful* sounds like *Americur, the beautiful*

Southern American.   The Southern American dialect is probably the easiest to identify and, until recently, is the most stable geographically. It is used in the region south of the Ohio River from the Atlantic to eastern Texas, with influences in portions of neighboring states. In part it is characterized by the lengthening of a single vowel sound into two or three sounds, so that:

big sounds like *bi-ug*
dog sounds like *daw-ug*
love sounds like *lu-uv*
can't sounds like *cay-unt*

Some diphthongs become single vowels, so that:

time sounds like *tom*
right sounds like *rat*
oil sounds like *all*
coal sounds like *call*

The vowel sounds in words like *ten* and *pen* are made to sound like those in *tin* and *pin*:

send sounds like *sinned*
lends sounds like *Lynd's*
Ben sounds like *bin*
get sounds like *git*

In some words the *r* sound is added, as in Eastern speech:

wash sounds like *warsh*
Cuba sounds like *cuber*
Martha sounds like *marther*
soda sounds like *soder*

However, the *r* is omitted from some words, especially when unstressed:

car sounds like *cah*
father sounds like *fathah*
door sounds like *doah*
sure sounds like *shuah*

Special American. Special American dialects are the speech patterns found in areas between the major dialect regions. These varieties are influenced by speakers in surrounding areas and are more individual and inconsistent than the dialect in the center of a region.

Appalachian. One of the largest special American dialects is Appalachian, which is spoken in the mountain sections of West Virginia, Virginia, Kentucky, Tennessee, and North Carolina, an area bordered by the Eastern, Southern, and Standard American regions. Its uniqueness is a result of the relative isolation of the area. In this dialect some vowel sounds are substituted for others:

pinch sounds like *peench*
ten sounds like *tin*
again sounds like *agin*
deaf sounds like *deef*
drink sounds like *drank*
judge sounds like *jedge*
such sounds like *sich*

rear sounds like *rare*
there sounds like *thar*
spill sounds like *spell*

Sounds are added, which produces *afishin, aknowed, abeen,* and *afixn.* Also,

it sounds like *hit*
bought sounds like *boughten*
across sounds like *accrost*
year sounds like *yaar*
scared sounds like *askart*

Sounds are omitted:

that sounds like *at*
about sounds like *bout*
afraid sounds like *fraid*
expect sounds like *spec*

Sounds are reversed:

apron sounds like *apern*
modern sounds like *modren*
children sounds like *childern*
introduce sounds like *interduce*

Syllable stress is different:

cigar sounds like *SEEgar*
directly sounds like *DIrectly*
Detroit sounds like *DEEtroit*
hotel sounds like *HOtel*

Big City. An evolving special American dialect is Big City, which is heard in parts of some metropolitan areas such as New York City, St. Louis, Chicago, Detroit, and Baltimore. The great melting pots and pressure cookers of middle- and lower-class metropolitan areas have merged foreign languages, local terms, and the surrounding dialects into a special variety of speech. Big City dialects are not consistent, but they are emerging as a special group of American dialects. In this group, generally, the *th* sound is replaced by *d* or *t*:

these sounds like *deze*
other sounds like *udder*
thanks sounds like *tanks*
bath sounds like *bat*

In some areas, the *er* sound is replaced by *oi:*

bird sounds like *boid*
thirsty sounds like *toisty*
New Jersey sounds like *New Joisey*
word sounds like *woid*

The *r* sound is omitted:

> *alarm* sounds like *alahm*
> *mustard* sounds like *mustad*
> *harp* sounds like *hahp*
> *air* sounds like *eh-uh*

As in Eastern American, the *r* is sometimes added:

> *drawing* sounds like *drawring*
> *Asia* sounds like *asiar*
> *Jamaica* sounds like *jamaicar*
> *saw* sounds like *soar*

Other special American dialects include *Mid-Atlantic* (including New Jersey, Delaware, and some parts of Maryland) and *Western Pennsylvanian*.

Socioeconomic Dialects

People speak variations of their regional dialect in accordance with their level of education, family economics, and social context. Although any classification scheme is highly arbitrary, four subcategories can be used for discussion purposes.

Formal Educated.   This dialect variety is used by college-trained speakers in formal settings. It is the dialect you expect to hear in the halls of Congress, at debate tournaments, and from the pulpit. Words are carefully chosen and pronounced; slang and colloquialisms are avoided. Contractions, such as *aren't* and *doesn't* are used infrequently, and reduced forms such as *gonna* and *meetcha* do not occur at all.

Informal Educated.   Educated people use this subcategory in conversation. Some words are contracted and some word endings are omitted, but the relaxation of articulation does not affect understanding, nor are radically different words and phrases used. *Going to* becomes *gonna, don't you* becomes *doncha, I'll be seeing you* becomes *be seein ya*. However, the main words are selected and articulated as in the formal educated variety.

Formal Uneducated.   This variety is used by people who are attempting to sound more knowledgeable than they are. Some words are overpronounced: *rigor* sounds like *rig-or, articulation* sounds like *artik-you-lation, pronunciation* sounds like *pronounce-ee-ation*. Long words are sometimes selected where short words are more appropriate. These may be interspersed with colloquial language, with which they sound incongruous.

Informal Educated.   This subcategory is "street talk" or, in the country, "down home." It is generally localized and difficult to understand outside its own speech community. Although all dialects can be understood outside of their regions by at least some people, this variety has the least general acceptance.

Ethnocultural Dialects

The United States is a nation of immigrants. Except for a small percentage of us who are descended from American Indians, we are all products of foreign cultures. Often English was not the first language of our ancestors. When their first language mixed with English in America, new dialects of English evolved.

Black American.   The Black American dialect is widely used, but it is not the dialect of all black Americans. As a result of its distinctive sound and its extensive use, it has been well studied.

The differences between Black American and Standard American are partly in structure and partly in sound. Structurally, for example,

> *He is going* becomes *He goin*
> *He is working* becomes *He be workin*
> *I am talking* becomes *I talkin*
> *What are you doing?* becomes *What you doin?*

Verb form is sometimes changed, resulting in:

> *He does it* becomes *He do it*
> *She has a bike* becomes *She have a bike*
> *They were going* becomes *They was goin*
> *I have one* becomes *I has one*

Double and triple negatives are used:

> He don't know nothin, no how
> Didn't nobody see it?
> He ain't here, is he?
> I ain't never had nothin!

Structural differences are significant, but sound differences are also obvious. By the omission of final consonants,

> *Laughs* sounds like *laugh*
> *gold* sounds like *goal*
> *left* sounds like *lef*
> *west* sounds like *wes*

By the conversion of *th* to *t* or *f,*

> *thanks* sounds like *tanks*
> *with* sounds like *wif*
> *bath* sounds like *bat*
> *birthday* sounds like *birfday*

By the omission of *r,*

> *smart* sounds like *smaht*
> *sister* sounds like *sistah*
> *bear* sounds like *beh*
> *car* sounds like *cah*

By the omission of *l,*

> *help* sounds like *hep*
> *toll* sounds like *toe*
> *feel* sounds like *fee*
> *children* sounds like *chidren*

Despite these differences, Black American English and Standard American English are substantially similar. Children reared with either dialect have a rich verbal heritage. Generally, Black American English has given new, vivid, functional words to Standard American English and has received more widely comprehended articulation from it.

Spanish American.   This category describes a number of dialects that are based on the Spanish language, such as Mexican American, Cuban American, and Puerto Rican American. These dialects are spoken by at least half a million people in California, Arizona, New Mexico, Texas, Colorado, Florida, and New York. Most of the differences between Spanish American dialects and Standard American result from the fact that the Spanish spelling system, unlike that of English, is basically *phonetic*: each letter usually represents a single sound. In addition, Spanish has five vowels and three diphthongs, whereas English has twelve vowels and five diphthongs. Thus, when Spanish-speaking people acquire English as a second language, they must learn additional sounds. In Spanish American, the letter *i* is often pronounced *ee*:

> *it* sounds like *eeat*
> *bit* sounds like *beat*
> *sit* sounds like *seat*
> *did* sounds like *deed*

Since the *th* is rare in Spanish, *t* or *d* is often substituted for it:

> *bath* sounds like *bat*
> *Thursday* sounds like *tursday*
> *cloth* sounds like *clot*
> *that* sounds like *dat*

Sometimes *sh* is pronounced like *ch*:

> *she* sounds like *chee*
> *shave* sounds like *chave*
> *washing* sounds like *watching*
> *cash* sounds like *catch*

Frequently, *z* is replaced by *s*:

> *his* sounds like *hees*
> *was* sounds like *wass*
> *is* sounds like *ees*
> *music* sounds like *mu-sick*

Spanish American dialects have enriched Standard American English with many words from Hispanic culture.

Asian American.   The Asian American category encompasses a number of dialects of English that are the result of immigration from the Orient. The Chinese, Japanese, Korean, Vietnamese, Thai, Cambodian, Laotian, and Filipino languages have intermingled with American English, especially in the western states, to produce several dialects that, though unique, have some common elements. These dialects are different from Standard American English, partly because English uses more sounds than Asian languages do, partly because words in many Asian languages are only one syllable, and partly because most Asian languages use tonal changes as well as different combinations of sounds to indicate word meaning. The sounds *l* and *r* must be learned by many Asians; otherwise:

> *fried rice* sounds like *flied lice*
> *let's read* sounds like *ret's lead*
> *good luck* sounds like *good ruck*
> *really* sounds like *reary*

Because the *th* sound is new to them, Asians tend to replace it with *t* or *d*:

> *author* sounds like *auter*
> *booth* sounds like *boot*
> *that* sounds like *dat*
> *father* sounds like *fodder*

In Vietnamese the *t* and *d* are not different at the ends of words, so:

> *need* sounds like *neat*
> *kid* sounds like *bit*
> *code* sounds like *coat*
> *bride* sounds like *bright*

Other differences stem from the fact that Filipino and Vietnamese do not distinguish *f* and *p* and from the fact that other languages confuse *l* with *n*, so that:

> *fine* sounds like *pine*
> *face* sounds like *pace*
> *light* sounds like *night*
> *load* sounds like *node*

The Korean language does not contain a *j* sound, so:

> *jump* sounds like *dzump*
> *Jim* sounds like *dzim*
> *danger* sounds like *dan-zer*
> *hedge* sounds like *heads*

Asian languages have fewer vowels and diphthongs than Standard American English does, so that:

meat sounds like *mitt*
mad sounds like *mod*
down sounds like *don*
caught sounds like *coat*

Euro-American.   The Euro-American group of dialects is generated by the differences between European languages and English. The relative mobility of European immigrants in America has tended to reduce such differences, except in parts of some big cities.

Nevertheless, some European languages still influence the pronunciation of English. These differences are usually caused by the fact that some sounds in English do not occur in some European languages and other sounds are produced differently. As in Big City dialects, the *th* may become *t* or *d*:

those sounds like *doze*
thing sounds like *ting*
other sounds like *udder*
with sounds like *wit*

The sounds *v* and *w* may be interchanged:

well sounds like *vell*
women sounds like *vimen*
very sounds like *wery*
voice sounds like *wois*

The *r* sound is produced variously. In some dialects it is trilled, in others, it is produced gutterally, and in still others, it is omitted.

Yiddish American.   This dialect has maintained its special sound, converted from ancient Hebrew and mixed with Germanic languages. Although 96 percent of Jewish Americans live in metropolitan areas and are influenced by regional and Big City dialects, Yiddish enclaves exist throughout the country and enrich the speech of the localities in which they are found.

With this brief introduction to language, accent, and dialect, you can now begin to diagnose your unique speech patterns and analyze your voice and articulation.

VOICE AND ARTICULATION ANALYSIS

To get to where you are going, you must first know where you are. Similarly, for you to develop clear speech, you must first analyze your present vocal and articulatory skills to determine those areas in which you need improvement. For this purpose we have provided speech analysis forms and appropriate test material in Appendix A. Your professor may use this or other material or a combination of both to establish the strengths and weaknesses of your speech production.

As a part of your vocal analysis, you may be asked to make recordings of your voice. The old adage "Things are not always what they seem" certainly applies here. It is normal when you hear your recorded voice to say, "Is that me?" You sound strange because the machine records only the sound waves transmitted through the air from your mouth and nose. As you talk, however, your voice is carried to your ear not only indirectly, through the air, but also directly, in the form of vibrations that are transmitted through the bones of your head. Therefore, your speech sounds different to you than it does to other people. You may rest assured that what you hear from a quality recorder is what others hear when you speak.

If you frequently record and listen to your voice, you will be able to recognize the areas on which you need to work and be prepared to make improvements. The analysis of your voice and articulation reveals the characteristics of your accent or dialect. These characteristics are the result of the processes of speech production.

SPEECH PRODUCTION

Speech production is learned behavior. Speaking involves a combination of muscular activities that shape the lips, position the tongue, open the jaw, vibrate the vocal folds, and control the breath (not necessarily in that order), so that sound and words can be produced. Mastery of each of the elements is required for effective oral communication.

Speech is produced, in part, by four processes that involve the speech mechanism.

1. Respiration—the inhalation of air that, when exhaled, provides controlled production of sound (see Chapter 2).
2. Phonation—the vibration of the vocal folds, which converts exhaled air into sound waves (see Chapter 3).
3. Resonation—the amplification and modification of sounds by the throat, mouth, and nose (see Chapter 4).
4. Articulation—the shaping of the sounds by the tongue, teeth, palate, lips, and nose into distinct vowels, diphthongs, and consonants (see chapter 5).

The structures used for speech (displayed in Figure 1.1) serve not one but two fundamental purposes: they contribute to the maintenance of life as well as being involved in the production of speech. The abdominal muscles assist digestion and evacuation of bodily wastes. The diaphragm, the lungs, and the trachea are used for breathing. The vocal folds keep foreign matter out of the lungs and expel contaminants and irritants from them. Air is filtered and warmed by the nasal passages before it moves into the lungs. The mouth, tongue, teeth, and lips are used for eating, chewing, and partially digesting food; these structures are also involved in swallowing, sneezing, and coughing. The life-sustaining functions of these structures are primarily automatic acts. The overlaid functions for speech are voluntary.

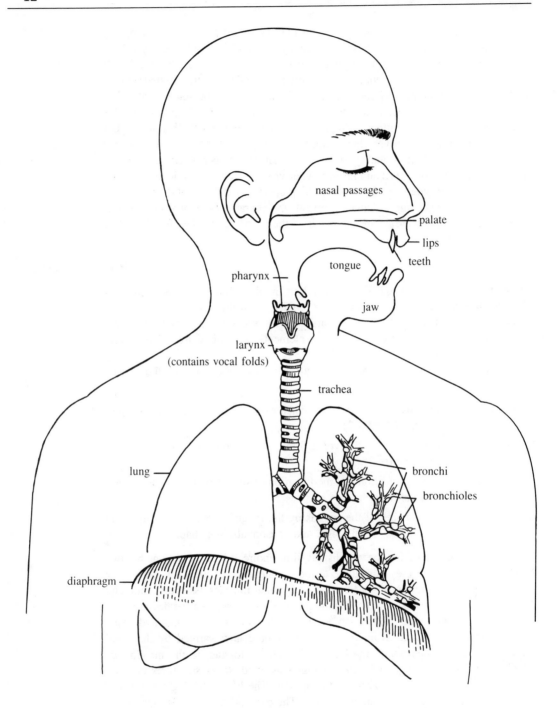

Figure 1.1   Structures for speech production.

SUMMARY

The parts of your body used for speech have the more basic purpose of sustaining life. Speech uses the same anatomical structures. It is, therefore, an overlaid function, which can be interrupted when life-sustaining functions become more important.

Your physical structure and your communication experiences have determined, in part, the way you control the basic processes of speech production—respiration, phonation, resonation, and articulation. In part, these processes are also affected by the speech you hear, the dialect spoken by those around you.

Regardless of your current dialect, the following principles apply.

1. All speakers have a dialect.
2. Each dialect is acceptable to other users of that dialect.
3. All dialects are constantly changing, influenced by neighboring speech patterns, education, and immigration.
4. Standard American is the most widely used and most widely understood dialect in the United States.
5. The acquisition of Standard American does not require an individual to give up his or her current dialect.
6. Many people have the ability to use more than one dialect; they are able to select from among several dialects the one appropriate to each speaking situation.

Obviously this discussion has been simplified. Many other variations and combinations of dialects exist. These are important but less widely spoken and so have not been mentioned. For more information on this subject, you may wish to consult appropriate references from the bibliography.

Although each language has many dialects, most have one that is considered the standard—the dialect used by most college-trained persons and by speakers on radio and television. In the United States, this dialect is called Standard American English. It is not necessarily better than other dialects; the standard is simply the most useful.

Following the analysis of your voice and articulation, you will be prepared to use the information and exercises in the following chapters to learn the skills necessary for speaking clearly.

2

Respiration

Our first act at birth is respiration. This lifelong process has two phases—inhalation and exhalation. It also has two purposes—breathing for life and breathing for speech.

We breathe for life whether we want to or not. If a child says, "I will hold my breath until I die," there is no need to worry. The body's demand for oxygen prevents any self-willed damage, and the child soon resumes breathing. This vital process takes place automatically, on the average about sixteen times a minute. Oxygen in the air moves into the body through the airways (nose, mouth, throat, trachea, windpipe, bronchi, and bronchioles) into the air spaces (ducts and air sacs, or alveoli) with the lungs. From there the blood in capillaries passing through the lungs absorbs oxygen and releases carbon dioxide. The oxygen is carried by the blood through 60,000 miles of vessels to convert food chemicals into energy. Carbon dioxide is exhaled from the air spaces through the lungs' airways. Adults breathe about 20,000 times a day, moving approximately 15,000,000 cubic centimeters of air. To understand the complex process of breathing, we need to know the parts of the body involved and how they work together.

ANATOMY AND PHYSIOLOGY OF RESPIRATION

The act of respiration, both as a vital function and as a part of speech production, involves the interaction of a number of body parts. Refer to Figures 2.1 and 2.2 as you read the definitions of the following terms.

Thorax (chest cavity):   The part of the body between the base of the neck and the diaphragm.

Rib cage: The bony structure of the thorax, which includes the backbone, the sternum, and twelve pairs of ribs (also called the costae).

Ribs (costae):   The twelve curved pairs of bones attached to the spine in the back. The seven upper pairs are attached in front to the sternum. The next three pairs are joined by cartilage to the rib above. The lowest two pairs, called floating

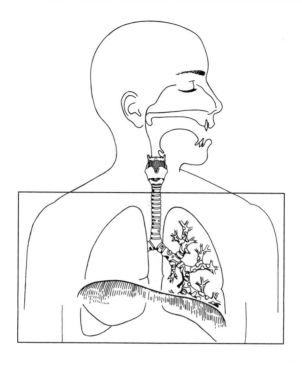

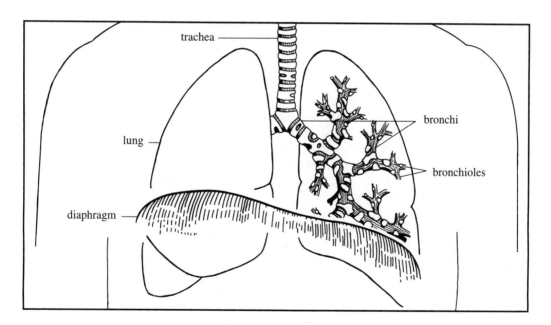

Figure 2.1 Respiratory system.

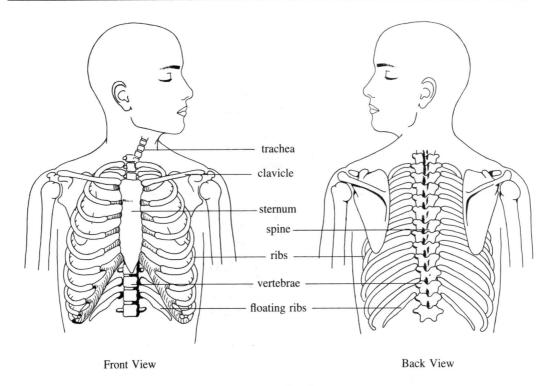

trachea
clavicle
sternum
spine
ribs
vertebrae
floating ribs

Front View   Back View

Figure 2.2   The thorax.

ribs, are not directly attached in front. This flexible structure becomes the framework of the thorax.

Sternum (breastbone):   The narrow, flat bone in the midline of the front of the thorax.

Vertebra: One of the thirty-three bones that make up the spine.

Spine (backbone):   The structure formed of the thirty-three vertebrae, which interlace with the ribs to form the main structure of the thorax.

Intercostal muscles: The muscles between the ribs. The *external intercostals* raise the ribs up and out (flaring increases the diameter of the chest cage) to aid inhalation; the *internal intercostals* pull the ribs down (which decreases the diameter of the chest cage) to aid exhalation.

Trachea (windpipe):   The round tube, on the average about 10 centimeters long, between the larynx (the voice box) and the bronchi. The trachea divides into two main bronchi, one for each lung, which subdivide into many additional smaller bronchi.

Lungs: Two large, elastic, spongy, cone-shaped organs in the thorax that contain some airways (bronchi and bronchioles) and air spaces (ducts and alveoli) as well as small blood vessels. They can hold about 500 cc of air when fully extended. Most persons use between 10 and 30 percent for speech.

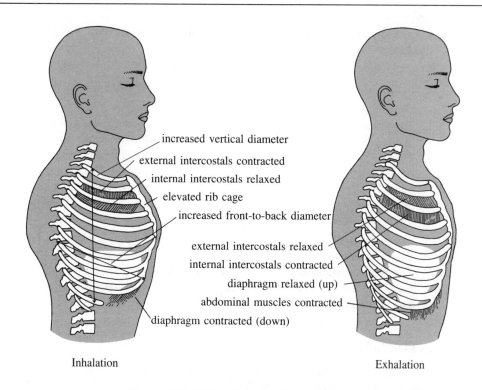

increased vertical diameter
external intercostals contracted
internal intercostals relaxed
elevated rib cage
increased front-to-back diameter

external intercostals relaxed
internal intercostals contracted
diaphragm relaxed (up)
abdominal muscles contracted
diaphragm contracted (down)

Inhalation

Exhalation

Figure 2.3   The rib cage during respiration.

Bronchi: Tubes lined with cartilage that branch from the trachea and reach into the lungs. Each bronchus subdivides within the lung into 20,000 terminal bronchioles, which further connect to air spaces containing ducts and alveoli. In these air spaces the transfer of oxygen and carbon dioxide occurs.

Bronchioles: The terminal portions of the bronchi.

Alveoli: The air cells in the lungs at the ends of the microscopic bronchioles.

Diaphragm: A sheath of muscles and tendons, dome shaped, separating the abdomen from the thorax. The esophagus, aorta, and nerves pass through it, but it provides an airtight separation between the chest and the abdomen.

Abdomen: The portion of the torso below the diaphragm that contains the stomach, liver, gallbladder, pancreas, spleen, intestines, bladder, and other organs.

Abdominal wall: The sheaths of muscles running vertically, horizontally, and diagonally in the lower front of the body.

RESPIRATION FOR LIFE

Normal breathing to sustain life requires little effort. About sixteen times a minute air goes in and out of the lungs. In this continuous rhythmical process inhalation is caused mostly by the lowering of the diaphragm (which in turn causes the lungs to expand), and exhalation results mostly from the elastic recoil of the lungs as the diaphragm rises to its resting position.

Watch a baby sleeping on its back and you will see the following phases.

1. In inhalation, the abdominal wall expands as the dome-shaped diaphragm flattens, pushing against the organs in the abdomen.

2. The thorax, particularly at the level of the floating ribs, expands, and the front of the rib cage rises. Almost all of the expansion occurs in the lower thorax. There is no movement of the shoulders, clavicles (collarbones), or upper chest. As a result the air pressure in the airtight thorax is reduced. The higher pressure outside causes air to flow in through the nose or the mouth and down the throat into the trachea, bronchi, and lungs. The lungs, somewhat like thousands of tiny interconnected balloons, are elastic and stretch as they are filled.

3. In exhalation, the diaphragm relaxes, the abdominal wall and thorax contract, the elastic lungs recoil, and the abdominal organs return to their normal positions. The pressure upon the air within the lungs becomes greater than that outside the body, and therefore it flows back out through the bronchi, trachea, throat, and mouth or nose.

RESPIRATION FOR SPEECH

When we need to, we can exercise precise control over the breathing process. For example, we can hold our breath for long periods of time to swim under water or to lift heavy weights. We can blow up balloons, blow out candles, cool off hot soup, sniff odors, and in countless other ways control the intake and outflow of air. The most remarkable use of controlled respiration, though, is for speech. We can change the inhalation-exhalation rhythm to match our speech needs. This ability is one of the reasons humans can speak understandably. Speech sounds occur normally only during exhalation. If we could not control exhalation, we would have difficulty speaking. At best, we would speak in jerky, robotlike phrases. As we breathe for speech, we inhale quickly and then exhale slowly. The length of exhalation depends on what we are saying. To support this longer, more controlled exhalation, the intercostal and abdominal muscles are especially important.

RESPIRATION FUNCTIONS COMPARED

Respiration for speech can be compared with life-sustaining respiration as follows:

Breathing for Life

1. Both inhalation and exhalation are involuntary.

2. Inhalation and exhalation take about the same amount of time.

3. Each breath is determined by the body's needs.

Breathing for Speech

1. Both inhalation and exhalation are voluntary.

2. Inhalation is quick. Exhalation is controlled and takes as much time as is needed for a phrase to be expressed.

3. The amount of air inhaled is determined by the length of the phrase to be uttered.

MUSCLE INTERACTION IN RESPIRATION

As is true of all muscles, those used for breathing actively pull in only one direction. Opposing muscles then return them to their original positions. Thus, the diaphragm actively flexes down, which draws air into the lungs and pushes out the passive abdominal wall muscles. At the same time the external intercostals pull the rib cage up, which stretches the passive internal intercostals. Then the active and passive roles reverse. The muscles of the abdominal wall push the abdominal organs against the passive diaphragm and move the latter up into its original position, while the internal intercostals contract, drawing the ribs down as the now passive external intercostals relax. Figure 2.3 illustrates this process.

This natural process, which we all possess at birth, may become distorted. We may learn to inhale by contracting the waist and lifting the thorax, which draws air into the upper chest. The shoulders and clavicles (collarbones) rise. These actions tense the muscles of the neck and hence alter the control of voice production. More importantly, this type of respiration, called clavicular breathing, is harder to regulate during exhalation than abdominal breathing. The combination of clavicular breathing and abdominal breathing may be appropriate for athletics and for other strenuous physical activity, but for speech and singing it is most inefficient. Clavicular breathing is more shallow than abdominal breathing. Therefore the speech rhythm may be jerky as the speaker stops frequently for air. Also, clavicular breathing occurs where the thorax can expand the least. The repeated attempt to get enough air often causes more tension in the neck and throat, which may make the voice become constricted. By learning to imitate the natural abdominal breathing of a baby, you will be able to maintain good breathing habits for life as well as effective respiration for pleasant speech.

The following relaxation and respiration exercises will help you to acquire or improve abdominal breathing for speech. They will strengthen not only your breath control but also your health and appearance.

RELAXATION

Your voice reveals your feelings. For example, if you are nervous, anxious or fearful, your defense mechanisms alert the muscles, making them tense and inflexible. This action and reaction in the thorax, neck, and jaw restrict and constrict your voice and articulation:

1. Your voice may go up in pitch.
2. Your vocal focus may become high in the head.
3. Your pitch range may decrease toward monotone.
4. Your articulation may be tight and incomplete.
5. Your breath may deplete quickly and you may inhale new air inadequately.

You can avoid these vocal problems if you can relax. Relaxation, however, means not sloppiness but the absence of muscle tension, which you can learn with practice.

Besides the "rag doll" exercise (explained later in this chapter), use the following exercises to make relaxation a habit.

RELAXATION EXERCISES

1. Lie on your back on the floor.
2. Lift your knees and point them to the ceiling with the feet slightly apart.
3. Spread your shoulders, back, and buttocks on the floor.
4. Stretch your spine along the floor, easing each vertebra apart.
5. Draw your head away from the body, stretching your neck.
6. Rotate your head, releasing the neck muscles.
7. Shake your elbows, wrists, and fingers; then let your arms gently drop.
8. Say aloud:
   Spread back
   Spread shoulders
   Stretch spine
   Free wrists
   Free elbows
   Free neck

As you become more self-aware, you will be able to induce this relaxed state whenever you wish. In this relaxed state you are ready to breathe easily and efficiently. Remember to inhale at the lower thorax, flexing the diaphragm down and expanding only at the floating ribs.

RESPIRATION EXERCISES

In-Class Exercises

The following exercises may be used in the classroom to increase your abdominal breathing ability.

The Yawner. Stand evenly with your hands on your hips. Lean your head back, look at the ceiling, and yawn. Let your jaw open completely and easily. Notice how the waist expands as the diaphragm flattens and draws in a large quantity of air. As the yawn becomes contagious, exhale and phonate the sound *ah*. Stretch out the sound as long as possible without discomfort.

The Waist Squeezer.   Place your open palms on the sides of your waist with your fingers in front and your thumbs behind. Squeeze slightly. Inhale slowly and feel the effect of the diaphragm pressing the abdominal wall forward against your fingers as the entire waist area expands. Hold the breath for five counts. Now count out loud and exhale slowly while you squeeze with your hands. Sense the resistance from the diaphragm, the ribs, and the costal muscles as they relax, expelling the air.

The Counter.   Do the following.

1. Breathe in to a mental count of *In, 2, 3.*
   Breathe *Out, 2, 3.*
   (Repeat a few times.)

2. Breathe *In, 2, 3.*
   Breathe *Out, 2, 3, 4, 5, 6.*
   Rest, *2, 3.*

3. Breathe *In,* quickly but smoothly.
   Breathe *Out, 2, 3, 4, 5, 6,*

4. Breathe *In, 2, 3, 4, 5, 6.*
   Breathe *Out, 2, 3,* and pause.
   Breathe *Out, 2, 3.*

5. Breathe *In,* quickly but smoothly.
   Breathe *Out, 2, 3,* and pause.
   Out, 2, 3, and pause.
   Out, 2, 3.

6. Breathe *In,* taking a good chest breath.
   Keep the ribs held out, and with only the diaphragm and abdominal muscles moving, pant very gently through the open mouth, being careful to ensure that the movement of the abdominal wall is correlated with the intake and output of the breath. At the end of the exercise breathe *Out,* letting the ribs come in.

7. Breathe *In,* taking a good chest breath.
   Keep the ribs held out and continue breathing with the diaphragm only.
   Take the breath in and out through the mouth.
   Breathe *Out, 2, 3.*
   Breathe *In, 2, 3.*
   Breathe *Out, 2, 3,* etc.
   Finally breathe out and let the ribs come in.

8. Breathe *In,* taking a good chest breath.
   Hold the ribs out, and with only the diaphragm and abdominal muscles working, breathe *Out, 2, 3.*

Renew the breath rapidly and gently through the mouth.
Repeat several times.
Finally, breathe out, letting the ribs come in.

Out-of-Class Exercises

These exercises should be practiced daily at home until abdominal breathing for speech becomes habitual.

The Rag Doll. Stand evenly on both feet. Let your arms hang loose. Lean your head and shoulders forward and slowly let your upper torso fall forward at the waist. Do not try to touch the floor with your fingers, but just allow the head, arms, and thorax to hang limp. Stay in this "rag doll" position for 1 minute; then slowly straighten and repeat the exercise. Notice how the air is naturally exhaled when you bend at the waist.

The Waist Relaxer. Lie on your back. Place a book on your upper abdomen. Clear your mind of external matters. Concentrate on directing each part of your body to relax. As you become aware that you are calm and relaxed, concentrate on the movement of the diaphragm. Inhale and watch the abdominal wall and the book rise. Then, as you exhale, flatten the abdominal wall as much as possible. The book should lower as the diaphragm relaxes and is pushed up by the abdominal muscles, which help pull the ribs down. Repeat this exercise until you habitually expand the waist on inhalation and contract it on exhalation.

The Yogi. Sit in an Indian, or lotus, position. Let your head rest forward with your chin on your chest. Look at your waist. Inhale. Feel your waist expand as you raise your head up and back until you have a full abdominal breath. Exhale and easily phonate *ah*. Now slowly lower your head and watch your waist contract.

The Reader. The following is a paragraph containing short and then longer sentences. Inhale only before each sentence, then control exhalation as you read aloud; try to read each sentence with one breath.

Begin here. Notice your posture. Stand evenly with straight knees. Concentrate on inhaling with the diaphragm. That means to expand only the waist and to leave the upper thorax relaxed. Open your mouth fully and inhale as deeply as you can. Begin to speak at the peak of inhalation, so that no air is wasted before you speak. During the exhalation, try to control the breath flow so that you will have enough breath to finish the sentences. Be sure to feel the contraction of the abdominal muscles as you firmly control the outgoing airstream. The muscular control is essential, because it helps you maintain a strong steady flow of air during phonation.

SUMMARY

Good inhalation involves four actions.

1. The upward and forward movement of the lower thorax.
2. The back-to-front expansion of the lower thorax.
3. The lengthening of the thoracic cavity as the diaphragm flattens.
4. The expansion of the waist and the upper abdominal wall. Proper exhalation involves the reverse of these actions.

Your efforts to improve habits of breathing for speech will be reflected in your breathing for life. You will be able to draw in larger quantities of air and to hold your breath for longer periods of time. More importantly, you will gain the ability to strengthen your voice and to give it force and flexibility.

3

Phonation

As we listen to people around us speak, we are amazed by the great diversity of vocal types. We may be impressed by the voices of network newscasters or cringe at the sound of the newspaper seller on the street corner. We wonder at the flexible voices of cartoon character actors and are put to sleep by the droning of poor lecturers. Voices vary almost as much as fingerprints do. Your voice is your own expression of yourself.

We learn to use our voices more or less by accident. We hear the speech of those around us, and as we begin to talk, we emulate those models. As we grow older, we develop vocal habits based on a combination of factors—our early learning, our physical structure and development, our experiences, and our expanding personality. Our voices tend to reflect our feelings for ourselves and those around us. Regardless of the influences that have established our current vocal habits, however, we can all improve our vocal behavior.

This chapter will help you to:

1. Learn the characteristics of the ideal voice.
2. Recognize your vocal strengths and correct your weaknesses.
3. Develop vocal efficiency and flexibility.

Vocal production can be divided into two main areas—phonation and resonation. *Phonation* is the process of producing vocal tones when the breath stream passes between lightly closed vocal folds, causing them to vibrate. *Resonation*, on the other hand, is the selective amplification and reinforcement of the vocal tone in the vocal tract (the airways of the throat, mouth, and nose). Resonation will be the topic of Chapter 4.

ANATOMY OF VOCAL PRODUCTION

To learn to improve your voice, you will first need to know how and where it is produced. The following terms will help you to understand the process of phonation (see Figure 3.1):

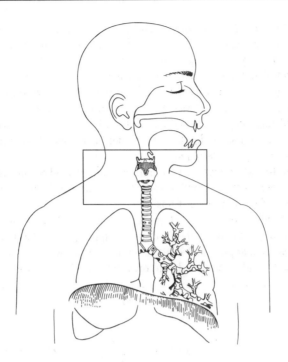

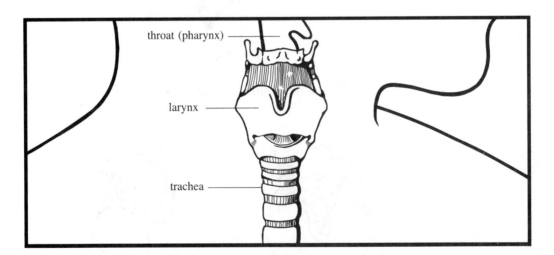

throat (pharynx) —

larynx —

trachea —

Figure 3.1.   Structures of phonation.

Larynx (the voice box):   the cartilagenous, hollow structure located in the center
of the front of the neck, made up of the *thyroid cartilage,* the *cricoid cartilage,*
the *arytenoid cartilage,* the *epiglottis,* and the muscles and tendons that connect
these structures, among which are the *vocal folds* (vocal cords). It rests on top

of the *trachea* (windpipe) and is connected above to the *hyoid bone,* which forms the base of the tongue. The upward frontal projection of the larynx is commonly called the "Adam's apple" (Figures 3.2 and 3.3).

Thyroid Cartilage: shaped somewhat like a shield (or the bow of a ship), it slopes down and back toward the trachea. It rests on and surrounds, on two sides, the cricoid cartilage. It is open in the back.

Cricoid Cartilage: shaped somewhat like a signet ring, with its "bank" toward the front and the broad, flat "signet" part toward the back, between the sides of the thyroid cartilage.

Arytenoid Cartilages: two small, pyramid-shaped cartilages that rest on the upper surface of the "signet" area of the cricoid cartilage. Each of these connects to one of the two vocal folds.

Vocal Folds: two folds of muscle tissue attached to the sides of the thyroid cartilage, joined in the front to the upper part of the thyroid cartilage near the "Adam's apple," and in the back to one of the arytenoid cartilages. When the vocal folds are closed, air pressure, coming up from the lungs through the

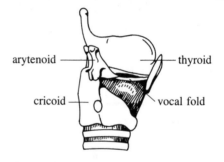

arytenoid —————— thyroid

cricoid —————— vocal fold

Figure 3.2. Structure of the larynx.

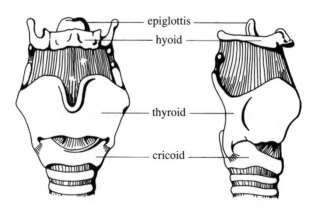

epiglottis

hyoid

thyroid

cricoid

Figure 3.3. The larynx, front and side view.

trachea, moves the arytenoid cartilages together, causing the vocal folds to vibrate.

Epiglottis: a leaf-shaped cartilage that attaches to the upper front border of the thyroid cartilage. During swallowing, it is pulled down and back, allowing solid and liquid matter to flow around it, keeping the airway clear.

Glottis: the opening or space between the vocal folds.

FUNCTIONS OF THE LARYNX

The larynx serves two major functions: *life maintenance* and *phonation* (the production of vocal tone).

Life Maintenance: The larynx is part of the respiratory system and connects the trachea to the airways of the throat, mouth, and nose; it allows air to move freely in and out of the body. It also serves to protect the breathing mechanism from contaminants and irritants and from larger pieces of matter. Because the vocal folds can close tightly, breath pressure can be built up below them and suddenly released, as in a cough. The larynx, therefore, is able to blast irritants out of the airway. Since they can form an airtight seal, the vocal folds also make it possible to hold the breath.

Phonation: The larynx also functions in the production of vocal tone. Because phonation and the life maintenance functions use the same structures, the processes are, for the most part, incompatible; for example, you cannot talk and cough at the same time. Almost always, a life maintenance function will take precedence over a phonatory one.

THE PROCESS OF PHONATION

During respiration the vocal folds are apart. The triangular space between them, called the *glottis,* allows for the free passage of air to the lungs. When the glottis is narrowed (that is, when the vocal folds are partially closed) and air is exhaled, the resulting air turbulence is heard as whispering. When the vocal folds are brought closer together and caused to touch lightly (that is, when the glottis is closed) and the breath is exhaled with sufficient pressure, the edges of the folds begin to vibrate, like the opening of a rapidly deflating balloon, in the process called phonation. This vibration is transmitted to the column of air within the vocal tract and through the outside air to the ear of a listener. Figure 3.4 illustrates the positions of the glottis corresponding to the processes of respiration, whispering, and phonation.

To better understand the process of phonation, imagine a single vibration of the vocal folds. At first, they are completely closed. Then, as the breath pressure beneath them builds up, they are forced open, allowing a puff of air to pass between them. This causes air pressure in the vocal tract and the outside air to increase slightly and the pressure in the trachea, below the vocal folds, to decrease. Since the vocal folds are elastic, they return to the closed position until air pressure beneath them increases and pushes them apart again, to repeat the cycle. The vocal

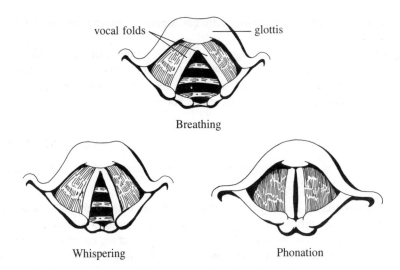

Figure 3.4. The vocal folds and glottis as seen through a laryngeal mirror in three actions. (The front of the neck is at the top of the drawing.)

folds are aided in closing each time by the fact that, as the puff of air rushes between them, it tends to pull the vocal folds along, drawing them together. As they close, the air pressure in the vocal tract and outside air decreases, to be increased again by the next puff of air as the vocal folds are pushed open again.

As long as sufficient breath pressure is maintained and proper closure of the vocal folds is continued, alternating increases and decreases of air pressure in the airways and the outside air will occur. These pressure changes are *sound waves*.

CHARACTERISTICS OF PHONATION

The sound waves produced by the vocal folds and modified in the vocal tract are responsible for the unique sound of each individual's voice. In attempts to describe these individual differences, various terms have been assigned to vocal characteristics, including *high, low, loud, soft, husky, harsh, aspirate, strident, strained, shrill, throaty, metallic, intense* and *musical*—to mention only a few. Such words have limited utility; each tends to mean different things to different people. What you think of as husky someone else may describe as hoarse. Additionally, none of these terms tells us anything about what the speech mechanism does to sound that way.

To explain the behavior of the phonatory mechanism as we describe individual voice differences, we will define eight separate, distinctive, and easily identifiable characteristics of phonation. These are *vocal pitch, vocal loudness, vocal fold mode, vocal tract dimension, vocal fold vibrance, vocal tract focus, vocal fold contact,*

Table 3.1 Vocal Characteristics and Voice Quality

SOME COMMON VOICE QUALITY TERMS	VOCAL CHARACTERISTICS							
	Vocal Pitch	*Vocal Loudness*	*Vocal Fold Mode*	*Vocal Tract Dimension*	*Vocal Fold Vibrance*	*Vocal Tract Focus*	*Vocal Fold Contact*	*Vocal Effort*
Ideal	Optimal with variety	Adequate with variety	Optimal	Open	Voiced	Balanced	Smooth	Little
Aspirate	May vary	May vary	Optimal	May vary	Breathy	May vary	May vary	May vary
Harsh	May vary	May vary	Optimal or light	Constricted	May vary	In throat	Rough	Much
Hoarse	Low	Soft	Optimal	Constricted	Breathy	In throat	Rough	Much
Strident	High	Loud	Optimal	Constricted	Voiced	In throat	Rough	Much
Thin	High	Soft	Optimal or light	Constricted	May vary	In throat	Smooth	Little

and *vocal effort*.[1] These characteristics interact to produce the unique sound of your voice. Table 3.1 demonstrates how voices can be described behaviorally rather than qualitatively. Commonly used voice quality terms appear in the leftmost column; corresponding descriptions for the particular voice characteristics appear to the right.

Vocal Pitch

Vocal pitch is the highness or lowness of your voice. Vocal pitch depends on the speed of vibration of your vocal folds. The faster they vibrate, the higher the pitch of the voice; the slower they vibrate, the lower the pitch of the voice.

A good way to understand pitch is to relate it to the musical scale on an instrument such as the piano. Most music is based on an eight-tone scale, the familiar do-re-me-fa-so-la-ti-do. The group of eight notes from do to do is called an *octave*.

Each of the keys on the piano has a note letter and an octave number. The lowest note on the piano is called A_1. Two white keys up from it is C_1 (Figure 3.5). To produce that note, the piano string vibrates at a rate of 32 vibrations per second, or 32 hertz (Hz).[2] C_2, eight notes or one octave up the keyboard, vibrates at a rate of 64 Hz, or double the rate for C_1. C_3 vibrates at 128 Hz; C_4, also called

---

[1] These eight vocal characteristics are variations on those described by Perkins (1971, 1977).

[2] The hertz is a unit named for Heinrich R. Hertz, an early investigator of electromagnetic radiation: 1 Hz is equivalent to 1 vibration per second.

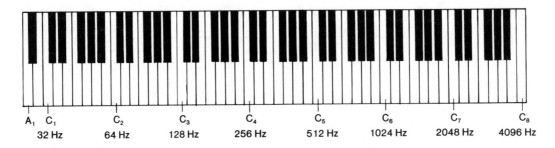

A₁	C₁	C₂	C₃	C₄	C₅	C₆	C₇	C₈

Figure 3.5. The piano keyboard with frequencies of various notes.

middle C, at 256 Hz. The highest note on a piano, C_8, vibrates at 4096 Hz. When you voice any of these notes, your vocal folds vibrate at the same rate, or frequency, as the corresponding piano string.

Determinants of Vocal Pitch. What determines the pitch of your voice? Knowing how tones are made by various musical instruments may help to answer this question. On the piano, different notes result from the striking of strings of different length; the longer the string, the lower the note. The notes of a trumpet are produced by the lip vibrations of the player; the less the tension, the lower the note. The notes of a xylophone depend on the striking of metal bars of different sizes; the thicker the bar, the lower the note. These three factors—*length, tension,* and *thickness*— operate in the same way in the human vocal folds to produce pitch changes. The greater the length of the vocal folds, the lower their tension, and the greater their thickness, the lower the pitch will be.

The musical instruments just discussed share a trait with the human voice: their design affects their sound. No one expects a spinet piano to have the tone of a concert grand. Trumpets and other brass instruments differ widely, and a child's toy xylophone sounds only slightly like the professional instrument. Similarly, different sizes and shapes of larynxes affect the sounds produced. Women's voices, generally, are pitched approximately one octave higher than men's because their vocal folds are usually shorter. A child's voice is higher than an adult's for the same reason. Normally, thick vocal folds produce a deeper voice than thin ones.

Pitch Range. Each voice is able to produce a number of different notes. The distance from the lowest to the highest note is called *pitch range*. Most voices have about a two-octave range; opera singers frequently reach three or more.

To establish your pitch range, count the notes from the lowest to the highest notes that you can produce on the musical scale.

Habitual Pitch. One of the notes in your pitch range is used most frequently in your speech. This is called your *habitual pitch*. You can locate your habitual pitch by repeating over and over, rapidly, a simple phrase, such as "Come for lunch." Identify on the musical scale the tone you voice most frequently.

Optimal Pitch. Like the musical instrument, voices sound best at certain pitch levels. For example, not only can the trumpet not reach as low a pitch as the trombone, its very low tones are not as effective as its higher ones. The player must blow much harder to produce a tone at the lower range in the instrument.

Voices operate in the same way. You have a pitch level, called your *optimal pitch,* that is relatively easily produced. It is normally found in the lower half of your pitch range. *Ideally your optimal pitch and habitual pitch will be the same.*

Vocal Loudness

A second phonation characteristic is loudness. Loudness refers to the power or volume level of the voice. Just as the loudness of a trumpet is determined by how hard the player blows, so the loudness of a voice is determined by how vigorously the speaker exhales. The greater the breath pressure, the greater the movement of the vocal folds when they are pushed apart. The larger their movement, the greater the pressure changes that are transmitted through the vocal tract to the outside air and to the listener. The greater the pressure changes, the louder the sound.

While pitch is measured by the number of vibrations per second made by the vocal folds, loudness is measured in terms of the sound energy produced. A sound level meter is used for this purpose; its unit of measurement is the *decibel.*[3] Typically, a conversational voice registers a sound pressure level of 60 decibels (dB). A loud voice might be measured at 90 dB, while screaming or yelling may reach 110 dB or more. The human ear reaches the threshold of pain at about 120 dB, but fortunately that is approximately the limit of the human voice as well.

Vocal Fold Mode

There are four distinct ways or *modes* of producing voice in the larynx—*optimal vocal mode, light vocal mode, pulsated vocal mode,* and *whispered vocal mode.* Most of our vocalization is done in the optimal vocal mode, but the three modes have important functions in our vocal behavior.

Optimal Vocal Mode. Optimal vocal mode is the way we usually phonate. The vocal folds vibrate over their entire length. This mode has the widest pitch range of the four and can usually be produced more loudly than the rest. It is used in most of our speech communication.

Light Vocal Mode. Light vocal mode (or falsetto voice) is produced when the vocal folds vibrate over only the front third of their length. This type of vocal adjustment is used to create the voices of Mickey Mouse and other cartoon characters; it is also used by singers to reach their highest notes and is heard in the

---

[3]The decibel is one tenth of a bel, a unit of sound energy named for Alexander Graham Bell, the inventor of the telephone. A decibel is the smallest difference that can be heard by the human ear.

voices of yodelers. The mode has a narrower and higher pitch range than the optimal vocal mode and is not normally as loud.

Pulsated Vocal Mode.   Pulsated vocal mode (also called glottal fry) contains the lowest pitch levels the vocal folds can produce, as low as 2 Hz. The vocal folds vibrate over their entire length but are moved much less vigorously than in either the optimal or light vocal modes. Similar to a Geiger counter, pulsated voice has the sound of a slowly turning wheel of fortune. Each vibration of the vocal folds is heard as a separate click. Pulsated voice is not normally used in speaking but may occur at phrase ends when the speaker is talking with relatively little energy.

Whispering.   Whispering is the result of the exhaled breath stream passing through narrowed, but not closed, vocal folds. The smooth airflow is interrupted, causing audible air turbulence.

Vocal Tract Dimension

Vocal tract dimension refers to the diameter of the vocal tract above the vocal folds. If the vocal tract is narrowed, the phonation sounds *constricted*. An unconstricted vocal tract sounds *open*.

Phonation with the vocal tract dimension at its widest dimension (vocal openness) can be experienced by voicing softly immediately after yawning. Your voice will flow more effortlessly than it does under most conditions.

Phonation with the vocal tract dimension narrowed (vocal constriction), on the other hand, can be experienced by placing a narrow cardboard tube to your lips and trying to speak through it. You will have effectively reduced the opening through which sound waves pass. Your voice sounds softer than it does without the tube.

Vocal constriction can occur at any point along the vocal tract *where excess tension is present.* For example, try talking and partially swallowing at the same time. You will feel the muscles of your throat become tense and hear your voice become softer and more constricted. For another example, phonate the sound *ah* as you slowly pull your tongue into the back of your mouth. You will notice that your voice becomes increasingly muffled as your tongue moves farther back.

Because vocal constriction reduces loudness, the vocally constricted speaker must use greater than normal breath pressure to be heard as loudly as the vocally open one. The vocal folds, therefore, are vibrated more vigorously than normal. Talking loudly or for long periods of time may cause them to become irritated or sore. Continual irritation can result in injury to the vocal folds; thus, vocal constriction is to be avoided. Vocal constriction is aptly termed the enemy of the voice. The ideal vocal tract dimension, therefore, is open.

Vocal Fold Vibrance

Vocal fold vibrance refers to the proportion of air passing through the glottis that results in vocal fold vibration.

You probably have heard an actress trying to sound "sexy" by speaking in a soft sigh. You may have spoken in a similar manner when you were quite tired. You and the actress were using a relatively small proportion of the breath stream to phonate. Your vocal folds were not completely closed during vibration, and air was leaking from the opening; you were speaking with a *breathy voice*. A *full voice,* on the other hand, is produced when most of the exhaled breath stream sets the vocal folds into vibration.

In the breathy voice the escape of air is heard as a rushing sound along with the voiced sound. Breathy persons, consequently, have lower loudness ranges than those with full voices. Because they have to breathe more frequently, they speak in short phrases. They may even seem to be out of breath. Extreme breathiness, in fact, is whispering.

Vocal Tract Focus

There are three main areas of the vocal tract where the sound of the voice is affected—the airways of the throat (pharynx), the mouth (oral cavity), and the nose (nasal cavity). Vocal tract focus refers to the balance among them.

Some voices seem to be trapped in the throat; others, manufactured in the mouth; and still others, nestled in the nose. The greater the effect in the throat area, the more the sound seems to be trapped there. The greater the mouth effect, the more oral the sound is. The more the nasal effect, the more nasal the sound is. The ideal adjustment is *balanced focus*—that is, with no tract area predominating.

The balanced focus voice feels as though it is floating in the head freely, not as though it is trapped or located in any specific area. There is no strain in the mechanism.

Vocal Fold Contact

Normally during phonation the vocal folds come fully together and vibrate smoothly. The effect is an easy contact that results in an even tone production. If for some reason the contact is not smooth, due either to distortions of the surface of the vocal folds or to vocal strain, the contact will be uneven and *roughness* will be perceived in the voice. Since the contact made by the two folds is dependent on other vocal characteristics (such as vocal tract dimension), vocal roughness normally disappears when other problems are reduced.

Vocal Effort

Ideally, the voice is produced with little *vocal effort*. The sound flows forth with little or no obstruction, and the energy used depends solely on the desired loudness level. If the vocal tract is constricted, and the focus is in the throat, much more energy is required to produce vocal tone and vocal effort is increased. The amount of effort is directly related to the amount of breath pressure necessary to initiate phonation.

Table 3.2　Ideal Vocal Characteristics

	VOCAL CHARACTERISTICS							
	Vocal Pitch	*Vocal Loudness*	*Vocal Fold Mode*	*Vocal Tract Dimension*	*Vocal Fold Vibrance*	*Vocal Tract Focus*	*Vocal Fold Contact*	*Vocal Effort*
IDEAL	Optimal with variety	Adequate with variety	Optimal	Open	Voiced	Balanced	Smooth	Little

THE IDEAL VOICE

Your goal for voice production is to use your speech mechanism to its best advantage. The vocal characteristics of the *ideal voice* (Table 3.2) result in *vocal efficiency*. An efficient voice is one that produces maximum output with minimum effort (Van Wye, 1936). It requires lower levels of breath pressure to produce a given loudness level than a less efficient voice does. It is characterized by open phonation, balanced vocal focus, and full vibrance. Vocal effort is low, therefore, and vocal contact is smooth.

Few students enter a speech class with an ideal voice. Most students have one or more characteristics that can be improved. Your professor may already have indicated to you those that require development.

PHONATION EXERCISES

Voice exercises should be done with care. The best vocal practice involves short periods, of 5 minutes or less, spaced frequently through the day, instead of one or two long sessions. In your desire to improve your vocal skills quickly, you may try to do too much for too long a time. Stop if your voice feels tired and especially if you feel roughness or scratchiness in your throat. This may indicate that you are performing the exercises incorrectly and need help from your professor. Remember, your goal is vocal efficiency, not vocal exhaustion.

Most students do not need to use all of these exercises. Select only those that pertain to the vocal characteristics that you need to develop. This section contains the following procedures to help you improve vocal efficiency.

1. Exercises to improve vocal tract openness.
2. Exercises to achieve and strengthen balanced vocal focus.
3. Exercises to improve vocal fold voicing.

Subsequent sections will provide exercises for the effective control of pitch and loudness.

The exercises in this and the following chapter have been used successfully in a large college program for voice and articulation (over 900 students per year) and also in clinical settings.

Exercises to Improve Vocal Tract Dimension

The Relaxer.   Lie down on a firm surface (e.g., the floor or a firm mattress). Use abdominal breathing to inhale and exhale slowly through your mouth. Let your lips and jaw hang loose, and concentrate on the feeling of relaxation that develops in them. Then concentrate on the feelings in your throat. Let this area now relax. Feel the movement of air through the throat and mouth. There should be no sensation of obstruction or blockage.

The Yawner.   Still lying down, pretend to yawn, or produce an actual yawn.

1. You should experience a stretching action as the mouth and throat are pulled open.
2. At the peak of the yawn these structures will normally be opened as widely as possible.
3. As the yawn concludes, you should feel the mouth and throat return to a relaxed, open state.

Study these findings as you repeat the yawn several times. Try to establish the stretched feeling in the throat and the return to the relaxed, open state. Also try to maintain the open feeling throughout the rest of these exercises.

The Sigher.   Inhale (by abdominal breathing) and try to produce a slightly breathy sigh as you say *ah*. If you feel yourself constricting somewhat, go back to the Yawner and repeat that exercise and this one until you produce an open-throated voice. When you obtain an unconstricted, breathy *ah,* repeat it several times.

The Counter.   Keep the same open, relaxed feeling, and with your sighing voice, count slowly up to five. Make sure that each number is said with the same open feeling (*three* and *five* seem frequently to produce constriction). Repeat this exercise until you can say each word with ease.

The Sitter.   Sit in a comfortable straight-backed chair and repeat the Counter. If you have a tendency to constrict somewhat in the new position, return to the Relaxer, the Yawner, and the Sigher before you go on. Do the exercises this time in the sitting position. Your goal, again, is to count to five in a sighing voice while maintaining vocal openness.

The Voicer.   Count to five again but in your full, optimal voice, and watch for evidence of constriction. If you have difficulty, do the Sitter again until you can make the full-voiced count with ease.

The Stander.   Repeat the Voicer in a standing position.

The Expander.   While standing, count to five again. Take a new breath (abdominal, remember), and count the rest of the way to ten. Be conscious of numbers that tend to cause constriction (especially *eight* and *nine*). Take a new breath and go on to fifteen, twenty, and so on, breathing after each five numbers, until you can reach a hundred while maintaining open phonation.

The satisfactory completion of these exercises is the first step in the achievement of vocal efficiency.

Exercises to Achieve and Strengthen Balanced Vocal Focus

Balanced vocal focus, the sensation of correct placement of vocal tone in the vocal tract, can be achieved through the following series of exercises. Concentrate on abdominal breathing and on open phonation as you do them.

The Ghost.   Phonate in your light vocal mode (the Mickey Mouse voice) and say the sound *oo*. Keep your loudness level soft; concentrate on keeping the vocal tract open and on using full voicing. Open and close your jaw slightly as you phonate. When the sound feels as though it were floating in the head, centered at the bridge of the nose, you will experience the sensation of balanced vocal focus.

The Balancer.   Concentrate on the balanced feeling, produce your light voice, and say *ah*. You may have to make several tries to get it. If you feel any constriction, go back to the Relaxer, the Yawner, and the Sigher again to fully establish the feeling of vocal openness, and repeat the Ghost.

The Balanced Counter.   Using your soft, light voice, count slowly from one to five. Concentrate on the feelings of openness and balanced focus. You may find that certain numbers cause a shift of focus, a change in openness, or both. Repeat the exercise until all numbers can be uttered consistently.

The Balanced Voicer.   In your optimal voice, produce the sound *ah*. Concentrate on the same feelings as those of the Balancer, and repeat several times. In your optimal voice, count slowly to five and maintain the same balanced feeling as before. Repeat the exercise several times.

The Balanced Expander.   In your optimal voice, slowly read the following limericks. Pause at the end of each line, take a new breath, and go on. Concentrate on maintaining the feeling of vocal balance.

> A gourmet dining in St. Lou
> Found quite a large mouse in his stew.
>   Said the waiter, "Don't shout
>   And wave it about,
> Or the rest will be wanting one too."

There was a young lady of Crete
Who was exceedingly neat.
    When she got out of bed
    She stood on her head
To make sure of not soiling her feet.

There was a young man from Kentuck
Who was always known for bad luck.
    When he bet on a horse,
    The result was, of course,
That the horse would get stuck in the muck.

There was an old person of Leeds,
And simple enough were his needs.
    Said he, "To save toil
    Growing things in the soil,
I'll just eat the packets of seeds."

The satisfactory completion of these exercises is the second step on the road to vocal efficiency.

An Exercise to Improve Vocal Fold Vibrance

This exercise is specifically for students whose voices demonstrate breathiness. If this is not your problem, go on to the following section, Exercises to Combine Openness, Balanced Focus, and Full Vibrance.

To improve vocal fold voicing, you need either a tape recorder or a willing listener to help you recognize the difference between your breathy voice and your full voice.

The Listener.   Produce a prolonged *ah* sound at moderate loudness while you record your voice or speak to your helper. The escape of air, which indicates breathiness, will be heard along with the vocal tone. Repeat the activity several times until you are able to identify these two elements in your voice—the tone and the rush of air.

Exercises to Combine Openness, Balanced Focus, and Full Vibrancy

With the ability to phonate in an efficient (open, balanced focus, fully vibrant) manner, you are ready to try your voice in a number of situations. The amount of effort required to phonate and the quantity of roughness in your voice should be as little as possible.

The Alphabetizer.   Say the letters of the alphabet slowly in your full voice. Watch for possible constriction, shift of focus, or breathiness on some letters. Say each letter slowly. Be aware of its sound and its feel before going on to the next.

The Calendar.   Recite the names of the days of the week and the months of the year. Again, go slowly, watching for instances of change in any of the characteristics.

The Reader.   From the selections in Chapter 11, choose a few of the shorter but more complex selections to read. Continue to concentrate on openness, focus, and voicing. Again, keep the rate slow at first; speed up only as you gain confidence in your ability to control the various elements of your voice.

The Talker.   Working for vocal efficiency, converse with several persons with whom you feel comfortable, especially members of your speech class. Ask your partners to help you recognize shifts in your old patterns.

With the ability to phonate continuously in your efficient voice, you should find little or no trace of roughness, and you are ready to work on the improvement of pitch and loudness problems. You may find it necessary, however, to refer back to these exercises frequently to maintain and strengthen your newly gained abilities.

The Full Voicer.   Concentrate on open, balanced focus phonation and produce louder and louder *ah* sounds while you record your voice or work with your helper. Unless you have a definite laryngeal problem, the rush of air should be heard to decrease markedly at some point in your loudness range. At that point you are fully voicing. As you repeat the *ah* sound at that loudness level, concentrate on the feeling as well as the sound of your voice. Then, keeping the same feel and sound, slowly reduce your loudness level. Listen carefully at each step for a return of the breathy sound. Should it appear, increase your loudness to the point at which you no longer hear it, and begin to lower your voice again. When you reach the conversational loudness level, repeat the fully voiced *ah* several times.

The Expander.   Return to the Expander (p. 36) and follow its instructions. If you can maintain your full voice throughout the count, you have achieved efficient voicing, and you are ready to extend your practice to conversational control.

Exercises to Improve Pitch

We have already discussed optimal and habitual pitch and their relation to your voice. The ideal voice, varying around its optimal pitch, will have a range of about one and a half octaves, with the optimal pitch located in the lower third (Figure 3.6). To determine how closely you approach the ideal, you first need to establish your pitch range, your current habitual pitch, and your optimal pitch.

Establishing Your Pitch Range.   The following procedure should be done with the aid of a piano, guitar, or other appropriate musical instrument. If these are not available, however, your professor or a classmate with a good musical ear can help you identify your pitch limits.

In your efficient voice, softly sing the *ah* at a comfortable pitch level. Starting from that point, sing the next lowest note on the musical scale. Continue singing

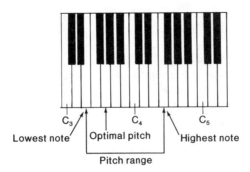

Figure 3.6. A typical vocal pitch range superimposed on the piano keyboard. The optimal pitch for this voice is approximately two keys (up the scale) from the lowest note.

downward, note by note, until you are unable to go lower without a decrease in efficiency. Then, beginning at that level, sing up the scale until you reach the highest note possible without a change in your vocal focus or openness. Count the total number of notes that you have produced. This represents your present pitch range. An eight- to twelve-note range is considered adequate for most speech purposes.

Establishing Your Optimal Pitch. In the evaluation of your voice, your professor may have indicated that your habitual pitch level was too high or too low. In either case you need to determine the pitch level most effective for your structure.

The Leveler. Read the following phrase in your optimal voice, at a comfortable loudness level: *a dozen doughnuts*. Repeat it several times, faster and faster each time. The faster you say it, the less pitch change there will be. Finally you will shift to a monotone. This is your present habitual pitch. Locate the position of this note on your total pitch range. If it is located approximately one fourth of the distance up from your lowest one, your optimal and habitual pitches are the same. You may skip ahead to the Range Stretcher.

The Optimizer. If your habitual pitch is in the upper half of your range or is on your first or second lowest note, you may wish to change to the pitch level best for your voice. To locate your optimal pitch, divide the number of notes in your pitch range by four. Count from the bottom of your range up to the number you calculated. That note is your optimal pitch. For example, if you have a twelve-note pitch range (one and a half octaves), the optimal pitch is the third note up from your lowest possible pitch.

The Optimal Counter. Using your optimal pitch (with abdominal breathing and open, balanced phonation, of course), practice counting from one to twenty. Repeat this several times. Then, as you count, vary your pitch with tones higher and lower than your optimal tone.

The Range Stretcher.   If your range is considered too narrow by your professor or if you wish to expand it for professional reasons, the following exercise is helpful.

1. Pick a note in the middle of your range and sing down to your lowest note. Repeat this action, but use a slightly breathy voice. You will probably be able to produce a lower note than before with no change in the critical vocal characteristics. Repeat this part of the exercise several times; then, in your full voice, try to reach the new low note. Repeat the entire exercise until no lower notes can be reached without a decrease in efficiency.

2. To extend your pitch range upward, follow the same procedure but reach for higher notes each time until you find the point at which you cannot do so without changes in openness or focus. When you reach the upper limit, you should then practice singing up and down your entire range several times a day.

3. Following practice in your singing voice, repeat the exercises in your talking voice, and explore the limits of your vocally efficient pitch range.

Exercises to Improve Loudness

Two problems are often noted with loudness:

1. Decreasing efficiency at high loudness levels.

2. Use of loudness levels are inappropriate for the situation—that is, talking too loudly or too softly.

This series of exercises is designed to help you make improvements in either of these areas if your professor has indicated a need.

Increasing the Number of Efficient Loudness Levels.   You are constantly required to change the loudness level of your voice. One minute you speak quietly to a friend in the library, and the next you shout across the athletic field. Later you try out for a part in a play just before you go to your job in a noisy pizza shop. Since there are so many levels of loudness you use each day, we have arbitrarily selected six, varying from very soft to loud, for purposes of discussion. They include:

1. Confidential conversation—the level you use if you do not want to be overheard while talking in a crowded room.

2. Quiet conversation—the level used when you talk with one to four persons under quiet conditions.

3. Classroom—the level needed to be easily heard by listeners in the back row of a typical classroom.

4. Large lecture hall—the level needed to be heard in all corners of a lecture hall.

5. Auditorium—the level required for speaking from the stage of an average-sized auditorium.

6. Large theater—the level required for speaking from the stage of a large, balconied theater, depending upon accoustical differences.

You may have noticed that in certain situations your voice tends to constrict, especially when you have to speak loudly. You may have noticed that you lose vocal tract balance as well. In fact, without training, most persons are able to maintain vocal efficiency only in a relatively narrow range of pitch and loudness levels. Some will experience vocal constriction and loss of balanced focus when trying to be heard in a classroom, especially at high or low pitch levels. More will have problems in a large lecture hall. Almost all, without training, will experience difficulty in larger structures—that is, at higher loudness levels. The farther you are from your optimal pitch and the louder you speak, the more likely you will lose focus and become constricted.

The ideal voice is able to maintain vocal openness and balanced focus over a wide range of pitch and loudness levels. It can respond efficiently regardless of the demands placed upon it. The typical speaker may show relatively efficient phonation at soft loudness levels but break down at the louder.

The Loudness Stretcher.   Your loudest efficient pitch level is now your optimal pitch. Use it to phonate the sound *ah* at confidential conversation loudness. Then produce louder and louder *ah* sounds until you feel yourself beginning to constrict or to change focus. At this level you have reached your loudness barrier. Back off two or three levels and then increase your loudness again, in smaller steps this time. Concentrate on the feelings of efficiency (especially on any increase in effort) as you slowly approach your loudness barrier, and try to move beyond it. You may need several trials before you succeed. Continue this process until you reach the greatest loudness level important to your needs. In most cases you will be surprised at the levels at which you can remain vocally efficient.

		LOUDNESS LEVELS				
		Confidential Conversation	*Quiet Convesation*	*Classroom*	*Large Lecture Hall*	*Auditorium*	*Large Theatre*
P	12						
I	11				vocal tract		
T	10				constriction		
C	9						
H	8		vocal				
	7		efficiency		change in		
L	6				vocal-tract focus		
E	5						
V	4	approximate region optimal pitch					
E	3						
L	2						
	1						

Figure 3.7   Pitch, loudness, and constriction in an untrained voice. (Adapted from Perkins, 1971, 1977.)

You may have difficulty in one aspect of this exercise—increasing loudness without increasing pitch. The use of a recording machine or a friend to monitor your voice helps guard against the tendency to increase pitch along with loudness.

The Loudness Extender. Once you have mastered this technique at your optimal pitch, you can extend your control over loudness to higher and lower levels. Be certain not to exercise for periods longer than a few minutes, particularly at first. You will be practicing at the extreme limits of your voice, and the chances of overworking it are high. Should you feel strain at any time, stop. Rest your voice for a while; then, using some of the basic breathing and constriction-reducing exercises, slowly work back to this exercise set.

You will find that there are certain times of the day and even periods of several days when you cannot seem to make any progress. Remember that your voice is a mirror of your emotional state. When you find yourself tired, uptight, irritated, or worried, the chances are good that your voice will suffer. Exercises designed to push your voice to its limits are very difficult, if not impossible, to do under these conditions. At such times, concentrate on efficiency at low loudness levels and wait until you are more in shape to continue practicing. It is also unwise to exercise with a cold, a sore throat, or any other irritation that affects your vocal mechanism.

The Loudness Controller. When you are able to say *ah* efficiently throughout your pitch and loudness ranges, extend your control to other activities by means of further practice of the exercises to combine openness, balanced focus, and voicing. This time, however, perform the tasks at all pitch and loudness levels.

The Loudness Adjuster. You use your voice in many situations each day. Use a recorder or a friend to determine how loud you need to be for the situations most important to you. Place the recording microphone or the friend at the distance you want your voice to carry. The distance, of course, varies with the situation for which you are practicing. Experiment with different loudness levels until you are satisfied that you have the right one for that distance. Then practice reading and talking at that level until you have a feel for the required loudness. Repeat this exercise for as many loudness levels as you need to use.

The Signaler. With a classmate, arrange a set of hand signals—one for "make it louder," one for "make it softer," and one for "okay." In your speech class or in other situations, adjust your voice until you obtain the "okay" sign, and then work to maintain that level.

SUMMARY

In this chapter we have discussed eight vocal characteristics—pitch, loudness, vocal fold mode, vocal tract dimension, vocal fold vibrancy, vocal tract focus, vocal fold contact, and vocal effect. Vocal tract openness and vocal tract focus along with vocal fold vibrancy are key factors in determining vocal efficiency. An open, balanced, full voice is the goal.

Exercises and practice material have been provided for the improvement of each vocal characteristic. As you strengthen your voice and expand your ability to use many pitch and loudness levels without increasing vocal effort, you will achieve the best voice of which you are capable. You may not wish to become a performer or to use your voice professionally, but with the speech mechanism you possess, you can develop an efficient voice that will meet any requirement you set for it.

4

Resonation

At the beginning of Chapter 3, we referred to the many types of human voices, some pleasant and some not. We indicated that many voice differences result from variations among the eight vocal characteristics (Chapter 2). This does not, however, account for all the variety of voices. Compare, for example, the voice of the typical radio or television announcer with that of a Lily Tomlin-like telephone operator. The first appears to be rich and full, while the second sounds as though it were produced in the nose. These and other vocal qualities are determined by *resonation, the selective amplification and reinforcement of the vocal tone.

The following topics will be covered in this chapter.

1. The process of resonation.

2. Resonance in the vocal tract.

3. Problems of resonation.

4. Exercises to improve resonation.

THE PROCESS OF RESONATION

Resonant Frequency

The process of resonation can best be understood by considering a familiar activity— blowing across the top of a bottle to produce a kind of whistling sound. When you blow, some of the air enters the bottle and pushes against the air already there. The air in the bottle is compressed. When the compression effect reaches the bottom of the bottle, the air is bounced back to the top; meanwhile, more air continues to be blown in. A series of pressure changes is thus set up in the bottle and is transferred to the outside air. The number of pressure changes per second (or the frequency of vibration) depends on the amount of time it takes for the compression to reach the bottom of the bottle and bounce back again. The shorter and narrower the bottle, the more rapid the bounce and, therefore, the higher the frequency. The vibration rate of a particular bottle is termed its *resonant frequency*.

Amplification and Reinforcement in Resonation

There are many sizes and shapes of resonators besides bottles. You probably are familiar with those of various stringed instruments, such as the guitar, the violin, or the banjo. The sound of each of these depends on the vibration of strings and the size and shape of the "box" to which they are attached. If a string were removed from a guitar, stretched tightly between two points, and plucked, you would hear a very soft tone. When the string is attached to the guitar, however, its sound is much louder. This difference is an effect of the guitar body, essentially a box with a hole cut in the top across which the string is stretched. As the string vibrates over the hole, it causes the air surrounding it to vibrate. This causes the air within the guitar body to vibrate as well (as in the example of the bottle). Because the sides of the guitar body are hard, these vibrations bounce back and forth within the structure. This bouncing around of sound waves within the guitar is communicated to the surrounding air by the vibration of the surface areas of the instrument, creating a much louder tone than the string plucked alone. The sound of the string is amplified, or made stronger, by the *resonant effect* of the guitar body.

Overtones in Resonation

Few vibrating objects produce pure tones. Most produce a basic or *fundamental tone* accompanied by *overtones*. An overtone is any multiple of the fundamental tone or frequency. A string vibrating at a frequency of 100 Hz, for example, would have overtones of 200 Hz, 300 Hz, 400 Hz, and so on. The overtones are produced because of the inability of most objects to vibrate smoothly. Most wiggle and shake in a variety of ways depending on their length, thickness, and shape. The resultant sound is called a *complex tone,* a combination of the fundamental frequency and its overtones. Since in general the fundamental frequency is much louder than its overtones, it is what we perceive.

Selection in Resonation

When a complex tone is presented to a resonator, both the fundamental frequency and the overtones are affected. A large resonator amplifies the lower overtones; a small resonator strengthens the higher ones. Consider again the stringed instruments. The size and shape of a guitar affect the overtones amplified when a string is plucked; even when the same note is played, a guitar and a ukulele sound quite different because of the overtones each is designed to resonate. The same complex tone presented to three differently sized and shaped resonators will result in three different sounds, because each will *select* those overtones that correspond to its resonant frequency to amplify and reinforce. Thus, resonation is the *selective amplification and reinforcement of a tone.*

RESONANCE IN THE VOCAL TRACT

In the human vocal tract, resonation takes place within the three airways through which the vocal tone passes: the throat, the mouth, and the nasal passages (Figure 4.1).

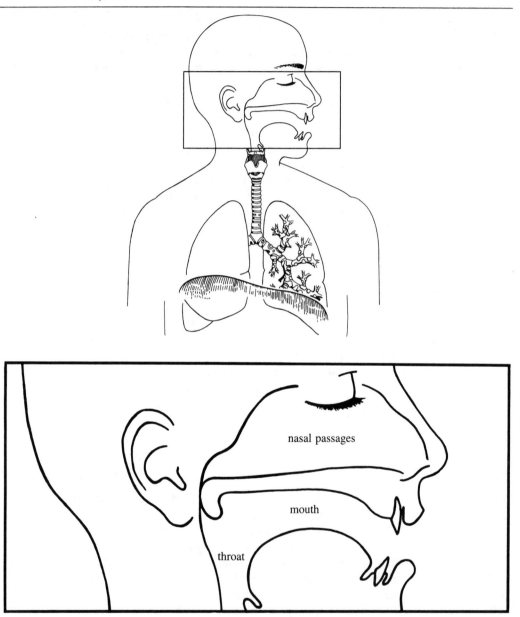

Figure 4.1   The resonators.

Throat Resonation

The throat (pharynx) lies just above the larynx and generates the initial resonation of vocal fold vibrations. When the interior and exterior throat muscles are relaxed, the airway is open wide and the inner surface is soft; the resonated tone is rich in low overtones. When the throat muscles are tense, the airway is narrower and its surface is harder; higher overtones are resonated more readily. Other than through relaxation and tongue positioning, we are able to exert little control over the dimensions of the throat and its resonance. When the vocal tract is open wide and vocal focus is balanced, throat resonance is ideal.

Mouth Resonation

In contrast to the throat, we have much greater control over the mouth and its resonance. Jaw and lip openings and tongue movements are infinitely variable. As with the throat, the lower overtones are emphasized when the mouth is more open than closed and also *when the tongue is more forward than back*. Here, too, the ideal resonance condition is obtained with the vocal tract open wide and vocal focus balanced.

Nasal Resonance

The nasal passages also serve as resonators. The sounds *m, n,* and *ng,* in fact, are emitted through the nose rather than the mouth.

The nose is the least variable of the resonators in that we have no control over the size and shape of the passageways. The amount of nasal resonance normally is governed by the action of the soft palate. If it is raised toward the back wall of the throat, most of the vocal tone passes through the mouth (see the diagram for the nonnasal sound of *ah,* in Chapter 6). If the soft palate is lowered, the sound can pass through both the nose and mouth at the same time. If the mouth is also blocked, the sound is emitted through the nose only (see the diagrams for the nasal sounds in Chapter 8). As in throat and mouth resonance, nasal resonance is best with the vocal tract open wide and vocal focus balanced. Balanced focus, in fact, allows a certain amount of nasal resonance on all sounds, providing the clearest of vocal tones.

RESONANCE PROBLEMS

The achievement of vocal tract openness and balanced focus usually results in effective resonance as well. Certain problems of resonance are persistent, however, and may require special attention. These include *jaw closure, tongue retraction, denasality,* and *nasality.*

Jaw Closure

Definite jaw openings are associated with each sound we articulate. If the mouth is not opened widely enough, especially during the production of vowel sounds, the resonant effect of the mouth is reduced and that of the nasal passages tends to be increased.

Tongue Retraction

Pulling the tongue back toward the throat, *tongue retraction,* leads to a resonance problem that is closely allied with unbalanced vocal focus. It deflects sound waves coming up from the larynx, reducing loudness. The voice feels trapped in the throat. Additionally, tension in the muscles that pull the tongue back may pull down on the soft palate, thus increasing nasal resonance.

Denasality

If there is no nasal resonance, the sounds *m, n,* and *ng* will seem more like *b, d,* and *g,* respectively; the voice will sound dull and flat. This quality may be the result of a physical problem such as a cold, the flu, or an allergy or a growth in the nasal passages. It can also occur when the soft palate is too high and tight against the back wall of the throat during speech or singing.

Nasality

With too much nasal resonance, sounds seem to be spoken through the nose. There are three types of nasality: (1) *general nasality,* in which all speech and singing are produced with excessive nasal resonance; (2) *nasal emission,* in which the flow of air through the nose is audible, especially on sounds like *sh, s, p, b, t,* and *d;* and (3) *assimilation nasality*, in which sounds are nasalized when they occur next to those that are normally nasal (i.e., *m, n,* and *ng*).

RESONANCE EXERCISES

Following are exercises designed to improve the resonance of your voice.

Exercises to Increase Oral Resonance

The following exercises are to free the action of the lower jaw and to allow for increased mouth opening during phonation.

The Chewer. Look in a mirror. With your head held erect, open your mouth widely, without forcing it. As it comes to a fully open position, say the sound *ah.* Observe the action of your tongue. If it stays mostly flat but is slightly raised in the back, you are moving it correctly. If it appears to be high in the back of your mouth, your mouth resonance will be poor. Flatten the tongue as much as possible as you say *ah*. Keep the tongue as flat as possible and begin a chewing action, as though you were starting a large piece of gum. As your mouth reaches its widest point for each chew, phonate the sound *ah*.

Concentrate on keeping the tongue as low in the mouth as possible as you perform the rest of these exercises.

The Chewing Counter.   Now repeat the chewing action while counting from one to five. Time your words so that you say the stressed vowel as your mouth reaches the full open position. Say: *o*ne, tw*o*, thr*ee*, and so on. Repeat this exercise several times.

Try "chewing" the days of the week in the same manner. As with the numbers, let your mouth come fully open on the stressed part of the word, for example— M*o*nday, T*ue*sday, W*e*dnesday. Do the same with the months of the year—J*a*nuary, F*e*bruary, M*a*rch, and so on.

The Reader.   Turn to page 85 and read the *ah* words listed there. Let your jaw open as you say the *ah* sound in these words, and allow your tongue, jaw, and lips to move only to make the other sounds. If you find yourself closing on the *ah* sound, place two fingers between your upper and lower front teeth to maintain an adequate opening.

Next, turn to the exercises for the sound *p* in Chapter 8. As you say the words, make certain that your mouth opens as you say the stressed vowel. Repeat this exercise with the *b*, *t*, *d*, *k*, and *g* sounds also in Chapter 8.

Turn to the collections of nursery rhymes and limericks in Chapter 11. As you read each of them, watch yourself in a mirror to ensure that your jaw opens easily for the vowel sounds in each word.

Expand your abilities by further reading and conversation practice.

Tongue Retraction Exercises

The Chewer II.   Repeat the Chewer I and concentrate on producing a forward and downward action of your tongue.

The Expander.   Count from one to a hundred as in the Chewing Counter, described earlier. Again, concentrate on forward tongue placement.

The Reader II.   Read the word lists on pages 73, 75, 77, and 79. The vowels in these words tend·to pull the tongue forward, Then, concentrating on the forward movement, read from the lists of pages 89, 91, and 93, which contain vowels that tend to pull the tongue back.

Watch yourself in a mirror for evidence of tongue retraction as you read from the sections of nursery rhymes and limericks in Chapter 11.

Improve your abilities at forward tongue placement by reading aloud from various selections in Chapter 11.

Denasality Exercises

If your professor has indicated that you have a problem with denasality, and if there are no physical or medical factors causing it, the following exercises are designed to help you alleviate it.

The Hummer.   Place the fingers of one hand on the bridge of your nose, and hum. Feel the vibration that is transmitted through the nose to your fingertips. Now open your mouth, look into a mirror, and produce the *ng* sound while you watch the back wall of your throat. You should see the soft palate somewhat low in the mouth and resting on the back of the tongue. As you watch, shift to the sound *ah*. You should observe that the tongue lowers and the soft palate rises. Repeat this action several times and concentrate on the sensations involved in lowering and raising the soft palate.

The Clouder.   To recognize when you are speaking through your nose and to correct the problem, you will find a small hand-held mirror invaluable. Refrigerate it for a few moments—long enough so that it clouds when you breathe on it. Place the cold mirror under your nose, against your upper lip. Hum (the sound *m*), and as you do, be certain that the mirror clouds. Do the same with the sounds *n* and *ng*. Try to feel the lowering action of the soft palate.

Turn to the exercise section of Chapter 8 for the three nasal sounds. Using the cold mirror, read the lists of nasal words. Make certain that the mirror clouds for the three sounds whenever they occur.

The Reader III.   Turn to the paired list in the Comparer exercise prescribed for assimilation nasality. Repeat each pair and be conscious of the difference between them. Using a recorder or a mirror, or working with a listener can help you note the particular words that cause difficulty. Repeat the exercise until you can produce all nasal sounds accurately.

Read the following nursery rhymes. Be certain to nasalize all *m*, *n*, and *ng* sounds.

> Mary had a little lamb.
>> Its fleece was white as snow,
> And everywhere that Mary went
>> The lamb was sure to go.
> It followed her to school one day,
>> Which was against the rule.
> It made the children laugh and play
>> To see a lamb at school.

> Little Tommy Tucker
>> Sings for his supper.
> What shall we give him?
>> White bread and butter.

Pussy Cat, Pussy Cat,
    Where have you been?
I've been up to London
    To look at the queen.
Pussy Cat, Pussy Cat,
    What did you there?
I frightened a little mouse
    Under her chair.

Jack be nimble.
    Jack be quick.
Jack jump over
  The candlestick.

Doctor Foster went to Gloucester
    In a shower of rain.
He stepped in a puddle up to his middle
    And never went there again.

Mary, Mary, quite contrary
    How does your garden grow?
With silver bells and cockleshells
    And pretty maids all in a row.

A diller, a dollar, a ten o'clock scholar.
    Why do you come so soon?
You used to come at ten o'clock,
    But now you come at noon.

Hickory, dickory, dock,
    The mouse ran up the clock,
The clock struck one;
    The mouse ran down.
Hickory, dickory, dock.

Hey diddle, diddle,
    The cat and the fiddle,
The cow jumped over the moon.
    The little dog laughed
To see such sport,
    And the dish ran away with the spoon.

The Talker.   Converse with a friend, using prearranged hand signals to indicate proper nasalization of the *m*, *n*, and *ng* sounds. Work until all of the nasal words receive the "okay" sign.

General Nasality Exercises

Use the cold mirror for the following exercises.

The Clouder II.   Place the mirror edgewise under your nose. Press it against your upper lip and exhale through your nose. You should see the mirror become cloudy directly under your nostrils.

The Lifter.   To improve the action of the soft palate so as to reduce nasality, you need to observe its action. In a mirror, watch the back wall of your throat as you breathe in and out through your nose. You will note that the back of the tongue is raised and the soft palate lowered. Then whisper the sound *ah*. You should see the soft palate lift and the tongue lower. Practice this action several times and concentrate on the sensation of movement of the palate.

The Raiser.   Place a cold mirror under your nose. Whisper the sound *p* while you concentrate on the feeling of raising the soft palate. The mirror should remain clear. If it does not, repeat the preceding exercise several times, and then try again. You may produce some clouding of the mirror at soft volume. If it does not clear at louder levels, you may need to consult with your professor before you proceed further. Use the mirror to check yourself on the remaining exercises.

The Contraster.   The following list contrasts nasal with nonnasal words. As you pronounce each pair, you should feel the air being emitted through the mouth for the nonnasal word and through the nose for the nasal one.

pay	may	dial	Nile
bet	met	cap	nap
bill	mill	coat	note
tap	nap	gas	mass
toll	knoll	gold	mold

The Worder.   The following words have no nasal sounds in them. As you say each word, concentrate on the action of your soft palate. Use a mirror to check for unwanted nasal resonance.

pack	bad	talk	dash	kick	gas
pie	bit	tell	did	cold	give
pot	boy	toast	dive	curve	gold

The Reader IV.   This exercise should be done with a recording machine, the cold mirror, or a willing listener to detect any instances of nasality. The following sentences contain no nasal sounds. Listen to your recording, watch the mirror, or consult your helper to find instances of nasality in your reading. Repeat this exercise until you can produce each word in a nonnasal manner.

1. Polly put out the cat.
2. Bills are paid with cash.
3. Ducks dive to catch fish.
4. Ruth's chocolate cake was delicious.
5. Pile all this paper by the back of the garage.
6. Give that girl eight quarts of Dr. Pepper.
7. I have left the car to be repaired.

The same instructions apply to the reading of the following nonnasal paragraph.

> Pete, a traffic cop, directed cars carefully. He saw a driver circle the block where he stood. She looked troubled. He stopped to ask her what the difficulty was. She said that she wished to get to the freeway but that she was lost. He showed her the way. A little later, she was back. He asked her if she was still lost. She said that the freeway was blocked. Pete looked to see which way she drove. "That's a real goof, lady," he said, "You've tried to get to the freeway through the driveway of a pizzeria."

If you do well with this paragraph, try reading the following selections. Underline all the words with the nasal sounds *m*, *n*, and *ng*. As you read, be careful with these sounds, since they can let you slide back into nasal production. At first, read almost word by word. Increase your reading rate as you gain confidence.

> I met a traveller from an antique land
> Who said, "Two vast and trunkless legs of stone
> Stand in the desert. Near them, on the sand,
> Half sunk, a shattered visage lies, whose frown,
> And wrinkled lip, and sneer of cold command,
> Tell that its sculptor well those passions read
> Which yet survive, stamped on these lifeless things.
> The hand that mocked them, and the heart that fed;
> And on the pedestal these words appear:
> 'My name is Ozymandias, king of kings;
> Look on my works, ye Mighty, and despair!'
> Nothing beside remains. Round the decay
> Of that colossal wreck, boundless and bare,
> The lone and level sands stretch far away."
>
>   Percy Bysshe Shelley

> How sweet the moonlight sleeps upon this bank!
> Here will we sit, and let the sounds of music
> Creep in our ears; soft stillness and the night
> Become the touches of sweet harmony.
> Sit, Jessica; look how the floor of heaven
> Is thick inlaid with patines of bright gold;
> There's not the smallest orb which thou behold'st,

But in his motion like an angel sings,
Still quiring to the young-eyed cherubins;
Such harmony is in immortal souls.
But whilst this muddy vesture of decay
Doth grossly close it in, we cannot hear it . . .

William Shakespeare

But as for certain truth, no man has known it,
Nor will he know it; neither of the gods,
Nor yet of all the things of which I speak.
And even if by chance he were to utter
Finality, he would himself not know it;
For all is but a woven web of guesses.

Xenophanes

We are the music-makers,
     And we are the dreamers of dreams,
Wandering by the lone sea-breakers,
     And sitting by desolate streams
World-losers and world-forsakers,
     On whom the pale moon gleams—
Yet we are the movers and shakers
     Of the world forever, it seems.
With wonderful deathless ditties
We build up the world's great cities.
     And out of a fabulous story
     We fashion an empire's glory;
One man with a dream, at pleasure,
     Shall go forth and conquer a crown;
And three with a new song's measure
     Can trample a kingdom down.

Arthur O'Shaughnessy

Assimilation Nasality Exercises

Your professor may have indicated that you have a problem with assimilation nasality. Some persons who have little trouble with general nasality and others who have conquered it have difficulty with vowel sounds that are close to nasal ones. For example, when you say the word *much,* your soft palate is lowered for the nasal *m.* It must then be raised for the *uch* part of the word. If the lifting action is slow, the vowel *u* is partially nasalized. Similarly, when you say the word *wrong* and you lower the soft palate early for the *ng* sound, the vowel *o* is affected.

The Comparer.   This exercise is designed to help you recognize words in which you nasalize vowels that are next to nasal consonants. As you read the following lists, note that the first member of each pair of words has no nasal sounds. The vowel in it and the vowel in the following nasal word should be made to sound alike. As in other exercises, the use of a recorder, a mirror, or a listener is helpful in noting the words with which you have difficulty. Repeat this exercise until all the vowels sound nonnasal.

bat	mat	cubbing	coming	cub	come
base	mace	ribbing	rimming	dub	dumb
bad	mad	lubing	looming	sub	some
bud	mud	raiding	raining	bird	burn
debt	net	rubbing	running	dub	done
dear	near	tugging	tonguing	hag	hang
dice	nice	wigging	winging	sag	sang
dough	know	bagging	banging	wig	wing

The Reader V. The following sentences are loaded with nasal sounds. As you read the sentences, follow the instructions for the Comparer. Repeat the sentences several times until you can produce all the vowels in a nonnasal manner.

1. My manager makes an unusual number of mistakes.
2. Many mighty men will run in the Olympic games.
3. Ann never notices the number of nickels in her change purse.
4. The newspaper salesman never comes near my home.
5. It makes me angry when no one listens to me.
6. Abraham Lincoln made most Americans notice their need for freedom.
7. The more fences we make, the more fences we mend.
8. Nervous Nelly needed nine driving exams to become licensed.
9. Florence Nightingale made nursing an outstanding profession.
10. When fishing, never tangle your lines into knots.

Using the preceding instructions, read the following paragraph, and work to avoid the nasalization of the vowels.

Nelly, the nervous nurse, worked evenings at Memorial Hospital. She never went there hungry, however, for she was a nut candy muncher. All night long, she munched on nut candy. If candy didn't contain nuts, Nelly wouldn't nibble on even the tiniest chunk. One evening, Manny, the manager of the candy emporium whence Nelly normally obtained her candy, was absent. His business wasn't open. Nelly became twice as nervous that night, for without her candy, her nerves naturally became jumpy. Nelly made more mistakes in ten minutes than any nurse had made since Memorial Hospital opened. Nelly was sent home and told never to return without her nut candy again.

Nasal Emission Exercises

Nasal emission occurs when nonnasal consonants are produced partially through the nose. Sometimes they are accompanied by a snortlike sound.

Problems with nasal emission are rare. For students whose professors have indicated that they have such a problem, however, these exercises will be of value. These exercises will help you to recognize when you nasalize consonants.

The Clouder III.   Place a cold mirror edgewise under your nose, against your upper lip. Whisper the sound *p*. If the mirror clouds, you are emitting part of the sound through your nose and need to work with the Lifter and the Raiser exercises prescribed for general nasality. If you cannot reduce the problem by means of this procedure, consult your professor.

Still using the mirror, read the following list of words and watch for evidence of clouding as you produce the consonants.

pay	tie	kick	see	ship	chop
pie	top	cave	sold	shell	chair
put	taste	cry	suit	shadow	chip
big	day	good	zebra	treasure	jazz
box	date	gravy	zoo	pleasure	joy
baby	dish	guys	zero	garage	judge

The Reader VI.   Still using the mirror, read the Contraster exercise for general nasality. Be certain that the mirror clouds for the nasal sound in each pair and remains clear for the nonnasal one.

Still using the mirror, read the Comparer exercise for assimilation nasality. Repeat it until you can produce all consonants except the *m*, *n*, and *ng* sounds without nasality.

Go through the rest of the exercises prescribed for general nasality and assimilation nasality. Concentrate on producing all consonants except the nasals through the mouth.

SUMMARY

The process of resonation, the selective amplification and reinforcement of the vocal tone, affects the complex sound produced by the process of phonation. The "bouncing around" of sound waves strengthens certain overtones and weakens others. You sound the way you do partly because of the size and shape of your resonators but mostly because of what you do with them.

Resonance problems, such as jaw closure, tongue retraction, denasality, and nasality have been discussed and exercises for their correction presented. The primary purpose for the exercises has been to strengthen the resonance of lower overtones and to control the activity of the soft palate.

5

Fundamentals
of Articulation

Each of the sounds of Standard American English is produced differently. The purpose of this chapter is to describe how each sound is formed and to provide you with activities that will help you produce them accurately.

A century ago, it was believed that sounds were articulated in fixed, static positions (Jesperson 1889). Modern fluoroscopic motion pictures of the speech organs, however, demonstrate that articulation is functional: the position for each sound is fairly consistent from utterance to utterance and from person to person, but it is influenced by several variables.

1. Variations in physical structure among persons require different articulatory adjustments for them to produce the same sound.
2. The articulation of any sound is affected by that of the sounds that precede and follow it.
3. Persons tend to show variations in their articulatory positions under different emotional states and different social situations.

Despite variations in articulation, speech sounds have enough in common to allow each to be described. A given sound can be produced differently in various contexts and by different people, but the similarities of different articulations far outweigh the dissimilarities. As you proceed, you should know that not all combinations of sounds are discussed. However, if you learn to produce each of the ones described in the following chapters to your professor's satisfaction, you will be on the road to accurate articulation.

ANATOMY OF ARTICULATION

The primary speech organs in the articulation of sounds are found in the oral cavity (mouth), the pharynx (throat) and larynx (voice box).

Description

Lips: Fleshy, muscular folds of tissue, surrounding the exterior of the mouth. For articulating sounds, they can spread, round, and purse.

Teeth: Bonelike, enameled structures, rooted in the upper and lower jaws. Principally used for biting and chewing, they serve as surfaces against which the tongue directs the breath stream. Most important are the upper front teeth.

Tongue: The large, fleshy, muscular structure reaching from the front of the lower jaw to the larynx. Capable of considerable variation in size and shape, it is the most important organ of articulation. For discussion and convenience, we have divided it into five areas:

1. Tip: The front edge of the tongue.
2. Blade: The top surface of the tongue, just behind the tip.
3. Front: The area of the tongue immediately behind the blade.
4. Center: The middle area of the tongue.
5. Back: The area of the tongue closest to the throat.

Hard Palate: The bony part of the roof of the mouth. It is typically divided into two areas:

1. Front Palate: The area immediately behind the gum ridge.
2. Central Palate: The area between the front palate and soft palate.

Soft Palate: The muscular structure behind the hard palate.

Gum Ridge: The portion of the upper gum protruding behind the upper front teeth.

Lower Jaw: The hinged lower framework of the mouth. In articulation it determines the size of the mouth opening.

Glottis: The space between the vocal folds.

CLASSIFICATION OF SOUNDS

For purposes of discussion, we have classified the sounds of Standard American English into the following, somewhat traditional, groups.

1. By type, denoting the manner of articulation
   a. Vowels such as ē, [i]
   b. Diphthongs such as ī, [aɪ]
   c. Consonants such as p, [p]
2. By tongue position
   a. By the part of the mouth in which the tongue is at its highest point
      1) High such as o͞o, [u]
      2) Mid such as ŭ, [ʌ]
      3) Low such as ä, [a]
   b. By the part of the tongue that is raised
      1) Front such as ĭ, [ɪ]
      2) Central such as ûr, [ɝ]
      3) Back such as ô, [ɔ]

3. By place of articulation (Figure 5.1), that is, by the body parts that approximate
   or contact to produce particular sounds
   a. Lip to lip such as m, [m]
   b. Lip to teeth such as f, [f]
   c. Tongue tip to teeth such as *th*, [ð]
   d. Tongue tip to gum ridge such as l, [l]
   e. Tongue blade to front palate such as sh, [s]
   f. Tongue center to central palate such as r, [r]
   g. Back of tongue to soft palate such as k, [k]
   h. Glottis such as h, [h]

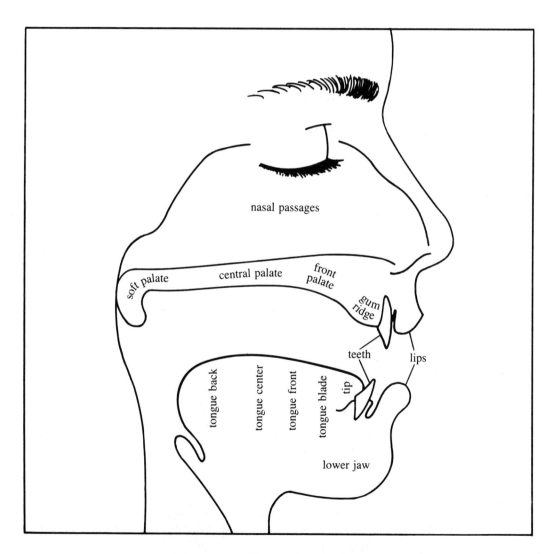

Figure 5.1   Places of articulation.

4. By mode of air emission, that is, by the modifications of the breath stream required to produce the intended sounds
   a. Stop-plosives such as t, [t]
   b. Fricatives such as s, [s]
   c. Affricates such as j, [dz]
   d. Glide such as hw, [ʍ]
   e. Glide such as y, [j]
   f. Lateral such as l, [l]
   g. Nasal such as ng, [ŋ]
5. By the voicing
   a. Voiceless such as th, [θ]
   b. Voiced such as v, [v]

We have used all these classifications in the succeeding chapters. Vowels, diphthongs, and consonants each have their own chapter, which indicates the strong distinction among these three types of sounds. The classifications of tongue positions and heights applies to vowels and diphthongs; the classifications of place of articulation, mode of air emission, and voicing apply to consonants. Carefully study the figures indicating the various sounds as they appear in the following chapters until you fully understand why each sound is classified the way it is. Such understanding will aid you in acquiring clear articulation.

DIACRITIC AND PHONETIC SYMBOLS

The English language contains more sounds than letters. Some letters, therefore, have multiple sounds. This has made it difficult for us to learn to spell and pronounce words easily. For example, notice the difference in the pronunciation of the underlined letters in these words:

though	face
through	fast
cough	father
enough	fall
bough	many
brought	about

You hear six different pronunciations of *ough* and six variations of *a* in these words.

Try pronouncing this new word: *ghoc*. It is pronounced *fish*. How? By pronouncing the letters as they are said in the following words: "Laughing women appreciate." Even the most basic study of English proves that spelling and pronunciation are often not directly related.

In order to represent the sounds of American English, various symbol systems have been devised. The most exact is the International Phonetic Alphabet (IPA), which consists of many familiar letters plus some unfamiliar symbols. The IPA is used by phoneticians, dialecticians, and linguists. It contains all the sounds of all spoken languages and delineates precisely the sounds of English.

Most American dictionaries use diacritic symbol systems that contain the familiar letters of the alphabet plus diacritic markings. Some of the commonest diacritic symbol systems are listed in Table 5.1.

Table 5.1 Diacritic and Phonetic Symbols

		International Phonetic Alphabet	American Heritage	Longman Dictionary of American English	Funk and Wagnall's	American College	Webster's New World
Vowels	bee	[i]	ē	iʸ	ē	ē	ē
	pit	[ɪ]	ĭ	ɪ	i	ĭ	i
	rotate	[e]	ā	eʸ	—	—	—
	pet	[ɛ]	ĕ	ɛ	e	ĕ	e
	pat	[æ]	ă	æ	a	ă	a
	father	[ɑ]	ä	ɑ	ä	ä	ä
	hot	[ɒ]	ŏ	ɔ	ŏ	ŏ	—
	caught	[ɔ]	ô	—	ô	ô	ô
	obey	[o]	ō	oʷ	o	—	—
	took	[ʊ]	o͝o	ʊ	o͝o	o͝o	oo
	boot	[u]	o͞o	uʷ	o͞o	o͞o	o͞o
	urge	ɝ	ûr	ɝr	û(r)	ûr	ʉr
	butter	[ɚ]	ər	ər	ər	ər	ər
	cut	[ʌ]	ŭ	ʌ	u	ŭ	u
	about	[ə]	ə	ə	ə	ə	ə
	vowel + r						
	care	—	âr	ɛər	—	—	—
	pier	—	îr	ɪər	—	—	—
Diphthongs	pay	[eɪ]	ā	—	ā	ā	ā
	pie	[ɑɪ]	ī	aɪ	ī	ī	ī
	noise	[ɔɪ]	oi	ɔɪ	oi	oi	oi
	out	[ɑʊ]	ou	aʊ	ou	ou	ou
	toe	[oʊ]	ō	—	ō	ō	ō
Consonants	pop	[p]	p	p	p	p	p
	bib	[b]	b	b	b	b	b
	tight	[t]	t	t	t	t	t
	deed	[d]	d	d	d	d	d
	kick	[k]	k	k	k	k	k
	gag	[g]	g	g	g	g	g
	fife	[f]	f	f	f	f	f
	valve	[v]	v	v	v	v	v
	thin	[θ]	th	θ	th	th	th
	this	[ð]	*th*	ð	t̶h	t̶h	*th*

Table 5.1 Diacritic and Phonetic Symbols (continued)

		International Phonetic Alphabet	American Heritage	Longman Dictionary of American English	Funk and Wagnall's	American College	Webster's New World
Consonants (continued)	sauce	[s]	s	s	s	s	s
	zebra	[z]	z	z	z	z	z
	ship	[ʃ]	sh	ʃ	sh	sh	sh
	vision	[ʒ]	zh	ʒ	zh	zh	zh
	hat	[h]	h	h	h	h	h
	church	[tʃ]	ch	tʃ	ch	ch	ch
	judge	[dʒ]	j	dʒ	j	j	j
	which	[ʍ]	hw	hw	hw	hw	hw
	with	[w]	w	w	w	w	w
	yes	[j]	y	y	y	y	y
	roar	[r]	r	r	r	r	r
	lid	[l]	l	l	l	l	l
	mum	[m]	m	m	m	m	m
	nine	[n]	n	n	n	n	n
	thing	[ŋ]	ng	ŋ	ng	ng	ŋ

For this text we have selected the diacritic symbols used in the American Heritage Dictionary (AHD) and the phonetic symbols of the IPA. Notice that the AHD system is very similar to that of the American College Dictionary.

To talk about sounds, you must know the names of the symbols. If you use diacritic symbols, you need to be familiar with their markings. Each marking has a name, as follows:

- ‾ is called a macron
- ˘ is called a breve
- ¨ is called an umlaut
- ^ is called a circumflex

Thus, the symbol ī may be called "i macron," ŏ may be called "o breve," and ä may be called "a umlaut."

CLEAR ARTICULATION

Three conditions must be fulfilled to articulate clearly.

1. The sound must be accurately formed.
2. The sound must be sufficiently supported by the breath.
3. The sound must be completely finished.

Movement of any of the parts of the speech mechanism affects the total sound. Since it is often difficult to feel physical action, we encourage you to look in a mirror while you practice, so that you can see your various articulatory positions, and to touch the articulators, if possible, to experience their mobility.

Accurate Formation

The formation of each sound is described in detail in Chapters 6 through 8. It is essential that these descriptions be followed as closely as possible when you practice them. To say *d* accurately, for example, the tongue tip must fully and firmly close with the gum ridge. Anything less than full closure produces an indistinct or unintelligible sound.

We have produced a series of exercises at the end of this chapter to strengthen your articulators, if necessary. After a few weeks of daily practice, you will gain forcefulness and suppleness in your articulators, which will enable you to learn to produce any sound accurately.

Sufficient Support

Breath supply and support are so important that Chapter 2 was devoted to that subject. To produce normal speech, air must be exhaled. To convert that airflow into sounds, the breath stream must be strong enough to withstand friction, redirection, and stoppage. If these articulatory modifications overcome weak breath support, incomplete and vague sound production results. Strength and accuracy in the use of the respiratory system are part of the skills that lead to clear articulation.

Complete Finish

One of the most noticeable articulation problems is incompleteness. Some sounds, such as *t* and *d*, should have an audible explosion of air when they end. Others, such as *l* and *r*, need a vowel-like finish. If those endings are absent, articulation is incomplete, and the indistinct sound can cause the listener to hear another word; for example, *trade* might become *tray*. It is not appropriate to be so obviously precise that people notice your manner of speaking more than your ideas, but complete articulation is essential to effective communication.

ARTICULATION EXERICSES

As we have said, articulation is a physical act that requires, for accuracy, the relaxation and dexterity of the speech muscles. They must be trained for speech as much as the leg muscles must be trained for running. As you do the following exercises, exaggerate the actions. Devote a few minutes every day to this activity. Remember to combine the elements of efficient phonation while you exercise.

Lip Exercises

1. Stretch the lower lip up over the upper lip, and then stretch the upper lip down over the lower lip. Alternate with increasing rapidity.

2. Pucker the lips as tightly as possible, and then widen them vigorously, as for an exaggerated *e* sound. Alternate ten times, at first slowly and then rapidly. Relax and repeat the exercise.

3. Repeat each of the following syllables many times, at first slowly and then more and more rapidly. Exaggerate the lip movements.

be-me-be-me-be-me-be-me	whee-whoo-wa-who
bo-po-bo-po-bo-po-bo-po	blee-bee-kee-blee-bee-kee
flee-flee-flee-flee-flee	mla-mla-mla-mla-mla-mla
vro-vro-vro-vro-vro-vro	flack-mack-flack-mack

4. Look in a mirror. Watch the different positions of the lips as you say *ah*, *aw*, *o*, *oo*, *e*. Repeat the exercise five times.

5. To make the lips more flexible, exaggerate and repeat "How are you?" several times.

6. With the jaw and tongue relaxed in normal position, use the lips only as you read the following vowels. Make a definite change between each.

ah-aw	ah-aw	ah-aw	ah-aw
ay-oh	ay-oh	ay-oh	ay-oh
ee-oo	ee-oo	ee-oo	ee-oo

   Now, with the lips and tongue relaxed, pronounce the following vowels by closing and opening the jaw.

oo-aw	oo-aw	oo-aw	oo-aw
ee-aw	ee-aw	ee-aw	ee-aw
ee-ah	ee-ah	ee-ah	ee-ah

Tongue Exercises

1. Double the tongue back against the soft palate as far as you can, and then stretch it out from the mouth as far as possible. Repeat the exercise ten times.

2. Push the tongue hard against one cheek and then against the other. Extend it up over the upper lip, down over the lower lip, and then from side to side. Repeat the exercise ten times. Relax, and repeat it again.

3. Round the lips tightly, and grooving the tongue, push it through the opening. Repeat the exercise.

4. Press as much as possible of the upper surface of the tongue against the hard palate, and then release it. Repeat the exercise, at first slowly and then more and more rapidly.

Jaw Exercises

1. Utter the following sounds with a broad movement of the jaws. Exaggerate and prolong the vowels. *Wee-ee-ee-ee-ee! Why-y-y-y-y! Wo-o-o-o-o-o-o! Wah-ah-ah-ah-ah-ah-ah!*

2. Utter the following syllables and firmly exaggerate the jaw movements. *Bah-bah-bah-bah-bah-bah! Fah-fah-fah-fah-fah! Mah-mah-mah-mah-mah! Pah-pah-pah-pah-pah! Wah-wah-wah-wah-wah! Bee-boh! Fee-foh! Mee-moh! Pee-poh! Wee-woh! Dee-doh! Gee-goh! Jee-joh! Kee-koh! Lee-loh! Nee-noh! Kwee-kwoh! Ree-roh! See-soh! Tee-toh!*

3. Utter the following syllables, and strongly exaggerate the tongue movement and jaw movement. *Dah-dah-dah-dah-dah! Gah-gah-gah-gah-gah! Jah-jah-jah-jah-jah! Kah-kah-kah-kah-kah! Lah-lah-lah-lah-lah! Nah-nah-nah-nah-nah! Qwah-qwah-qwah-qwah-qwah! Rah-rah-rah-rah-rah! Sah-sah-sah-sah-sah! Tah-tah-tah-tah-tah! Thah-thah-thah-thah-thah!*

4. Make sure that the jaw is completely relaxed, with the tongue resting normally in the bottom of the mouth. Pronounce these syllables, and return to that relaxed position between each one.

sah	say	see	so	soo
zah	zay	zee	zo	zoo

Soft Palate Exercises

Pronounce these words and sense the movement of the soft palate.

angry	finger	longer	hunger

ARTICULATION PRACTICE

In your articulation practice, you should follow these guidelines.

1. Watch yourself in a mirror.
2. Practice for short periods several times a day rather than trying to do it all at once.
3. Relax.
4. Breathe deeply and abdominally.
5. Concentrate on vocal efficiency.
6. Read aloud.
7. Read slowly.
8. Repeat difficult words and phrases several times.
9. Check with your professor to insure that you are making the sounds correctly. Incorrect practice is worse than no practice at all.

SUMMARY

In this chapter, we have discussed the locations and the parts of the articulators, the requirements for exactness in articulation (accurate formation, sufficient support, and complete finish), the classification of speech sounds and their symbolization, and exercises for articulatory flexibility. With strong, flexible articulators, you are now ready to begin a study of the individual sounds of Standard American English.

6

Vowel Articulation

Vowel sounds are the main building blocks of clear speech. They are voiced sounds; that is, the vocal folds vibrate to produce them. They are emitted from the mouth freely and without friction. By changing the jaw opening and the position of the tongue, we change the resonant frequencies of the mouth, resulting in the different vowel sounds (Figure 6.1).

FORMATION OF VOWELS

Vowel sounds are determined by four factors.

1. *The opening of the jaw*. The size of the mouth can be changed by differences in the opening of the jaw, which causes clearly different sounds. Pronounce *heat* and *hat*. Notice that the jaw opens wider for *hat*. Do the same thing with *hoot* and *hot*.

2. *The shape of the lips*. Changing the shape of the lips affects vowel sound production. Look in a mirror and notice the change as you say *tote* and *tot*: the lips become less rounded. Do the same with *soak* and *seek*: the lips become more spread.

3. *The position of the tongue*. For almost all vowels, the tongue rests behind the lower teeth. The front, center, and back of the tongue, however, rise by different amounts to produce different vowels. Open your mouth wide. Place your finger on your tongue and your tongue tip slightly behind your front teeth. Pronounce the first part of the words *hat, hit,* and *heat*. You will feel the tongue rise progressively from sound to sound. A similar action takes place with the back of the tongue as you say *hot, hook,* and *hoot*.

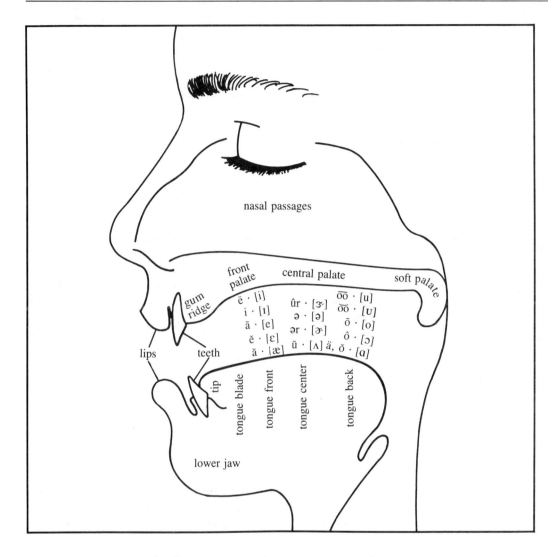

Figure 6.1 Places of vowel articulation

4. *The tension of the tongue*. The firmness of the tongue surface also affects vowel articulation. Concentrate on the tip of your tongue and place it behind your lower teeth. Say *mitt* and *meet*. Notice how much more firm and tense the tongue is in the production of the vowel sound in *meet*. Do the same with *fat* and *fought*, and with *pull*, and *pool*. The second word in each pair is produced with greater tongue tension.

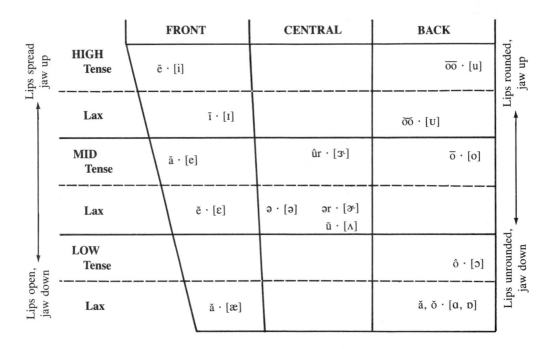

Figure 6.2   Position of vowel sounds

Figure 6.2 represents one system for classifying vowels. The top line represents the hard palate and the bottom line represents the flattened tongue. The vertical lines on the left and right represent the front and back of the mouth, respectively. The figure shows tongue positions for the 12 key vowel sounds of Standard American English. It also shows positions for two sounds that function as vowels in unaccented syllables and before voiceless consonants. These are ā [e], as in *rotate*, and ō [o], as in *opaque*. These two sounds become diphthongized at the ends of words or when followed by voiced consonants.

Between the diacritic and phonetic symbols in this diagram is a dot (·). It represents the approximate position reached by an area of the tongue for each sound. To produce the sounds located below the front palate, the tongue front rises to the indicated position. The sounds below the center palate are made with the tongue center. The sounds closest to the soft palate are produced with the tongue back. The tongue front, therefore, rises to the middle of the mouth to make ĕ [ɛ]; the tongue back rises nearly to the soft palate for the sound o͞o [u].

In Figure 6.2, notice that the vowels can be classified according to whether the tongue is raised at the front, center, or back of the mouth, by how high it is raised in the mouth (indicated by the terms *low*, *mid*, and *high*), and by the shape of the lips (open or spread, rounded or unrounded).

CHARACTERISTICS OF VOWELS

The following characteristics of vowel sounds are necessary for clear articulation.

1. The tongue, lower jaw, and lips are important in vowel articulation.
2. The tip of the tongue is placed behind the lower teeth for almost all vowel sounds.
3. The front of the tongue humps or bunches forward toward the front palate for the front vowels.
4. The center of the tongue humps or bunches toward the center palate for the central vowels.
5. The back of the tongue humps or bunches toward the soft palate for the back vowels.
6. High vowels are articulated with the jaws close together.
7. Mid vowels are articulated with the tongue and jaw lower.
8. Lower vowels are made with the tongue and jaw lowest of all.
9. The lips are more spread in the high front vowels than in the low front vowels.
10. The lips are more rounded in high back vowels than in low back vowels.
11. The soft palate is raised for all vowels.
12. The vocal folds vibrate for all vowels.

The rest of this chapter provides descriptions of the vowel sounds of Standard American English. To help you discriminate among them, lists of word pairs are provided in which the only difference between the two paired words is a change in the target vowel. With some words, however, the nature of the target vowel makes it impossible to provide such pairs; lists of practice words will be found instead. For most sounds you will see six columns of Single Words. The first two have the target sound in the *initial* (beginning) position in the words. The second two have it in the *medial* (middle) position and the third two in the *final* (ending) position. Some sounds do not occur in all positions.

The Word Pairs for all sounds are arranged in the same order as the vowels and diphthongs are presented in this book, of course without the target sound paired with itself. We have included only "pure" pairs.

A blank area on a practice page indicates that the target sound does not occur in that position, in English words.

(ē) Diacritic   **Phonetic [i]**

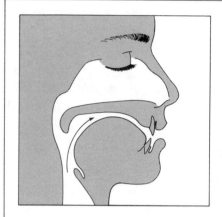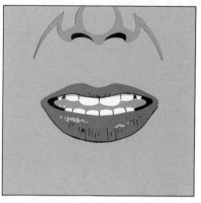

Formation

The front of the tongue is lifted very high toward the front palate. The muscles of the tongue are tense; the jaw is almost shut; the lips are unrounded. The soft palate is raised, and the vocal folds vibrate.

Definition

ē [i] is a high front tense vowel.

Misarticulation

Since ē [i] is a high front, tense vowel, some speakers make it nasal. Most misarticulation is caused by the substitution of other vowel sounds; for example,

1. If ē [i] is replaced by ĭ [ɪ], then *seat* becomes *sit*.

2. If ē [i] is replaced by ĕ [ɛ], then *league* becomes *leg*.

Some speakers insert the neutral vowel, ə [ə], after ē [i], particularly if it is followed by l [l]; then *reel* becomes *ree-ul*.

Correction

To form the sound accurately, try the following procedure: prepare to whistle the highest possible note; then relax the lips, hold the tongue high, and sound the tone. Practice pronouncing ē [i] while you hold your nose closed. Project the sound out the mouth. Look in a mirror, pronounce *real*, and be sure the lips and the jaw do not move in pronouncing the final l [l] sound; it should be formed by an independent movement of the tongue to the gum ridge. Once the ē [i] sound is set, the lips and the jaw need not move.

(ē)   [i]

Single Words

eager	easy	female	need	agree	he
eagle	Egypt	green	peace	be	me
ease	either	keep	please	fee	sea
east	equal	leaf	real	flea	ski
eastern	evening	meeting	steel	free	three

Word Pairs

itch	each	chip	cheap		
Evan	even	fell	feel		
at	eat	fat	feet		
ox	ekes	stop	steep		
all	eel	walk	weak	saw	see
		soot	seat		
		soon	seen	true	tree
		work	week		
utter	eater	hut	heat		
		mail	meal	may	me
I've	eve	side	seed	shy	she
		boys	bees	toy	tea
		fouled	field	cow	key
oval	evil	slope	sleep	no	knee

Sentences

1. She seemed to seek heat on the beach.
2. He feels beat as he reaches the steep heap.
3. Leave the easy eating for an Easter meal.
4. Each seamstress was eager to agree.
5. We react morally and see cheating as cheap.
6. Eager to please, Eve seized the weak leader.
7. The bees flee from the evil fleas.
8. Wheat can't be beat to eat with peaches.
9. Eve's feet reeked of seawater.
10. We are completely defeated when we leave reality.

Tongue Twister

An extremely freethinking tea leaf reader named Tina told me to beware of an eager Eastern wheat farmer, whom I would meet while eating my evening meal at Shakey's. I took heed of what the beaded tea leaf reader, Tina, told me and meekly seated myself at Shakey's while my ego reeled. You see, I seek pizza-eating freakies, even if they are wheat farmers.

(ĭ) Diacritic   **Phonetic [ɪ]**

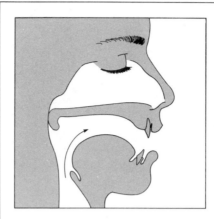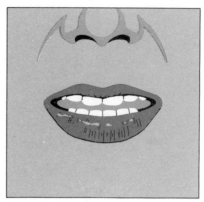

Formation

The front of the tongue is high but more relaxed than it is for ē [i]. The lips are unrounded and relaxed. The soft palate is raised, and the vocal folds vibrate.

Definition

ĭ [ɪ] is a high front lax vowel.

Misarticulation

Most misarticulation is caused by the substitution of other sounds; for example,

1. If ĭ [ɪ] is replaced by ē [i], then *still* sounds like *steel*.
2. If ĭ [ɪ] is replaced by ā [e], then *sin* sounds like *sane*.
3. If ĭ [ɪ] is replaced by ĕ [ɛ], then *pin* sounds like *pen*.
4. If ĭ [ɪ] is replaced by ŭ [ʌ], then *rim* sounds like *rum*.

Another error is to allow the ĭ [ɪ] to be nasal, especially near nasal sounds, such as in *dim*, *sin*, or *ring*. Some speakers insert ə [ə] after ĭ [ɪ], so that *skill* sounds like *ski-ul*.

Correction

If you have much difficulty in production of the ĭ [ɪ] sound, place two fingers between the teeth on one side of your mouth and try to say it. The exaggerated mouth opening usually helps produce the sound. Before proceeding with the exercises, check with your professor for the exactness of your sound. Practice with an expert to gain feedback to hear the difference between ĭ [ɪ], and ē [i]. Look in a mirror and allow the lips to be more relaxed for ĭ [ɪ], while you pronounce the word pairs on the next page. Touch your jaw and be sure it does not move as you shift from the ĭ [ɪ] to the consonant following it.

(i)   **[ɪ]**

Single Words

important	insurance	acid	finger
impulse	interest	been	fit
industry	into	brick	grip
insect	introduce	business	history
instrument	invention	committee	women

Word Pairs

ease	is	beet	bit
etch	itch	ten	tin
as	is	bask	bisque
odd	id	drop	drip
off	if	tall	till
		took	tick
		stool	still
err	ear	churn	chin
		love	live
ail	ill	pain	pin
eyes	is	ripe	rip
oink	ink	moist	mist
out	it	mouse	miss
own	in	grope	grip

Sentences

1. Bill injected the India ink into the Israeli pen.
2. Inca Indians hid in the hills from Spanish explorers.
3. The pills killed the intolerable pain in her finger.
4. Little lambs and kids mill about the inlet.
5. The imminent insults filled Ishmael with pity.
6. To sing diligently is to fulfill your ambition.
7. The Indonesian rings were singly the most interesting.
8. If the bin were filled with bing cherries, why did it linger?
9. The linguist from Chile mimicked Finnish singers.
10. I'll introduce Ichabod to Mr. Miller in a minute.

Tongue Twister

Millie killed the dill weeds on the hill. Her fingertips were nearly filled with grit and were beginning to itch. "Ick," she insisted, "I wish the idiotic ingrates from the windy city would have helped kill these dill weeds. They mill around here in these hills drinking and singing incessantly every day but won't linger a single minute when work is imminent.

(ā) Diacritic   **Phonetic [e]**

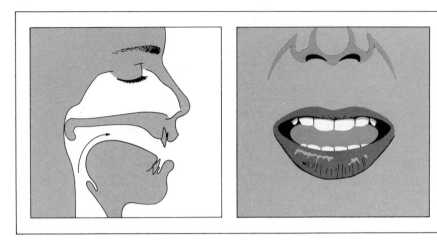

Formation

The front of the tongue is at the upper mid front position and is tensed. The lips are unrounded and lax. The soft palate is raised and the vocal folds vibrate.

Definition

ā [e] is a mid front tense vowel. Note that the diacritic symbol is the same as that for the diphthong ā (p. 106). This is because the American Heritage Dictionary makes no distinction between the vowel ā [e] and the diphthong ā [eɪ], whereas the International Phonetic Alphabet does.

Misarticulation

The vowel ā (e) is short. It occurs occasionally in unstressed syllables and, when stressed, before the consonants, *p*, *t*, and *k*. Most misarticulation is caused by the substitution of other sounds; for example,

1. If ā [e] is replaced by ĕ [ɛ], then *bait* sounds like *bet*.
2. If ā [e] is replaced by ī [aɪ], then *mate* sounds like *might*.
3. If ā [e] is replaced by ŭ [ʌ], then *ape* sounds like *up*.

If the tongue doesn't rise to produce the second element of the diphthong, the vowel ā [e] results. Some speakers allow the ə [ə] sound to follow the diphthong, so that *late* sounds like *lay-ut*.

Correction

Look in a mirror and pronounce the words containing the ā [e] sound on the next page. Be certain that the lips are slightly spread and that the tongue is in the mid front position.

(ā) [e]

ache	apron	bait	gate
acorn	ate	bake	great
acre	eight	cake	lake
acreage	eighteen	date	state
ape	eighty	fate	weight

eat	ate	seek	sake
it	eight	tick	take
		get	gait
at	ate	rat	rate
ox	aches	box	bakes
ought	eight	pauper	paper
		put	pate
		hoot	hate
irk	ache	jerk	Jake
ups	apes	Tucker	taker
Ike	ache	gripe	grape
		Coit	Kate
out	eight	lout	late
oak	ache	coat	cape

1. Kate baked a tasty cake.
2. Fate made Jake take the ape to the lake.
3. Nate was irate when his date was late.
4. She tasted the best grapes in the state.
5. It takes great bait to catch fish at the cape.
6. Eight paper plates were taken.
7. The rake may break if it's not taped.
8. She ate eight cakes by 8:18 A.M.
9. The ape's mate paced stately by the gate.
10. They pasted and taped paper for eight days.

Nate, a great gate maker, makes only great gates. His highly rated wife, Kate, had taken a newly baked cake to Nate as he was making great gates. Said Nate to the jaded gate maker, Jake, "Get two plates and we'll taste this great cake baked by Kate."

(ĕ) Diacritic   **Phonetic [ɛ]**

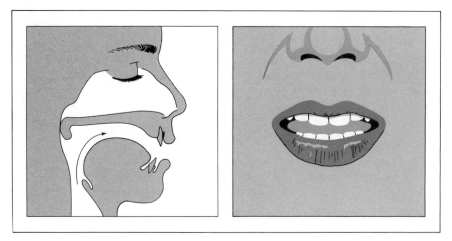

Formation

The front of the tongue is at mid front level and is relaxed. The lips are unrounded and lax. The soft palate is raised, and the vocal folds vibrate.

Definition

ĕ [ɛ] is a mid front lax vowel.

Misarticulation

Most misarticulation is caused by the substitution of other sounds; for example,

1. If ĕ [ɛ] is replaced by ĭ [ɪ], then *get* sounds like *git*.
2. If ĕ [ɛ] is replaced by ā [e], then *leg* sounds like *laig*.
3. If ĕ [ɛ] is replaced by ă [æ], then *set* sounds like *sat*.
4. If ĕ [ɛ] is replaced by ŭ [ʌ], then *met* sounds like *mutt*.

   If ə [ə] is incorrectly added after ĕ [ɛ], then *head* becomes *he-ud*. If nasal sounds are nearby, ĕ [ɛ] is sometimes nasalized as in *pen*, *hem*, or *men*.

Correction

Watch yourself in a mirror and practice aloud the words on the next page. Keep the front of the tongue raised halfway in the mouth. Transfer quickly to the following consonant with no jaw movement.

(ĕ)

[ɛ]

Single Words

any	ever	attention	heifer
edge	every	breath	Leonard
education	example	connection	suggestion
engine	exchange	digestion	thread
error	existence	guess	yesterday

Word Pairs

each	etch	bead	bed
imminent	eminent	sinned	send
and	end	bag	beg
odd	Ed	stop	step
audible	edible	sought	set
		bull	bell
		roost	rest
urge	edge	word	wed
umpire	empire	nut	net
Abe	ebb	sale	sell
I'm	em	pine	pen
oil	ell	foil	fell
hour	error	pout	pet
over	ever	toast	test

Sentences

1. Ed, the eldest, led the headman to the well.
2. Every deckhand stood at the edge of the wreck.
3. The beggar ate the wretched eggs.
4. Mr. Evans emigrated from Edinburgh.
5. Ted etched Betty's beautiful head on the edge of a ledge.
6. Fred's head felt like lead when he needed rest.
7. The error of Mel's ways wrecked his wedding to Nedra.
8. Ben said he'd bet the bread was ready to eat.
9. Two men led the deadly leopard to the net.
10. I met Betty in the shed and fell over the red doorstep.

Tongue Twister

Mr. Feldman celebrated his tenth wedding anniversary on the eleventh of February. His redheaded wife, Emily, felt like an egghead, home alone in bed, while Mr. Feldman celebrated elsewhere. "Every wedding event is wrecked by my wretched husband," Emily lamented while shedding tears. "I meant to set that lecher straight on the eleventh, but he headed out the exit before I was set to deck him."

(ă) Diacritic   **Phonetic [æ]**

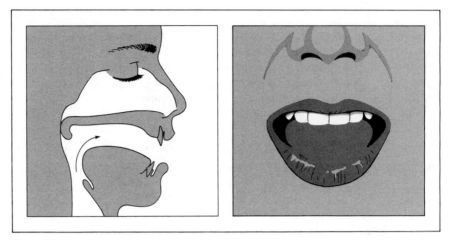

Formation

The front of the tongue is low and relaxed. The lips are unrounded and drawn back a bit at the corners. The soft palate is raised, and the vocal folds vibrate.

Definition

ă [æ] is a low front ax vowel.

Misarticulation

Most misarticulation is caused by the substitution of other sounds; for example,

1. If ă [æ] is replaced by ĭ [ɪ], then *can* sounds like *kin*.
2. If ă [æ] is replaced by ĕ [ɛ], then *bag* sounds like *beg*.
3. If ă [æ] is replaced by ä [ɑ], then *hat* sounds like *hot*.
4. If ă [æ] is replaced by ŭ [ʌ], then *cat* sounds like *cut*.

The ə [ə] sound is sometimes incorrectly added following ă [æ], so that *bad* becomes *ba-ud*. The ă [æ] sound is often nasalized in Mid-Western America.

Correction

Look in a mirror. Relax the tongue, lips, and jaw. Watch them as you say the word *Ed*. Then say *odd*. The jaw opening is the same for ă, [a] as for the vowel in *odd*. Now say *Ed, odd, ad*. Note that the jaw is as open for *ad* as it is for *odd*.

For some, ă [a] is difficult to say when followed by nasals. Say *Tom-tam, Don-Dan, bong-bang*.

(ă)   **[æ]**

Single Words

acid	angry	attack	family
actor	animal	balance	language
actual	appetite	camera	laugh
after	apple	chance	plaid
angle	ask	damage	that

Word Pairs

ease	as	beak	back
in	an	sit	sat
Ed	add	beg	bag
ox	axe	bond	band
on	Anne	caught	cat
		look	lack
		moon	man
Earl	Al	bird	bad
umber	amber	dud	dad
aim	am	pain	pan
idol	addle	bite	bat
oyster	aster	coin	can
out	at	hound	hand
opal	apple	post	past

Sentences

1. At the crack of dawn she sang in abject misery.
2. Anthony's addled cat lacked intelligence.
3. Black cats are bad luck when they pass across your path.
4. I sat on a tack that Sam had set for Sally.
5. Patty was sad when she crashed into her pal at the bank.
6. Fatcats carry masses of cash.
7. The bag of sap Anne banged into an alleyway aggravated her.
8. The lad padded his ankles before he sat on the raft.
9. As you know, Brad is a bad athlete.
10. The asters attracted mad sapsuckers.

Tongue Twister

Sam and Patty graduated on Saturday. Sam was an actor, but dancing was Patty's bag. After graduation the gang traveled to Sam and Patty's pad, where they chatted, chanted, danced, and gnashed mashed radishes.

(ä) Diacritic **Phonetic [ɑ]**

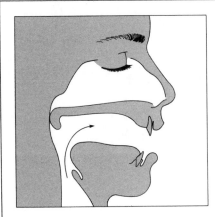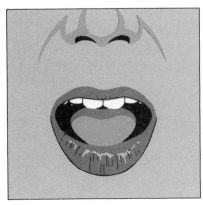

Formation

The back of the tongue is low and lax. The mouth is fully open. The lips are unrounded. The soft palate is raised, and the vocal folds vibrate.

Definition

ä [ɑ] is a low back lax vowel.

Misarticulation

The main reason for the misarticulation of ä [ɑ] is failure to open the jaw sufficiently. Most misarticulation is caused by the substitution of other sounds; for example,

1. If ä [ɑ] is replaced by ă [æ], then *calm* sounds like *cam*.
2. If ä [ɑ] is replaced by ô [ɔ], then *pod* sounds like *pawed*.
3. If ä [ɑ] is replaced by ŭ [ʌ], then *hot* sounds like *hut*.

If ə [ə] is added after ä [ɑ], then *pond* becomes *pah-und*. Some people add r [r] and cause *wash* to be *warsh*. The ä [ɑ] sound is sometimes nasalized, particularly near nasal sounds, as in *don* or *nominal*, especially under conditions of vocal constriction.

Correction

Look in the mirror. Assume that a physician has just told you to open your mouth and say *ah*. Produce the sound. Note that the lips and the jaw are open wide but not tense. The tongue is lax in the lower part of the mouth. Repeat the sound. Try it in the word *father*. If you are still unable to produce it correctly, your professor will provide you with a model to imitate. When your sound production is approved, practice the words on the next page.

(ä)

[ɑ]

ah	arm	balm	harbor	shah
archer	army	bard	llama	spa
ardor	arson	calm	palm	
argue	art	dark	swat	
ark	article	father	watch	

		seem	psalm	me	ma
ear	are	wish	wash		
Ed	odd	feather	father		
add	odd	mare	mar		
		gourd	guard		
		wood	wad		
		swoon	swan	boo	bah
irk	ark	hurt	heart		
		bum	bomb		
		came	calm	spay	spa
		pine	palm		
		goiter	garter		
		pout	par		
		toad	Todd	show	shah

1. The car was guarded by her odd father.
2. She swatted the swan in the pond on a balmy day.
3. The farmer's shack was far from the spa.
4. Ma read the Psalms while she asked for alms.
5. Hardhearted Papa pushed the shark onto the rocks.
6. Are the arks full of aardvarks?
7. Art's arms are on a par with Todd's.
8. Arlene's palm got hot as the guard watched.
9. The cart of tar paper was barred from the farm.
10. He chartered a yacht to take him to Hawaii.

Ma and Pa farmed the far part of the Barbary Coast. Their only problem was the heartless loan shark, Mr. Garfield. Mr. Garfield tried to jar Ma and Pa into farming afar, but the barking dogs stopped him. An artless arm wrestler was in love with Ma, and Pa tarred and feathered him. Calmly, Ma and Pa continue to farm the far part of the Barbary Coast.

(ŏ) Diacritic   **Phonetic [ɒ]**

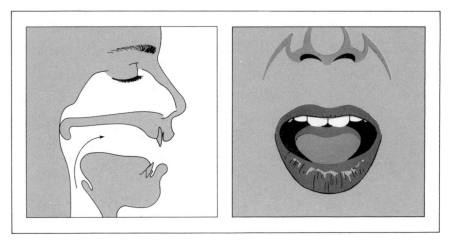

Formation

The back of the tongue is low and lax. The lips are unrounded, the mouth open. The soft palate is raised, and the vocal folds vibrate.

Definition

ŏ [ɒ] is a low back lax vowel. The International Phonetic Alphabet, used by John S. Kenyon and Thomas A. Knott in the *Pronouncing Dictionary of American English*, distinguishes between ŏ [ɒ] and ä [ɑ], but for some these sounds tend to be indistinguishable in Standard American Speech. We encourage you to say the ä [ɑ] sound wherever either symbol is used.

Misarticulation

Misarticulation of ŏ [ɒ] is the result of the same errors discussed in the case of ä [ɑ].

Correction

Follow the procedure described for ä [ɑ].

(ŏ)

[ɒ]

Single Words

object	opera	body	copy
occupy	operator	bottle	cotton
octane	optometrist	collar	pocket
ominous	opportunity	common	possible
oncology	oxygen	copper	property

Word Pairs

		beam	bomb
id	odd	click	clock
		neck	knock
active	octave	cap	cop
auks	ox	nought	not
		could	cod
		shoot	shot
		hurt	hot
		sub	sob
		rake	rot
		ride	rod
		join	John
		cloud	clod
		coat	cot

Sentences

1. The doctor locked the expensive clock in his car.
2. Do not sob on the odd cot.
3. The dock began to rot when it became oxidized.
4. The obstinate octopus was not ominous.
5. Osmosis is not an obstacle to the odyssey of a cell.
6. She chose an add onyx ring to wear to the opera.
7. The ominous bomb in a pod was dropped on a large lock.
8. It is not proper to mock a sot.
9. Todd was an odd operator.
10. To block a shot is possible but not probable.

Tongue Twister

If a Hottentot got a Hottentot tot to talk before the tot could totter, should the Hottentot tot sob or not? Or should the tot opt to play hopscotch with the top-notch optimists? The obsequious doctor allotted the Hottentot tot the proper opportunity to calm down, and then, oddly, the Hottentot tot knocked the doctor from the cot.

(ô) Diacritic   **Phonetic [ɔ]**

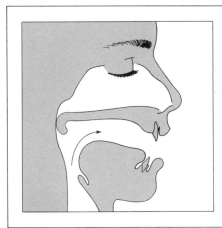

Formation

The back of the tongue is at low level and is tense. The lips are very slightly rounded in an oblong fashion. The soft palate is raised, and the vocal folds vibrate.

Definition

ô [ɔ] is a low back tense vowel.

Misarticulation

The sound is produced incorrectly if the tongue does not rise to the appropriate level. Faulty articulation can result from the substitution of other vowel sounds; for example,

1. If ô [ɔ] is replaced by ä [ɑ], then *naught* sounds like *not*.
2. If ô [ɔ] is replaced by ō [o], then *bought* sounds like *boat*.
3. If ô [ɔ] is replaced by o͞o [ʊ], then *fall* sounds like *full*.
4. If ô [ɔ] is replaced by ŭ [ʌ], then *bought* sounds like *but*.

If ə [ə] is added, then *caught* is pronounced *caw-ut*. Adding an r [r] sound changes *saw* to *sawer*. The ô [ɔ] sound can become nasalized near nasal sounds, as in *song* or *naught*, especially under conditions of vocal constriction.

Correction

Look in a mirror. Relax the lips, and jaw. Watch them as you say *hah*. Then say *ho*. The position of ô [ɔ] is midway between the positions of the vowels in *hah* and in *ho*. Now say *haw*. Try saying *hah, haw,* and *ho*. Make certain that each vowel is different. If you are still unable to produce the sound accurately, your professor will provide you with a model to imitate. When your production is approved, practice the words on the next page.

(ô)   [ɔ]

almost	or	across	loss	caw	law
audible	orb	because	salt	claw	maw
august	order	cloth	small	craw	paw
automatic	organization	cough	talk	flaw	raw
autumn	ornament	fault	walk	jaw	saw

Word Pairs

ether	author	beat	bought	see	saw
if	off	fit	fought		
edit	audit	net	nought		
at	ought	back	balk		
odd	awed	sod	sawed		
		wool	wall		
		pool	Paul	coo	caw
irk	auk	girl	gall	slurr	slaw
		fun	fawn	stray	straw
ate	aught	mail	maul	may	maw
Ike	auk	file	fall	rye	raw
oil	all	boil	ball	joy	jaw
hour	or	gown	gone	now	gnaw
oat	ought	cold	called	low	law

Sentences

1. The naughty child sawed the wrought-iron altar rail.
2. The ballpark draws mighty tall crowds in August.
3. Audrey saw Paul draw on the wall in awe.
4. While auditing the fall sales, I gnawed on toffee.
5. How does that awkward hawk balance on the straw?
6. The law states that no audible talking is allowed in the auditorium.
7. Not one hallway in that awful mall was without a flaw.
8. The auk often was caught gnawing on coleslaw.
9. Aubrey's jaw often went wrong when he called for raw auk.
10. Paul cautiously caught crawfish last August.

Tongue Twister

The audacious music hall operator fought often with songwriters. His austere musical arrangements aroused his audiences to unlawful actions. Maude, the songstress, sought to crawl cautiously out of the hall to avoid a jaw-breaking brawl. The drawling hawkers on the lawn found more raucously because of her loss.

(ō) Diacritic   **Phonetic [o]**

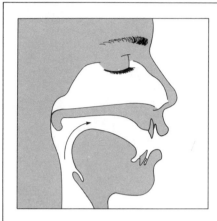

Formation

The back of the tongue is in the upper mid back position and is tensed. The lips are rounded and lax. The soft palate is raised and the vocal folds vibrate.

Definition

ō [o] is a mid back tense vowel. Note that the diacritic symbol is the same as that for the diphthong ō (p. 114). This is because the American Heritage Dictionary makes no distinction between the vowel ō [o] and the diphthong ō [oʊ], as does the International Phonetic Alphabet.

Misarticulation

The vowel ō [o] is common in other languages. It occasionally occurs in unstressed syllables in American English, and in stressed syllables before the consonants p, t, and k. Sometimes, it is made as a combination of two sounds, the ĕ [ɛ] and the oo [ʊ], making it into an unusual diphthong. Other sounds are sometimes incorrectly substituted for ō [o]; for example,

1. If ō [o] is replaced by ô [ɔ], then *coat* sounds like *caught*.
2. If ō [o] is replaced by ōō [ʊ], then *croak* sounds like *crook*.
3. If ō [o] is replaced by ŭ [ʌ], then *boat* sounds like *but*.

Correction

Look in a mirror as you pronounce the words containing the ō [o] sound on the next page. Be certain that the lips are rounded and that the tongue starts the sound in the mid back position.

(ō) [o]

oak	Oklahoma	broken	quoted
oaken	okra	choke	rope
oatmeal	open	hope	spoken
oats	opened	joke	throat
okay	opening	photo	wrote

eats	oats	speaks	spokes
it	oat	knit	note
		best	boast
at	oat	flat	float
		sop	soap
ought	oat	nought	note
		brook	broke
		boot	boat
irk	oak	perk	poke
		mutt	moat
ache	oak	cape	cope
Ike	oak	type	taupe
		Coit	coat
out	oat	gout	goat

1. I hope that this rope isn't broken.
2. She wrote a note about the taupe goat.
3. The soap floated on the moat like a boat.
4. They quoted the joke about the oaken spokes.
5. She opened the oatmeal box and it choked her throat.
6. He hoped to have the broken coat buttons replaced.
7. Motels and motor hotels are open late.
8. Her photos of the floats were coated with soap.
9. A frog croaked a sour note when it was choked by a rope.
10. The open soap box was near the broken oak tree.

A colt and a goat were tied with a rope. The colt hoped that the rope would be broken, for being roped to a goat was no fun. "This goat needs a soapy bath and a float in the moat," thought the colt. He saw a broken oak spoke poking through the wall. He hoped to rub the rope on the spoke and leave the goat. When the rope broke, the colt bolted and left the goat to mope.

(ōō) Diacritic   **Phonetic [ʊ]**

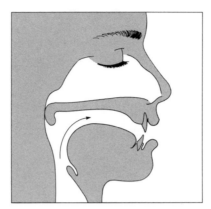

Formation

The back of the tongue is high and somewhat lax. The lips are moderately rounded. The soft palate is raised, and the vocal folds vibrate.

Definition

ōō [ʊ] is a high back lax vowel.

Misarticulation

Most misarticulation is caused by the substitution of other sounds; for example,

1. If ōō [ʊ] is replaced by ô [ɔ], then *full* sounds like *fall*.
2. If ōō [ʊ] is replaced by ō [o], then *cook* sounds like *coke*.
3. If ōō [ʊ] is replaced by ōō [u], then *soot* sounds like *suit*.
4. If ōō [ʊ] is replaced by ŭ [ʌ], then *book* sounds like *buck*.

If ə [ə] is inserted after oo [ʊ], then *wool* sounds like *woo-ul*. The ōō [ʊ] sound can become nasalized near nasal sounds, as in *nook*, especially under conditions of vocal constriction.

Correction

Look in a mirror. Pronounce the word *pool* and prolong the vowel sound. Note the position of the lips and the jaw, and note the feel of the back of the tongue. Now unround the lips slightly and relax the back of the tongue. Say the word *pull*. Make certain that you pronounce the vowel shorter than that of *pool*. Try to keep the same sound in words like *hood* and *good*. If you are still unable to produce the sound correctly, your professor will provide you with a model to imitate. When your sound production is approved, practice the words on the next page.

(o͞o)

[ʊ]

Single Words

bush	push
cook	rook
cushion	should
good	sugar
look	woman

Word Pairs

feet	foot
pit	put
well	wool
back	book
lock	look
hawk	hook
pool	pull
word	wood
crux	crooks
fail	full
hide	hood
boil	bull
cowed	could
broke	brook

Sentences

1. I took the book from the crook and shook it.
2. You should put a hook in the nook by the wooden bookcase.
3. You can pull the wool over a rookie's eyes.
4. Mr. Brooks should look out for the bull in the woods.
5. Cook took the bookie's Brooks Brothers suit.
6. She stood, fully balanced, on one foot.
7. I pulled the wooden bookcart to the library's nook.
8. She looked at the book back before hooking the brook trout.
9. I'll lead a fuller life by hook or by crook.
10. The hood of her full-length coat looked crooked.

Tongue Twister

The bookseller took a look at the hooks for the bookshelves. "I should put a good supply of cookbooks in the window, but the hooks for the bookshelves are crooked. Womanhood and brotherhood, bullets and bullfighting—so many books to pull from—but the hooks for the bookshelves are crooked," said the good bookseller. "Should I put uncrooked hooks on the wooden bookshelves?" asked he. "I could put out dozens more cookbooks for people to look at."

(o͞o) Diacritic   Phonetic [u]

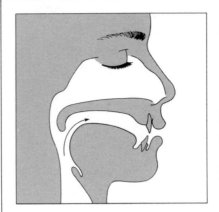

Formation

The back of the tongue is high and tense. The lips are puckered and rounded. The soft palate is raised, and the vocal folds vibrate.

Definition

o͞o [u] is a high back tense vowel.

Misarticulation

The o͞o [u] sound is sometimes ended too quickly, so that it approximates the oo [ʊ] sound instead. It should be held a bit longer than the front or the central vowels. Most misarticulation is caused by the substitution of other sounds; for example,

1. If o͞o [u] is replaced by o͝o [ʊ], then *fool* sounds like *full*.
2. If o͞o [u] is replaced by ŭ [ʌ], then *duel* sounds like *dull*.

Allowing ə [ə] to be added changes *cool* to *coo-ul*. The o͞o [u] sound can become nasalized near nasal sounds, as in *moon* or *room*, especially under conditions of vocal constriction.

Correction

Look in a mirror. Pronounce the word *cool* and prolong the vowel sound. Note the position of your lips and jaw during the pronunciation of that sound. The back of the tongue should feel tense. Repeat that sound. Concentrate on the lifting action of the back of the tongue. Next, say the word *too*. Be sure to stretch the o͞o [u] sound at the end of the word. Then try the words *glue, fool,* and *you*. If you are still unable to produce the sound correctly, your professor will provide you with a model to imitate. When your sound production is approved, practice the words on the next page.

(o͞o)   [u]

approval	movie	blue	true
beautiful	news	do	value
foolish	smooth	screw	view
fruit	spoon	shoe	who
group	tooth	through	you

beam	boom	see	sue
sip	soup		
fell	fool		
fad	food		
lot	loot		
bought	boot	draw	drew
pull	pool		
lurk	Luke		
skull	school		
raid	rude	slay	slew
might	moot	tie	two
join	June	toy	too
crowd	crude	now	new
moan	moon	glow	glue

1. Sue threw her shoes into the pool.
2. Do your duty; it's foolish to be untrue to the crew.
3. The feuding dude seemed crude to Luke, the mule skinner.
4. The dune grew as soon as the noon breeze blew.
5. June thought the blue hula hoop was a beauty.
6. Give a hoot, toot your flute, and don't pollute.
7. The fool got loose from the noose and looted the roost.
8. Luke hooted like a coot when he was wounded by the goofy crew.
9. The hooves on the roof were proof that Yule was soon due.
10. Judy brooded over the gooey glue.

The new balloon tycoon Rangoon soon knew that who cared a sou would not be a goon. He was no baboon. He knew the proof of the soup was in the spooning. So, in his new blue shoes, he soon sent platoons of balloons to the moon, fooled the dragoons, and crooned a new tune.

(ûr) Diacritic   **Phonetic [ɝ]**

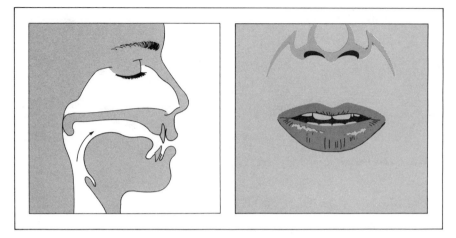

Formation

The central part of the tongue is raised toward the central palate and is tensed. The tongue tip and blade may be curled back slightly but should not touch at the front palate. The lips may be slightly rounded and pursed. The jaw is slightly open. The soft palate is raised. The vocal folds vibrate.

Definition

ûr [ɝ] is a mid central tense vowel. It occurs in stressed syllables.

Misarticulation

In Standard American Dialect, this sound is misarticulated if the tongue center does not reach high enough toward the palate. ŭ [ʌ] results instead. For example, if ûr [ɝ] is replaced by ŭ [ʌ], then *bird* sounds like *bud*. Persons for whom English is a second language tend to treat the ûr [ɝ] as a glide. For example, if ûr [ɝ] is replaced by âr [ɛr], then *her* sounds like *hair*.

Correction

Look in a mirror. Open your mouth and raise the center of your tongue toward the center palate. Raise the tongue tip and the tongue blade toward the front palate. Tense the tongue, without any tightening of other structures. Let the jaw close slightly. Round the lips slightly, protrude them partially, and phonate. You are in position to produce the sound ûr [ɝ]. Try it again, and stretch the sound out as long as possible. Repeat it again; this time, break the sound up by stopping and starting the breath stream without moving the articulators. Move the articulators to the position described. Produce the sound f [f] and blend it into the ûr [ɝ] sound. You will have said the word *fur*. If you are still unable to produce the sound accurately, seek assistance from your professor before going on to the following exercises.

(ûr)

Single Words

early	erstwhile	certain	curve	blur	fur
earth	Erwin	church	dirt	concur	incur
earthen	herb	circle	expert	confer	infer
earthquake	urban	curl	journey	defer	prefer
ermine	urge	curtain	learn	deter	were

Word Pairs

eve	Irv	bead	bird	bee	burr
in	earn	hid	heard		
egg	erg	wed	word		
an	urn	batch	birch		
honest	earnest	cot	curt	spa	spur
auk	irk	walk	work	paw	purr
		pook	lurk		
		tune	turn		
		gull	girl		
agent	urgent	pale	pearl	pay	per
I've	Irv	file	furl	sly	slur
oil	Earl	voice	verse	coy	cur
		shout	shirt	how	her
owner	earner	boast	burst	so	sir

Sentences

1. Myrtle heard the urchins' mirth, and it hurt her.
2. Earl, in earnest, slurred his words while he recited verse.
3. The erstwhile girl conferred with the ermine shirtmaker.
4. The bird perched in earnest on a worthless pearl.
5. The cat purred while I stirred her preferred food.
6. When searching for earthenware, refer to Woolworth's.
7. Were the purses worth pursuing?
8. One word would urge Erwin on to infer the worst.
9. Curving dirt roads cause my eyes to blur.
10. The Urban League heard words of encouragement.

Tongue Twister

Further and further, worthy Erwin searched for the burden he had nervously cursed. He erred by turning left when he should have searched right. He shirked not, however, spurning no work until the burden, an ermine fur, was returned. Urged on by its worth, working like the early bird, he earned his reward when he searched it out. Then Erwin, with his ermine fur burden, earned a purse of great worth.

(ər) Diacritic   **Phonetic [ɚ]**

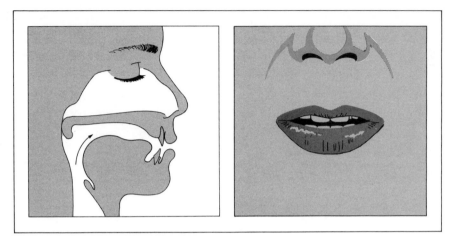

Formation

The center of the tongue is raised toward the center palate and is relaxed. The tip
and the blade of the tongue may be raised up toward the front palate. The lips may
be partially rounded and slightly protruded. The jaw is slightly open. The soft palate
is raised, and the vocal folds vibrate. The sound is produced with reduced loudness
and length in comparison to ûr [ɝ].

Definition

ər [ɚ] is a mid central lax vowel. It occurs in unstressed syllables.

Misarticulation

In Standard American Dialect, this sound is misarticulated if the tongue does not
rise far enough toward the palatal surface. ə [ə] is then substituted for ər [ɚ]. For
example, if ər [ɚ] is replaced by ə [ə], then *father* sounds like *fatha*. Some persons
for whom English is a second language incorrectly stress the syllables containing
ər [ɚ].

Correction

The same instructions given for ûr [ɝ] can be applied to the production of ər [ɚ].
However, caution must be used in the amount of stress given to the sound. Persons
who characteristically omit the sound or substitute for it have to pay the greatest
attention when it occurs at the ends of words.

(ər)   [ɚ]

Practice Words

cupboard	surmount	answer	fewer
performance	surprise	barrier	mother
perfume (verb)	surrender	better	neater
perfunctory	survey (verb)	brighter	shorter
permit (verb)	survive	collar	sister
pertain	undermine	catcher	smother
purloin	yesterday	color	summer
surmise (verb)	actor	father	treasure

Sentences

1. The performing actors and actresses are better than most.
2. His mother was shorter than his sister.
3. Yesterday, I was permitted to visit the underprivileged children.
4. Does this survey pertain to insurmountable sewer problems?
5. Father surmised that the catcher was surmounting his difficulties.
6. There are fewer and fewer good actors performing in the theater.
7. The barrier his brother uncovered was under surveillance.
8. That fabric is brighter and smoother than Esther's.
9. It's a perfunctory statement to say that your hair is neater than hers.
10. Perfume ofttimes pursuades younger men to fall in love.

Tongue Twister

After the theater performance, the doctor and the sailor decided to go to dinner. They entered a restaurant that featured saltwater fish. The doctor ordered lobster, but the sailor preferred red snapper. The waiter told them that it was a pleasure to serve these, and they overtipped him by five dollars. When the dinner was over, they surmised that they had never eaten better.

(ŭ) Diacritic   **Phonetic [ʌ]**

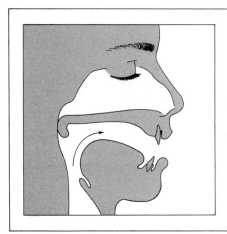

Formation

The center of the tongue is mid central and relaxed. The lips are unrounded. The soft palate is raised, and the vocal folds vibrate.

Definition

ŭ [ʌ] is a mid central lax vowel. It occurs in stressed syllables.

Misarticulation

Most misarticulation is caused by the substitution of other sounds; for example,

1. If ŭ [ʌ] is replaced by ä [ɑ], then *cut* sounds like *cot*.
2. If ŭ [ʌ] is replaced by ô [ɔ], then *nut* sounds like *naught*.
3. If ŭ [ʌ] is replaced by ō [o], then *hum* becomes *home*.

The ə [ə] sound is sometimes incorrectly added after the ŭ [ʌ] sound, which causes *son* to become *su-un*. It can also become nasalized, especially under conditions of vocal constriction.

Correction

Often, when we are asked a question for which we are unsure of the answer, we say *uh . . . uh . . .* before we give it. Some people frequently insert *uh* in their speech when they are nervous. This sound is the vowel ŭ [ʌ]. Practice saying *uh* several times (but don't use it in public speaking). Try it in the words *up, come,* and *under.* If you are still unable to produce the sound correctly, your professor will provide you with a model to imitate. When your sound production is approved, practice the words on the next page.

(ŭ)

[ʌ]

Single Words

of	upper	among	enough
ugly	upward	blood	from
umber	us	brother	love
umpire	udder	color	rough
up	utter	country	tongue

Word Pairs

either	other	bean	bun
inset	unset	tiff	tough
ember	umber	pep	pup
ankle	uncle	span	spun
opt	upped	dock	duck
		wrought	rut
		crooks	crux
		boon	bun
		third	thud
ace	us	mail	mull
Ivan	oven	bike	buck
		point	punt
outer	utter	shout	shut
		stroke	struck

Sentences

1. Not one crumb of that bun is under the rug.
2. The gull spun above the duck and then struck.
3. The nuts were tucked away for munching after supper.
4. The thud that the tough thug made stunned me.
5. Mr. Lum got stuck in the mud and became utterly unconscious.
6. My luck would come if I could just shuck him out of a buck.
7. Our clucking hen leads a dull, ugly life.
8. The sun struck the hut as the puppies jumped.
9. Unless the stud horse is bucking, rub him with a glove.
10. One rug was cut by the Huckleberry Rugcutters.

Tongue Twister

The ugly duckling was stunned when he thudded against the hull of a summer sailer's love boat. Seagulls spun above the hull and tucked their umber wings under the now-ulcered duckling. "Come, be one with us," sang the seagulls. "Our cult is unlike any other." Unluckily, a dull, dumb sailor, rubbing his gun, misfired it toward the sun. Of the ugly duckling, there is nothing, save a dent in the hull near the gunwale.

(ə) Diacritic   **Phonetic [ə]**

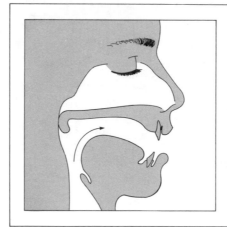

Formation

The tongue is low and relaxed. The lips are unrounded. The jaw is relaxed, and the mouth is slightly open. The soft palate is raised, and the vocal folds vibrate.

Definition

ə [ə] (schwa) is a mid central lax vowel. The schwa sound only occurs in unstressed syllables.

Misarticulation

Few speakers cannot make the ə [ə] sound. It is a short, unstressed vowel utterance that is the most common sound in American English. The main problem, in fact, is that it is incorrectly added after the other vowels or after diphthongs. Most misarticulation is caused by the substitution of another sound; for example,

1. If ə [ə] is replaced by ŭ [ʌ], then *alone* becomes *a-lone*.
2. If ə [ə] is replaced by ā [e], then *about* becomes *a-bout*.

Correction

Practice the difference in strength and length of ŭ [ʌ] and ə [ə]. Say *utter* and then *alone*. Notice how the first sound in *alone* is almost half as long as the first sound in *utter*. Contrast the words *unsure* and *under*. If you are still unable to produce the sound correctly, your professor will provide you with a model to imitate. When your sound production is approved, practice the words on the next page.

(ə)   [ə]

about	animal	arena
above	apparent	aroma
account	beautiful	bacteria
across	beneficent	camera
again	business	cinema
against	common	data
alone	decision	idea
among	dependent	petunia
amount	education	pizza
approval	immediately	pneumonia
attack	machine	Sahara
attention	medicine	strata
awake	support	Tina
occasion	system	umbrella
opinion	together	viscera

Sentences

1. Be alert to the abuse the petunias may receive from the juveniles.

2. My horoscope says that I adore pizzas.

3. The accident across the arena is the fault of the circus owner.

4. Aloha is the equivalent of hello or good-bye.

5. The immature, mischievous accountant adored riding his galloping stallion.

6. Alone in Austria, she felt abandoned.

7. I'm going across the Sahara Desert to gather data on its flora and fauna.

8. Coconut is edible in Australia.

9. Above you, around you, and about you are data on the earth's strata.

10. Her implacable beauty caused her to run amuck in wild abandon.

Tongue Twister

On this occasion, I will be above the abuse and immature ravings of the accountant. The items to account for are above me. I galloped around assessing the flora and fauna of the Sahara, but I accidentally lost the total a long time ago. The data that emanated will cause me to abandon my job, but, alone, I will enjoy consuming edible herbs sprinkled upon Chicago-style pizza.

SUMMARY

Vowel sounds are the basic building blocks of our speech. With an understanding of their formation and production, you are ready to study the combinations of some of them, which form the diphthong sounds.

7

Diphthong
Articulation

A diphthong is a continuous blending of two vowels into a single syllable. Since it is a combination of vowel sounds, it is voiced and is emitted through the mouth with no obstruction.

CHARACTERISTICS OF DIPHTHONGS

There are five diphthongs in American English. These diphthongs are produced by the blending of vowel sounds in the following patterns (represented by both diacritic and phonetic symbols).

Diphthongs	Diacritic	Phonetic
ā [eɪ] as in *pay*	ā = ā (vowel) + ĭ	[eɪ] = [e] + [ɪ]
ī [aɪ] as in *pie*	ī = ä + ĭ	[aɪ] = [ɑ] + [ɪ]
oi [ɔɪ] as in *noise*	oi = ô + ĭ	[ɔɪ] = [ɔ] + [ɪ]
ou [aʊ] as in *out*	ou = ä + o͞o	[aʊ] = [ɑ] + [ʊ]
ō [oʊ] as in *no*	ō = ō (vowel) + o͞o	[oʊ] = [o] + [ʊ]

Note: [aɪ] and [aʊ] are written with the symbol [a]. This is a low-central vowel and is not used typically in standard American English. It does occur in Eastern speech, however. Thus, [aɪ] and [aʊ] do not necessarily begin from the [a] position, but with the center of the tongue slightly raised.

Some writers describe ā [e] and ō [o] as diphthongs and some as vowels. We have elected to indicate that each is a vowel when it is in an unaccented syllable or before a voiceless consonant, and diphthongal at the ends of words or before voiced consonants. For this reason we include these two sounds as diphthongs in this chapter.

FORMATION OF DIPHTHONGS

Diphthongs are determined by three factors.

1. *The movement of the jaw.* For each diphthong, the jaw is first opened to its position for the first of the two vowels and then closes to its position for the second. Pronounce *ice* and *ace*. Notice that the jaw is opened widest at the beginning of *ice* but that it is at the same position at the end of both words. Now say *now* and *know*. The jaw opens wider for *now* but ends in the same position for both words. For all diphthongs, the pattern is the same: the jaw opens widest at the beginning and closes during production.

2. *The movement of the lips.* Like the jaw, the lips move during diphthong production, from their position for the initial vowel to that for the ending vowel. Say *oil* and *owl*. Notice that in the first word the lips start in a rounded position and move to a spread position. In the second word they move from an unrounded position to a rounded one. In general, the lips move from a more open position to either a rounded or spread position for diphthongs.

3. *The movement of the tongue.* The tongue also changes position during the production of diphthongs. Say *buy* and *bow* (of a ship). Notice that the tongue starts from the same position (low back for both words) but ends up in different locations (high front for *buy* and high back for *bow*). In general, the tongue moves from a lower position to a higher one for diphthongs.

Figure 7.1 illustrates the articulation movements required to produce the diphthongs. This figure should be compared with Figure 6.1, which illustrates the production of vowels.

Diphthongs have the following features in common.

1. The first vowel element is always stressed.

2. The jaw always closes between the first and second vowel elements.

3. The lips close (either by spreading or rounding) during production.

4. The tongue rises (either to the high front or the high back position) between the vowel elements.

DIPHTHONG ARTICULATION PRACTICE

The following pages provide practice material for the five diphthongs of Standard American English. As with the vowel sounds, paired words are included to help you discriminate between the target diphthong and other sounds.

If you are from a dialect area in the Southern United States, or speak with a foreign accent, you probably make the diphthongs too short or triphthongize them. The word *boy* sounds like boǝ [bɔǝ] and *house* sounds like häǝs [haǝs]. Pay particular attention to instruction number one below.

1. Stress the first element in each diphthong, but be certain that you finish the second. Many speakers do not raise the tongue high enough toward the palate at the end of diphthongs. For those with ĭ [ɪ] as the second element, the tongue

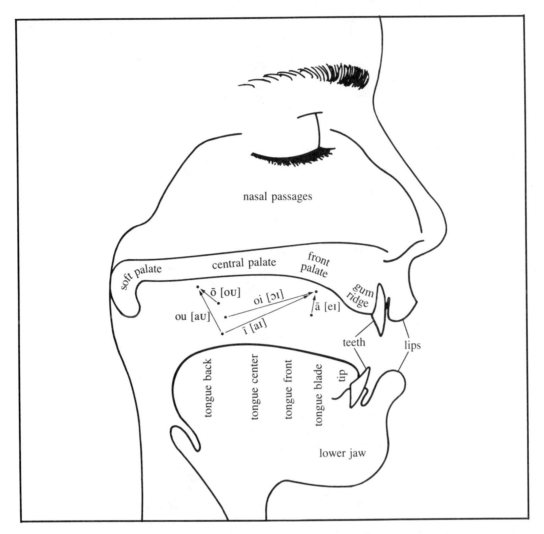

Figure 7.1 Places of diphthong articulation.

must reach the position for ĭ [ɪ]. For those ending in o͞o [ʊ], it must reach the o͞o [ʊ] position.

2. Practice in frequent short periods rather than one long one.

3. *Be conscious of both breath control and vocal efficiency.*

4. Read all exercises aloud and do so slowly.

5. Check your articulation of new sounds with recorded models, friends, or your professor.

6. Remember, practice is only practice. You must consciously use your new sounds conversationally to make them habitual.

(ā) Diacritic = ā + ĭ   **Phonetic [eɪ]**

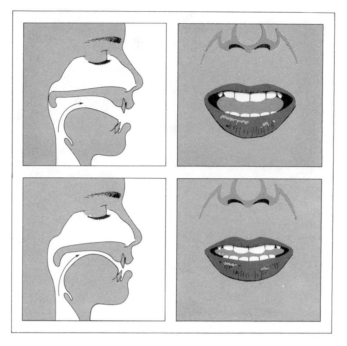

Formation

The front of the tongue starts at the mid front level and rises to the high front region. The lips are unrounded and relaxed. The jaw closes slightly. The soft palate is raised, and the vocal folds vibrate.

Definition

ā [eɪ] is a continuous combination of the vowels ā [e] and ĭ [ɪ].

Misarticulation

ā [eɪ] is a diphthong, but in certain contexts, it has a more vowel-like quality. The vowel ā [e] is short and sometimes unstressed, as in *rotate* or *chaotic*. The diphthong ā [eɪ] is a combination of the vowel ā [e] and ĭ [ɪ]; it is usually stressed, as in *obey*, *enable*, and *heinous*. Most misarticulation is caused by the substitution of other sounds; for example,

1. If ā [eɪ] is replaced by ĕ [ɛ], then *fail* sounds like *fell*.
2. If ā [eɪ] is replaced by ī [aɪ], then *trail* sounds like *trial*.
3. If ā [eɪ] is replaced by ŭ [ʌ], then *maid* sounds like *mud*.

   If the tongue does not rise to produce the second element of the diphthong, the vowel ā [e] results. Some speakers allow the ə [ə] sound to follow the diphthong, so that *late* sounds like *lay-ut*.

(ā)   **[eɪ]**

Abe	ailment	amaze	page	away	pay
able	alien	baby	parade	gray	play
age	alienate	cable	rain	lay	today
aid	aorta	fade	same	may	tray
aim	aviary	name	table	neigh	weigh

eels	ails	mean	main	see	say
immoral	amoral	mid	made		
edge	age	fell	fail		
am	aim	cam	came		
odd	aid	palm	pain	spa	spay
all	ale	tall	tale	raw	ray
		wood	wade		
		pool	pale	stew	stay
urges	ages	surge	sage	were	way
		numb	name		
		tried	trade	pie	pay
oiled	ail	soil	sale	boy	bay
		proud	prayed	prow	pray
ode	aid	toll	tail	grow	gray

1. Yesterday the instant replay enabled us to call it a fair play.
2. The ape played with the stranger.
3. The stately patient takes medication daintily.
4. Do not alienate the flagrant vagrant.
5. The swain, who claimed the Milky Way was fake, awakened mistaken.
6. Amos, the amiable astronaut, aided in an amazing undertaking.
7. At the age of 88, Jane flew to Maine.
8. "I hate to be late," related the staid knave.
9. The famous bantamweight railed at the gale and the hail.
10. The Navy laborer praised the Asian paper.

In Spain, a sane dame owned a lame crane, the bane of her days. One day in May, when it was raining on the plain in Spain, a Great Dane chased the lame crane. Across the plain came a grain-laden train endangering the crane. The crane was saved from a terrible fate when the rain turned to hail, the train derailed, and the Great Dane was chased from the plain.

(ī) Diacritic = ä + ĭ **Phonetic [ɑɪ]**

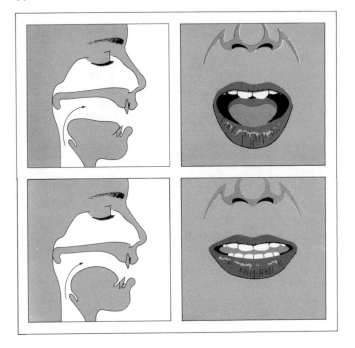

Formation

The lax tongue starts in the low back position and moves toward the high front region. The lips are unrounded, and the jaw closes. The soft palate is raised, and the vocal folds vibrate.

Definition

ī [ɑɪ] is a continuous combination of ä [ɑ] and ĭ [ɪ].

Misarticulation

If the tongue does not rise to the ī [ɪ] position, ä [ɑ] replaces ī [ɑɪ]. Commonly, *I* is then pronounced *ah*, as in *ah know that*. Most misarticulation occurs because another sound is substituted; for example,

1. If ī [ɑɪ] is replaced by ā [eɪ], then *ice* sounds like *ace*.

2. If ī [ɑɪ] is replaced by oi [ɔɪ], then *buy* sounds like *boy*.

3. If ī [ɑɪ] is replaced by ŭ [ʌ], then *mice* sounds like *muss*.

If ə [ə] is allowed after ī [ɑɪ], then *ride* sounds like *ri-ud*.

(ī)   **[ɑɪ]**

icing	ideal	bright	quiet	by	my
icon	idol	fight	society	cry	rye
Ida	Iowa	guide	surprise	deny	sky
Idaho	island	line	tired	fly	try
idea	Ivan	price	violent	lie	why

eave	I've	seat	sight	tee	tie
ill	aisle	bit	bite		
Ed	I'd	lead	lied		
atom	item	hat	height		
ox	Ike's	dock	dike	spa	spy
awe	eye	caught	kite	draw	dry
		book	bike		
oodles	idles	pool	pile	do	die
earn	iron	heard	hide	sir	sigh
us	ice	rum	rhyme		
ale	I'll	main	mine	pray	pry
oil	isle	poise	pies	boy	buy
hour	ire	found	fined	how	high
ohm	I'm	dome	dime	go	guy

1. I like fried rice.
2. I cried when my pie smashed on my thigh.
3. Myra reads the Bible at tribal rites.
4. I am likely to go to Thailand if I'm enticed by the right price.
5. Imbibing cider twice is, precisely, a vice.
6. Bryce Canyon will suffice for the mile-long hike with my tyke.
7. The ties on the kite's line were made with fine fiber.
8. At the height of the summertime, they took pride in biking.
9. The spider was mortified at the impolite fly.
10. I complied with the statewide signs on driving.

Heidi attended a prize fight at midnight. As a new writer, she had to clarify precisely and to qualify delightfully the details of the fight. The bright lights, shining in her eyes, blinded her sight for a while, and she missed the right cross that ended the fight. Another scribe supplied her with the right details, so that she could write the fight news right.

(oi) Diacritic = ô + ĭ   **Phonetic [ɔɪ]**

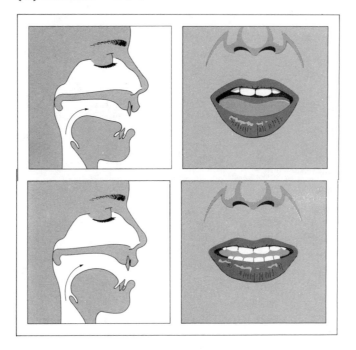

Formation

The tongue starts in a mid back position and moves to the high front region. The lips move from slightly rounded to unrounded. The soft palate is raised, and the vocal folds vibrate.

Definition

oi [ɔɪ] is a continuous combination of ô [ɔ] and ĭ [ɪ].

Misarticulation

If the tongue does not rise to produce ĭ [ɪ] as the second element, the vowel ô [ɔ] results, so that *all* and *oil* sound alike. The diphthong becomes more like a vowel. Most misarticulation results because another sound is substituted; for example,

1. If oi [ɔɪ] is replaced by ī [aɪ], then *boy* sounds like *by*.
2. If oi [ɔɪ] is replaced by ûr [ɝ], then *oily* sounds like *early*.

(oi)   **[ɔɪ]**

Single Words

avoid	noisy	alloy	enjoy
boiling	pointed	annoy	joy
join	poison	cowboy	ploy
joint	spoil	destroy	soy
loin	voice	employ	toy

Word Pairs

eel	oil	reel	royal	bee	boy
		mill	moil		
Esther	oyster	fell	foil		
ankh	oink	can	coin		
Ollie	oily	dolly	doily		
all	oil	tall	toil	saw	soy
		bull	boil	clue	cloy
		news	noise		
early	oily	curl	coil	curr	coy
		must	moist		
ailing	oiling	bays	boys	jay	joy
aisle	oil	pint	point	pie	poi
owl	oil	joust	joist	plough	ploy
old	oiled	pose	poise	toe	toy

Sentences

1. Joyce embroidered the doilies joyfully.
2. His voice annoyed the coy West Pointer.
3. Ms. Hoyle was employed as a needlepointer in Detroit.
4. Disappointment in his broiled sirloin destroyed his appetite.
5. Hardboil the oysters in tinfoil before they spoil.
6. That tenderloin steak is devoid of moist flavor.
7. The tabloid avoided the counterpoint of the argument.
8. She toyed with the soil by the royal oyster bed.
9. In my viewpoint, we should reappoint Mr. Voight in Des Moines.
10. The foyer of the building was destroyed by the oil leak.

Tongue Twister

Roy, the oily boy with the royal blue toy, avoided the noise of his sister's voice, which annoyed him. His joy was in tinfoil and corduroys. Joyce, his boisterous sister, exploited his joy as she spoiled or destroyed all the tinfoil and corduroys. Joyce, on the other hand, coyly embroidered her needlepoint while she ate oysters.

(ou) Diacritic = ä + o͞o   **Phonetic [ɑʊ]**

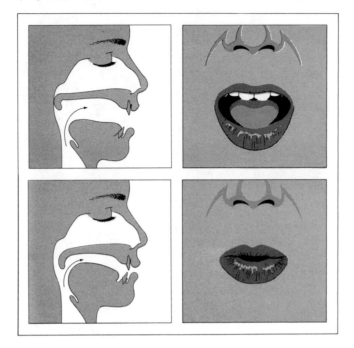

Formation

The tongue starts in the low back position and moves to the high back region. The lips are lax and unrounded for the first element of the diphthong; they become tense and rounded for the second element. The jaw moves from open to closed.

Definition

ou [aʊ] is a continuous combination of ä [ɑ] and o͞o [ʊ].

Misarticulation

Some speakers place the tongue too far forward for the first half of this diphthong and produce ă o͞o [æʊ]. If the tonuge does not rise for the second element, the ou [ɑʊ] sound is incomplete, and *hour* sounds like *are*. Misarticulation can occur if other sounds are substituted; for example,

1. If ou [aʊ] is replaced by ă o͞o [æʊ], then *town* sounds like *ta-own*.
2. If ou [aʊ] is replaced by o͞o [u], then *now* sounds like *new*.
3. If ou [aʊ] is replaced by ŭ [ʌ], then *gown* sounds like *gun*.

(ou)   **[ɑʊ]**

Single Words

ounce	outcome	about	flower	bough	plow
ourselves	outdo	account	fowl	chow	pow
outage	outfield	amount	house	endow	prow
outboard	outfit	brown	loud	how	thou
outcast	outgrow	cloud	mouth	landau	wow

Word Pairs

eater	outer	sheet	shout	see	sow
ill	owl	bit	bout		
etch	ouch	mess	mouse		
aster	ouster	lad	loud		
are	hour	dot	doubt	bra	brow
ought	out	fall	foul	paw	pow
		poor	power		
		shoot	shout	who	how
err	ow!	hearse	house	curr	cow
		gun	gown		
ate	out	rained	round	allay	allow
ire	out	cried	crowd	ply	plow
oil	owl	void	vowed	boy	bough
		groaned	ground	row (a boat)	row (fight)

Sentences

1. The highbrow from Moscow somehow landed in the hoosegow.
2. How do the snowplows overpower snow showers?
3. The hour to devour the cauliflower has come about.
4. The gunpowder allowed the Brower brothers to shake down the tower.
5. The howling of the owl aroused Mr. Powell.
6. The hand-me-down flowered gown was a dowdy brown.
7. Mr. Lowry was proud of the crowds his clam chowder aroused.
8. Sourly, the wallflower cowered while avowing a showdown.
9. When the plowman had gout, he would carouse and shout.
10. From a proud tower in the town, the powerful loudmouth looked down.

Tongue Twister

Minnie Mouse powdered her nose as the sour-faced cowboy sat outside her door. She loudly vowed that she would not allow him to take her downtown through the crowds of highbrows here. Instead, she wished to powwow with the howling Indians outside the town. After the powwow, the powerful chief cowered, and the hour of doubt came around. The Indians who had surrounded the town were gone, and the plowman and the cowboys shouted.

(ō) Diacritic = ō + o͞o Phonetic [oʊ]

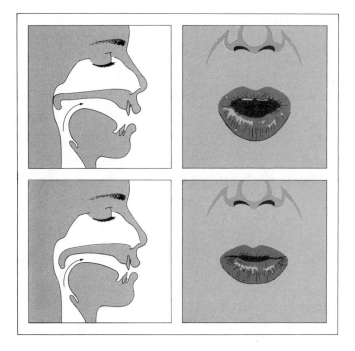

Formation

The tongue starts in a mid back position and moves to the high back region. The lips move from a slightly rounded to a fully rounded position. The palate is raised, and the vocal folds vibrate.

Definition

ō [oʊ] is a continuous combination of ō [o] and o͞o [ʊ].

Misarticulation

Although the vowel ō [o] is common in other languages, and although it occasionally occurs in unstressed syllables in American English, ō [oʊ] is a diphthong in Standard American speech; that is, when used in a stressed syllable, ō [oʊ] is longer and contains o͞o [ʊ] as a second element. If the tongue does not rise to produce o͞o [ʊ], the vowel ō [o] is heard. Other sounds are sometimes incorrectly substituted for ō [oʊ]; for example,

1. If ō [oʊ] is replaced by ô [ɔ], then *owe* sounds like *awe*.
2. If ō [oʊ] is replaced by o͞o [ʊ], then *showed* sounds like *should*.
3. If ō [oʊ] is replaced by ŭ [ʌ], then *code* sounds like *cud*.

(ō)   [ou]

oboe	omen	bold	moan	blow	though
ode	only	coal	prose	go	toe
odor	oval	control	road	narrow	tomato
ogre	over	gold	soul	potato	window
olio	owner	home	throne	snow	yellow

evil	oval	bean	bone	see	sew
in	own	rid	rode		
elder	older	red	road		
and	owned	can	cone		
odd	ode	job	Job		
awe	owe	gnaws	nose	law	low
		bulls	bowls		
		pool	pole	do	dough
		stern	stone	fur	foe
udder	odor	fun	phone		
aid	owed	main	moan	ray	row
I'm	ohm	rhyme	roam	shy	show
oiled	old	boiled	bold	boy	bow
		town	tone	now	know

1. Joan rode the roan to Rome alone.
2. The golden oldie was solely owned by Rosa.
3. Over and over the old hobo sewed his old chapeau.
4. The rogue loaned the robe to Lola.
5. Joey rode the old Olds home over the toll road.
6. The bold noble's odor was an odious omen.
7. The grown owner throws bones at the foe.
8. Moses' clothes were sewn by Navajos.
9. Job towed the golden oboe home.
10. Flo rowed and rowed over the flowing foam.

Hello! I'm Joe Schmo. I grow wild roses and bestow them on the Joneses before they decompose. I will not disclose to what plateaus my rose growing has exposed me, but, if the hobo's nose is the color of the rose, and if the hobo's hose have holes in the toes, and if the hobo hoes where tomatoes grow, do you suppose a Schmo could go to shows?

CORRECTIONS

(ā) Diacritic = ā + ĭ / Phonetic [eɪ]

Look in a mirror and pronounce the words containing the ā [eɪ] sound on page 107. Be sure that the front of the tongue rises, that the jaw closes slightly, and that the lips become more spread in passage from the first to the second element.

(ī) Diacritic = ä + ĭ / Phonetic [ɑɪ]

Look in a mirror as you pronounce the words containing the ī [ɑɪ] sound on page 109. Be sure that the front of the tongue rises on the second element, that the jaw closes, and that the lips spread slightly. Sometimes it helps to go from a serious mouth for ä [a] to a smiling mouth for ĭ, [ɪ].

(oi) Diacritic = ô + ĭ / Phonetic [ɔɪ]

Look in a mirror as you practice the words on page 111. Be sure that the tongue rises to the position of the second element, that the jaw closes, and that the lips move from a slightly rounded to a spread position.

(ou) Diacritic = ä + o͞o / Phonetic [ɑʊ]

Look in a mirror as you practice the words on page 113. Be sure that the tongue rises to the second element, that the jaw closes, and that the lips become rounded.

(ō) Diacritic = ō + o͞o / Phonetic [oʊ]

Look in a mirror as you pronounce the words containing the ō [oʊ] sound on page 115. Be certain that the back of the tongue rises on the second element of the sound, that the jaw closes, and that the lips become more rounded.

SUMMARY

Diphthongs are particularly important in Standard American English. Their accurate production requires the use of both vowel elements in each. Try to maintain effective control of your vowel and diphthong sounds as you study the production of consonants.

8

Consonant Articulation

FORMATION OF CONSONANTS

There are 25 consonants in Standard American English. Each consonant is identified by three characteristics.

1. *Place of articulation.* The place of articulation is the location in the vocal tract where the emitted air is partially or completely obstructed. For example, the lips come together and part in producing the sounds p [p], b [b], hw [ʍ], and m [m]; the lower lip touches the upper teeth in producing f [f] and v [v]; the tongue touches the upper teeth to make the th [θ] and *th* [ð] sounds; the tip of the tongue touches the gum ridge to create t [t], d [d], l [l], and n [n]; the blade of the tongue comes close to the gum ridge for s [s] and z [z]; the tongue blade rises to the front palate for sh [ʃ], zh [ʒ], ch [tʃ], j [dʒ], and y [j]; the tongue blade rises to the center palate for r [r]; the back of the tongue closes with the soft palate to make k [k], g [g], and ng [ŋ]; and the glottis is partially closed for the h [h].

2. *Manner of articulation.* The manner of articulation is the manner in which the air leaves the vocal tract, that is, whether it is completely or partially obstructed and the movement of the articulators. Such obstruction either stops the breath stream momentarily (for *stop-plosives*), restricts it so that air turbulence is heard (for *fricative* sounds), or redirects its passage (for the *lateral* or *nasals*). Other consonants (the *glides*) are the result of movement of the articulators from one position to another.

3. *Voicing.* Voicing is the vibration of the vocal folds during consonant production. The *voiced consonants* are phonated; that is, the vocal folds vibrate during their production. Voiced consonants include b [b], w [w], m [m], v [v], *th* [ð], d [d], l [l], n [n], z [z], zh [ʒ], j [dʒ], y [j], r [r], and ng [ŋ].

   The *voiceless consonants* have no vocal tone; that is, the vocal folds do not vibrate during their production. They include p [p], hw [ʍ], f [f], th [θ], t [t], s [s], sh [ʃ], ch [tʃ] and h [h].

   Two consonants that are made at the same place of articulation and with the same mode of emission but that differ only in voicing are called *cognates*.

Table 8.1   Definition of Consonants

	PLACE OF ARTICULATION	VOICING	MANNER OF ARTICULATION
p [p] b [b]	lip to lip	voiceless voiced	stop-plosive
t [t] d [d]	tongue tip to gum ridge	voiceless voiced	stop-plosive
k [k] g [g]	back of tongue to soft palate	voiceless voiced	stop-plosive
f [f] v [v]	lower lip to upper teeth	voiceless voiced	fricative
th [θ] *th* [ð]	tongue tip between teeth	voiceless voiced	fricative
s [s] z [z]	tongue blade to gum ridge	voiceless voiced	fricative
sh [ʃ] zh [ʒ]	tongue blade to front palate	voiceless voiced	fricative
h [h]	glottis	voiceless	fricative
ch [tʃ] j [dʒ]	tongue blade to front palate	voiceless voiced	affricate
hw [ʍ] w [w]	lip to lip	voiceless voiced	glide
y [j]	tongue blade to front palate	voiced	glide
r [r]	tongue center to central palate	voiced	glide
l [l]	tongue tip to gum ridge	voiced	lateral
m [m]	lip to lip	voiced	nasal
n [n]	tongue tip to gum ridge	voiced	nasal
ng [ŋ]	back of tongue to soft palate	voiced	nasal

There are nine cognate pairs: p [p] and b [b], hw [ʍ] and w [w], f [f] and v [v], th [θ] and *th* [ð], t [t] and d [d], s [s] and z [z], sh [ʃ] and zh [ʒ], ch [tʃ] and j [dʒ], and k [k] and g [g].

The tables arrange the same information about consonants in two ways for your study. In Table 8.1 (on page 119), they are arranged by category (stop-plosives, fricatives, glides, etc.). In Table 8.2, they are arranged by description and the cognate pairs are indicated.

Table 8.2 Classification of Consonants

PLACE OF ARTICULATION		MANNER OF ARTICULATION						
	Voicing	Stop-Plosive	Fricative	Affricate	Glide	Lateral	Nasal
Lip to lip	Voiceless	p [p]			hw [ʍ]		
	Voiced	b [b]			w [w]		m [m]
Lower lip to upper teeth	Voiceless		f [f]				
	Voiced		v [v]				
Tongue tip between teeth	Voiceless		th [θ]				
	Voiced		*th* [ð]				
Tongue tip to gum ridge	Voiceless	t [t]					
	Voiced	d [d]				l [l]	n [n]
Tongue blade to gum ridge	Voiceless		s [s]				
	Voiced		z [z]				
Tongue blade to front palate	Voiceless		sh [ʃ]	ch [tʃ]			
	Voiced		zh [ʒ]	j [dʒ]	y [j]		
Tongue center to center palate	Voiced				r [r]		
Back of tongue to soft palate	Voiceless	k [k]					
	Voiced	g [g]					ng [ŋ]
Glottis	Voiceless		h [h]				

ARTICULATION PRACTICE

The rest of this chapter consists of practice material for each of the 25 consonant sounds. As much as possible, word pairs are presented that contrast the target sound with a common substitution.

For example, those who have Big City, Southern, or Appalachian dialects or accents often differ in their articulation of the *th* [ð] from Standard American English. Most will substitute the d [d] sound some the z [z]. The pairs as often as possible, therefore, contrast those sounds instead of less likely substitutions.

As with vowels and diphthongs, certain instructions will help you in your practice.

1. Be certain that the voiced consonants are made with vocal fold vibration and that the voiceless ones have none. You can check yourself by placing a hand on your throat while articulating. You can feel the vibration with your fingertips for voiced sounds. Voiceless sounds will produce no sensation.

2. One of the most common faults of speakers is leaving off ending consonants. *Pay careful attention to completing the production of final consonants.*

3. Keep practice periods short but frequent.

4. Remember both breath control and vocal efficiency.

5. Do all practice aloud.

6. Once you learn a new sound, use it in reading aloud and in conversation as much as possible.

(p) Diacritic   **Phonetic [p]**

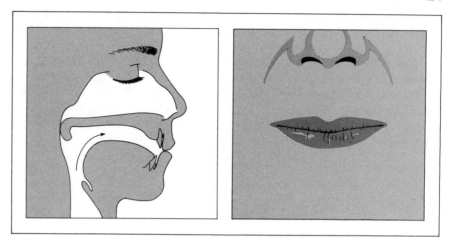

Formation

With the lips closed, the soft palate is raised, and air is exhaled to create gentle pressure behind the lips. The lips are then separated quickly, and the air is exploded through. The tongue is relaxed. The vocal folds do not vibrate.

Definition

p [p] is a lip-to-lip, voiceless, stop-plosive consonant.

Misarticulation

The p [p] sound is improperly formed by failure to bring the lips together evenly and firmly. Without complete closure, the air is not blocked, sufficient pressure cannot develop, and the proper explosion does not occur. Occasionally, when English is a second language, b [b] is substituted for p [p]. In some dialects of English and in many foreign accents, the final p [p] is omitted.

Correction

Pronounce the p [p] sound as you look in a mirror. Be sure that the lips are pressed together. Exhale to push air into the mouth. Feel the pressure of the exhaled air. Hold your fingers in front of the lips, quickly open the lips, and feel a puff of air on your fingers. Exaggerate p [p] as a final sound in words such as *step, tap,* and *jump,* and alternate the syllables *pa, ba, pa, ba, pa, ba.*

(p)

Single Words

paper	please	apple	respect	cheap	lip
part	possible	copy	responsible	deep	ship
peace	price	example	separate	help	sleep
picture	prose	expert	space	jump	soap
play	pull	open	special	keep	top

Word Pairs

feel	peel	seemed	seeped	chief	cheap
bill	pill	differ	dipper	tiff	tip
bet	pet	lever	leper	stem	step
fad	pad	rabid	rapid	cab	cap
bomb	palm	cobs	cops	lob	lop
fall	Paul				
bull	pull				
fool	pool	suiter	super	who'd	hoop
birch	perch	churning	chirping	churn	chirp
but	putt	utter	upper	putt	pup
face	pace	taking	taping	cane	cape
buy	pie	diver	diaper	rife	ripe
boys	poise				
bout	pout				
foes	pose	robing	roping	moat	mope

Sentences

1. Never play Ping-Pong with Pete.
2. Please draw a picture on this paper.
3. Ben gave Peter the bag of peanuts.
4. He played baseball for a private school.
5. After the party, there were cups on the carpet.
6. Put the beans, the peas, and the chip dip on the back porch.
7. He was punished for peeping at the ripped tapestry.
8. Polly played the piano at the shop.
9. Bob placed the cap and the pail beside the sleeping pup.
10. Perry had been stationed at an army post near Budapest.

Tongue Twister

Paul and Polly planned a supper on the patio. Playing the piano and supplying the pie was Paul's part. Polly prepared pink porridge plus participation in Ping-Pong. Help was provided by Pete, who pleaded that they partake of pumpkins, peaches, and poi. Pleased, he put cups and plates on top of the napkins and leaped into the pool.

(b) Diacritic   **Phonetic [b]**

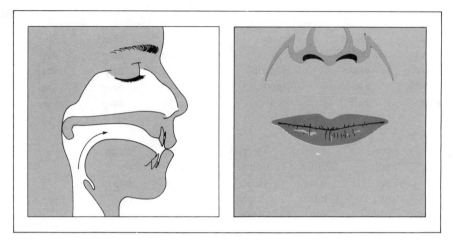

Formation

With the lips lightly closed, the breath is exhaled, and the vocal folds are vibrated. The soft palate is raised, which causes pressure to build up behind the lips. The lips are then quickly separated, resulting in a voiced explosive sound.

Definition

b [b] is a lip-to-lip, voiced, stop-plosive consonant.

Misarticulation

Some American dialects and foreign accents fail to voice the b [b] sound, which results in the p [p] sound, particularly at the ends of words. In some cases, the lips do not completely block the air, which results in a sound like v [v].

Correction

Lightly touch the larynx with the fingers and feel the vibration when you voice the sound. Watch yourself in a mirror while you produce *ba, ba, ba*. Be certain that the lips come into complete contact. Repeat the sound *ab, ab, ab* several times. Be certain that the voicing (vibration of vocal folds) continues through the release of the b [b] sound.

(b)

baby	black	able	possible	bib	knob
ball	body	about	probable	cab	nab
because	boot	harbor	public	dub	rub
been	bread	library	table	jab	stub
between	building	number	trouble	job	sub

peak	beak				
pit	bit	river	ribber	rip	rib
vet	bet	egging	ebbing	wed	web
vat	bat	rapid	rabid	tap	tab
palm	bomb	rotten	rotter	sop	sob
pall	ball	dogging	daubing	doff	daub
push	bush				
plume	bloom	tooling	tubing	loop	lube
turn	burn	curving	curbing	curd	curb
puck	buck	summing	subbing	rug	rub
vase	base	anal	able	bale	babe
vie	by	jiving	gibing	tripe	tribe
poi	boy				
vow	bough				
vote	boat	loads	robes	rove	robe

1. The baby bunny is in the blue crib.
2. The bear grabbed the box and broke it.
3. Bob built the biggest building in this suburb.
4. Behind the barn are the blackbirds and the blueberries.
5. Grab the scrubbing brush behind the cupboard.
6. Better be a baker than a sobbing bobby-soxer.
7. A book about bears is worth about a bushel of beans.
8. A babbling baby may want a big shrub or a bunch of bananas.
9. The boy built a cabin before he began his job.
10. Please buy a rubber ball and a basket of berries.

Betty Batter bought a tub of butter. "But," she said, "this butter's bitter. If I put it in my batter, it will make my batter bitter. Even a rabid rabbit wouldn't bite bitter batter. But a dab of better butter will make my batter better." So Betty Batter bought a tub of better butter and made batter better.

(t) Diacritic   **Phonetic [t]**

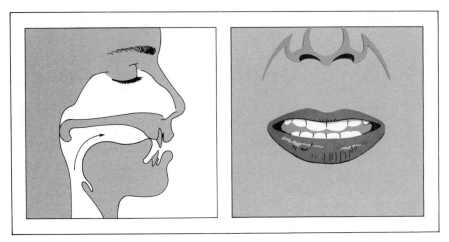

Formation

The tip of the tongue is lightly pressed against the gum ridge behind the upper teeth. The sides of the tonuge should touch the side teeth. The soft palate is raised, and the air is stopped. The tongue is dropped quickly, and the air explodes out of the mouth. The vocal folds do not vibrate.

Definition

t [t] is a tongue-tip-to-gum-ridge, voiceless, stop-plosive consonant.

Misarticulation

If the tip of the tongue does not press tightly against the gum ridge, the t [t] sound is not properly exploded, so that s [s] is produced instead. If the tonuge is too low and touches the teeth, this results in the production of the th [θ] sound. In some cases, the final t [t] is omitted in words. Some persons allow too much air to escape between the t [t] sound and the following vowel, which gives it an aspirate quality.

Correction

Extend the tongue with different amounts of pressure against the gum ridge to vary the blockage of air. Place a hand in front of the mouth. As the tongue is moved down, release the air and say *tah, tah, tah.* Feel the exploded air against the hand. Repeat the syllable *at, at, at,* and feel the exploded air against the hand at the end of the word. With the hand in front of the mouth, feel the explosion of the t [t] sound in *to, to, to.* Produce the shortest possible explosion to eliminate wasted air between the t [t] and the o͞o [u] sounds.

(t)

Single Words

tail	time	after	interest	almost	minute
tall	tired	butter	metal	complete	picked
teaching	tomorrow	country	potato	debt	private
test	tongue	detail	stretch	fact	receipt
tight	tooth	history	water	list	tossed

Word Pairs

three	tree	ether	eater	seethe	seat
thin	tin	pithy	pitty	kiss	kit
sell	tell	lesser	letter	less	let
sack	baths	bats	path	pat	
tack					
sop	top	rocks	rots	hop	hot
thought	taught	dauber	daughter	sauce	sought
cook	took	pulling	putting	puss	put
suit	toot	roofing	rooting	booth	boot
surf	turf	squirreling	squirting	hearse	hurt
sub	tub	supple	subtle	bus	but
sable	table	racing	rating	ace	eight
thigh	tie	writhing	writing	nice	night
soy	toy			coif	quoit
down	town	dousing	doubting	bowed	bout
soul	toll	dosing	doting	both	boat

Sentences

1. Touch the tip of the tongue to the gum ridge.
2. The transit authority pressed him into a tight spot.
3. Do not explode it; tap it.
4. "Liberty, equality, and fraternity" was a revolutionary motto.
5. Do not touch the teeth on the *t* sound.
6. The rules on substitutions are not consistent.
7. There is no substitute for drill to develop accurate articulation.
8. Whenever you talk, try to do your best.
9. Do not limit your practice to laboratory sessions.
10. The ticket taker took the stub and cut it into bits.

Tongue Twister

Little Todd Tinker and his sister, Tina, tasted the salt water at the beach. "Terrible," said Todd, "the taste is disgusting!" Tina replied with a twinkle in her eye, "It's too much like Aunt Tessie's taffy." "Aunt Tessie's taffy tastes tearfully terrible," said Todd. As they talked, a terribly tall wave crashed over the tiny tots' heads. Todd and Tina splashed to safety and stated that they wished to have more taffy and less water.

(d) Diacritic   **Phonetic [d]**

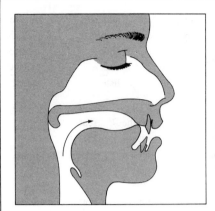 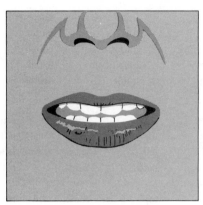

Formation

The d [d] sound is produced in the same way as the t [t] sound, except that the tongue touches the gum ridge with slightly less pressure and the vocal folds vibrate.

Definition

d [d] is a tongue-tip-to-gum-ridge, voiced, stop-plosive consonant.

Misarticulation

Sometimes d [d] is left out of the middle of such words as *blinding* or *grandfather*. Often it is not pronounced on the end of such words as *tried* or *had*. If the vocal folds are not vibrating, t [t] replaces d [d], so that *sudden* sounds like *sutten*. It is also incorrectly produced with the tongue in contact with the upper teeth, or even with it protruding between the teeth, as with the voiced *th* [ð], so that *ladder* sounds like *lather*.

Correction

Watch yourself in a mirror and repeat the words on the next page. Press the sides of the tongue against the sides of the upper teeth and repeat *do, do, do, do* quickly, one after the other over the tip of the tongue, while you raise and lower the tongue tip to and from the gum ridge. Rapidly contrast the sounds t [t] and d [d] by repetition of the syllables *tie-dye*.

(d)

Single Words

dark	door	body	reading	and	kind
day	doubt	building	ready	card	lend
dead	drain	idea	sudden	field	red
dear	drop	middle	under	friend	tired
do	dust	order	window	good	word

Word Pairs

zeal	deal	liter	leader	breathe	bread
zip	dip	bitter	bidder	his	hid
then	den	betting	bedding	set	said
tab	dab	lather	ladder	sat	sad
		father	fodder	rot	rod
taunt	daunt	causal	caudal	pause	pawed
		ensuring	enduring	shook	should
zoom	doom			soothe	sued
shirt	dirt	worthy	wordy	birth	bird
tusk	dusk	butting	budding	mutt	mud
tale	dale	lazy	lady	spate	spade
time	dime	rising	riding	size	side
		voicing	voiding	boys	Boyd
town	down	pouter	powder	clout	cloud
toe	dough	coating	coding	colt	cold

Sentences

1. Dizzy Lizzie was a delightful redhead.
2. The deed he did was disastrous.
3. She was the darling of downtown Denver.
4. Do delay the dance.
5. The dentist decided to drill the decay from the cavity.
6. The dress was a dark shade of red.
7. The odor of the daffodils was delightful.
8. The din from the wind and thunder was deafening.
9. Did you know Donald was a dream analyst?
10. According to the teacher, David received a *D* on the drill.

Tongue Twister

David Doolittle didn't dare divulge the details of his devious deed to his buddy, Darren. "Detective Dinkeldorf has an idea that David lied about his grades," Darren told Douglas while he drove downtown, "but, to this day, David denies doing anything that dastardly." "I don't desire discussing David Doolittle's indiscretions," Douglas said. "I'd rather depart for the desert," which he did suddenly.

(k) Diacritic   **Phonetic [k]**

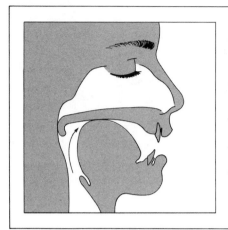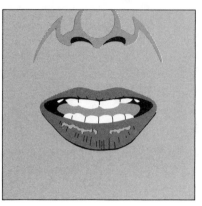

Formation

The back of the tongue is raised and pressed against the soft palate, so that it stops
the passage of air through the mouth. The soft palate is raised. The breath is blocked
momentarily. The tongue is then lowered suddenly, allowing the air to escape. The
vocal folds do not vibrate.

Definition

k [k] is a back-of-tongue-to-soft-palate, voiceless, stop-plosive consonant.

Misarticulation

If the back of the tongue does not actually touch the soft palate, a weak, tongue–
soft palate fricative is produced instead. In some cases, a puff of air is heard between
the k [k] sound and the following vowel, which gives it an aspirate quality. In other
cases, the sound is omitted from the ends of words.

Correction

Press the back of the tongue quite firmly against the soft palate. Exhale without
dropping the tongue, and you will hear an explosion of air as it leaves the mouth.
Now produce a series of k [k] sounds—*kaw, kaw, kaw, kaw, kaw*. To eliminate
extra airflow, place the hand in front of the mouth and produce *kaw, kaw, kaw* with
the smallest possible puff of air hitting the hand. Now read the series of words that
begin with this sound. With the hand in front of the mouth feel the small explosion
of air after each k [k]. Then try to use the ending k [k] sounds—*ak, ak, ak*. Again,
feel the explosion of air following each k [k].

(k)   **[k]**

card	cope	across	liquid	awake	public
cat	cotton	act	school	black	sock
clear	cough	affect	secret	brake	stomach
color	keep	because	ticket	milk	walk
copy	kick	equal	walking	music	work

Word Pairs

glean	clean	seating	seeking	league	leak
gill	kill	pits	picks	wig	wick
petal	kettle	debts	decks	net	neck
gam	cam	bagger	backer	sap	sack
got	cot	rotter	rocker	lot	lock
gall	call	bogs	balks	tag	talk
took	cook				
tool	cool	dudes	dukes	flute	fluke
certain	curtain	lurching	lurking	erg	irk
sup	cup	bulgy	bulky	bug	buck
gave	cave	mates	makes	ate	ache
tight	kite	bites	bikes	light	like
toy	coy				
sow	cow				
gold	cold	ocean	oaken	coat	coke

Sentences

1. The cock crows at the break of day.
2. The cook baked a cake for the picnic.
3. Kiss me, quick!
4. Dick took the milk to the kitchen.
5. Take the carrots and cabbages from the basket.
6. Carolyn cooked creamed corn for Kevin.
7. Kirk kicked the football clear over the backstop.
8. Can you come when I call?
9. Coca-Cola and coffee contain caffeine.
10. Ken controlled the snake with a forked stick.

Tongue Twister

"Can you corral kangaroos?" asked Kathy's cackling cousin. "Certainly I can," said the canny cowpoke, "if the crazy kangaroos are kept from hopping back out." Keeping kangaroos in a corral is practical when you lock canvas collars around their necks. Of course, caged kangaroos react by boxing careless cowpokes.

(g) Diacritic   **Phonetic [g]**

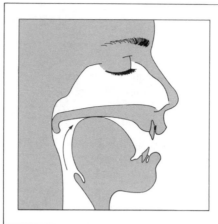

Formation

The back of the tongue is raised and in contact with the soft palate. The soft palate is elevated. Exhalation is begun, building up pressure, and the vocal folds are vibrated. The tongue is quickly lowered, producing a voiced plosive sound.

Definition

g [g] is a back-of-tongue-to-soft-palate, voiced, stop-plosive consonant.

Misarticulation

If the back of the tongue does not press hard enough against the soft palate, a voiced, tongue–soft palate fricative sound occurs. As also happens with the k [k] sound, some persons allow a puff of air to come between the g [g] sound and the following vowel. Others omit the sound from the ends of words. Some speakers unvoice the g [g] sound, which produces a k [k] sound instead.

Correction

Place the tip of the tongue against the gum ridge, and then shift gradually until the back of the tongue contacts the soft palate. With the tongue in that position, exhale, blocking the air with the tongue. At the same time, vibrate the vocal folds, and then release the blocked air. To reduce extra airflow following the explosion of air, place a hand in front of the mouth and lower the tongue quickly from the soft palate while you say *ga, ga, ga*. Reduce the amount of air hitting the hand as much as possible. To be certain of voicing the g [g] sound at the ends of words, place a hand lightly on the larynx, so that you can feel some vibration while the sound is being produced in words such as *log, big,* and *dog*.

(g)

Single Words

garden	government	again	finger	dig	leg
gird	grass	against	language	drug	pig
give	great	angry	regret	egg	rug
gland	group	begin	regular	flag	sag
gold	growth	eagle	together	league	tag

Word Pairs

clean	glean	leaks	leagues	lead	league
till	gill	picks	pigs	wick	wig
debt	get	bedding	begging	led	leg
crass	grass	lax	lags	back	bag
cot	got				
call	gall	lauding	logging	dawn	dog
would	good				
duel	ghoul				
curl	girl	birds	burgs	urge	erg
come	gum	mudding	mugging	luck	lug
cave	gave				
die	guy	timer	tiger		
coy	goy				
doubt	gout				
dough	go	loco	logo	rose	rogue

Sentences

1. The dog began to growl at the goat.
2. They were grimacing at the gray gun.
3. She was giddy from the golden gown he gave her.
4. Grace has gone to the garden to get some grapes.
5. The dog and the pig played tag.
6. Gwendolyn tugged the golden goblet from the bag.
7. Golda was the girl who gigged the frog.
8. They gladly gave the bagged groceries to the rogue.
9. What's good for the goose is good for the gander.
10. The guest gave her evening gown to Grandma Gloria.

Tongue Twister

Three gray geese were grazing in the green grass. Giddy from the great glee of grazing so greedily, their eyes became glazed and glassy. A gloomy but glamorous girl grimaced at the glassy-eyed, grazing gray geese and gathered gladioli in a grocery bag. Glancing down, she gazed at a gorgeous, gleaming, golden egg one of the grazing geese had laid. "Oh, goodness," she giggled, "I'll give this glorious egg to my grandmother, and we'll never beg for food again."

(f) Diacritic   **Phonetic [f]**

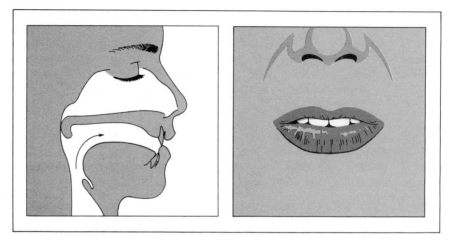

Formation

The lower lip is brought up under the edge of the upper teeth, and the soft palate is raised. The breath comes out in a continuous stream between the lower lip and the upper teeth, and the vocal folds do not vibrate.

Definition

f [f] is a lower-lip-to-upper-teeth, voiceless, fricative consonant.

Misarticulation

If the lower lip does not touch the edge of the upper teeth firmly, the f [f] sound is distorted. If the lips are brought together, the p [p] sound results.

Correction

Look in a mirror. Determine that the lower lip closes firmly with the upper teeth. Practice biting the lower lip gently while you exhale through the mouth. As the teeth contact the lip, the f [f] sound will be heard. Contrast the sounds f [f] and p [p] by repeating the words pit-fit, put-foot, per-fur and pat-fat.

(f)

Single Words

fact	field	after	elephant	belief	rough
fall	first	beautiful	left	chief	self
family	floor	before	lift	enough	shelf
father	phone	comfort	offer	if	stiff
female	photo	different	office	off	tough

Word Pairs

peal	feel	leaps	leafs (verb)	beep	beef
pill	fill	dipper	differ	tip	tiff
said	fed	leapt	left	death	deaf
pat	fat	lapping	laughing	cap	calf
pox	fox	prop it	profit		
thought	fought	sauced	soft	call	cough
pull	full	hooking	hoofing	hook	hoof
pool	fool	rooting	roofing	root	roof
purr	fur	serves	surfs	serve	surf
pun	fun	cups	cuffs	rut	rough
pace	face	sanely	safely	wave	waif
might	fight	lighter	lifer	night	knife
boil	foil	coil	coif	coin	coif
pound	found				
poled	fold	oaths	oafs	loath	loaf

Sentences

1. Fred's father takes him fishing every fall.
2. Feel the fine grain of this fabric.
3. Did you find enough coffee for breakfast?
4. The fancy frills on her frock gave her flair.
5. Phillip was not afraid of the funny faces.
6. The judge fined Frank a fee of forty dollars.
7. The farmer had beef before he left, laughing.
8. Let's feed our fine-feathered friends.
9. The fires burned fiercely for fifteen hours.
10. "Fee, fie, foe, fum," the fierce, fat giant laughed feverishly.

Tongue Twister

Fannie Finch fried flounders and fritters for Francis Fowler's father. Feeling fine, he fiddled with his fine felt furs. "Of all the felt I ever felt, I never felt any felt that felt the same as that felt felt when I first felt the felt of that felt fedora!" said Francis Fowler's father. "Enough," fumed Fanny. "If you fool around for fifteen foolish minutes with your soft felt fedora, I'll feel like feeding these fine fritters to the first waif I find."

(v) Diacritic   **Phonetic [v]**

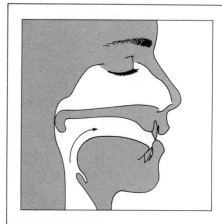 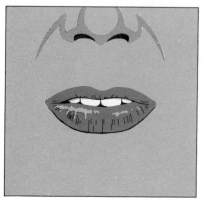

Formation

The lower lip touches the edge of the upper teeth, as is done to produce the f [f] sound, and the soft palate is raised. The breath comes out between the lower lip and the upper teeth in a continuous stream. The sound is voiced.

Definition

v [v] is a lower-lip-to-upper-teeth, voiced, fricative consonant.

Misarticulation

If the lips are brought together so that the lower lip contacts the upper lip instead of the upper teeth, the b [b] sound is substituted for the v [v] sound. If the lips are slightly rounded and do not contact the upper teeth, then the w [w] sound is substituted for the v [v].

Correction

Look in a mirror. Determine that the lower lip is firmly touching the edge of the upper teeth. Bite the lower lip to sense where it closes on the teeth. At the same time, vibrate the vocal folds to generate a phonated sound. Touch the vocal folds, the jaw, and the lips lightly with the fingertips to become sensitive to their vibrations. The voice breath stream should flow between the upper front teeth and the lower lip. Repeat the contrasting words berry-very, bat-vat, boat-vote, or wet-vet, wick-Vic, wine-vine.

(v)   [v]

Single Words

value	vessel	behavior	government	curve	move
vane	view	cover	level	give	nerve
vein	violent	division	oven	glove	of
verse	vital	even	over	have	save
very	voyage	every	private	love	wave

Word Pairs

feel	veal	weeper	weaver	leaf	leave
bicker	vicar	ribber	river	lip	live (verb)
berry	very	leather	lever		
ban	van	cabs	halves	cab	calve
folly	volley				
fault	vault				
		whose	hooves	proof	prove
		lubbing	loving	dub	dove
base	vase	safes	saves	waif	wave
buy	vie	nights	knives	strife	strive
Boyce	voice				
bough	vow				
boat	vote	lobes	loaves	cope	cove

Sentences

1. Loaves of baked bread will be served with the veal.
2. Victor advises that the river is violently wavy.
3. Virginia is vying with Vivian for Vinnie's love.
4. Her velvet dress unraveled in the cave.
5. Viola's new van is very valuable.
6. The waves in her hair gave her an oval-shaped face.
7. I believe Vicki saves doves from diving into the river.
8. Not very long ago, the vat of vinegar was in a cave.
9. Varicose veins never leave vicariously.
10. Herbert Hoover was not a vegetarian.

Tongue Twister

Velma was a very vivacious vagrant. She viewed life as a vast voyage. Since she intended vigorously to write volumes of books about her views, she drove her van to the river every day. There she gave vast quantities of victuals to starving children of the village, whose food was eaten by ravenous vermin. She vowed to save the victims of the vermin and invested in a vast vat of poison. With the vermin vying for the poison instead of the food, starvation was staved off, and Velma's volumes were eventually written.

(th) Diacritic   **Phonetic [θ]**

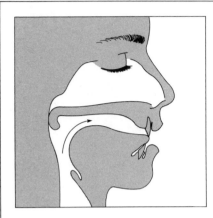

Formation

The flattened tip of the tongue is placed lightly between the edge of the upper and the lower front teeth. The breath stream passes between the tongue tip and the upper teeth in a continuous flow. The soft palate is raised. The vocal folds do not vibrate.

Definition

th [θ] is a tongue-to-teeth, voiceless, fricative consonant sound.

Misarticulation

A common problem in producing the th [θ] sound is placement of the tongue on the gum ridge or in back of the teeth instead of forward on the edge of the teeth. What occurs is usually the t [t] sound or, rarely, the s [s] sound. Some speakers bring the lower lip up to the upper teeth and produce an f [f] sound in the middle or at the end of a word. Some speakers place the articulators correctly, but pull the tongue back before starting the breath stream, resulting in a t [t]-like sound.

Correction

Look in a mirror. Place a forefinger in front of the lips. Push the tongue between the teeth, so that it touches the finger and the upper teeth. Breathe out, so that the air passes between the upper teeth and the tongue, and the sound is complete. Practice the th [θ] sound several times. Then take your finger away from the lips and try it again. Be certain that the upper lip does not touch the tongue, or a sound like t [t] will result. If you are still unable to produce the sound correctly, your professor will provide you with a model to imitate. When your sound production is approved, practice the words on the next page.

(th)

[θ]

Single Words

theory	thirty	anything	mathematics	birth	health
thief	thought	arithmetic	method	breath	month
thin	thousand	authority	nothing	death	north
thing	throat	bathtub	something	cloth	south
think	thunder	healthy	wealthy	growth	with

Word Pairs

tree	three	eater	ether	teat	teeth
tick	thick	pitty	pithy	wit	with
heft	theft	breadless	breathless	set	Seth
tank	thank	catty	Cathy	bat	bath
saw	thaw			brought	broth
true	through	rcots	Ruth's	toot	tooth
heard	third			worse	worth
some	thumb				
tie	thigh	pylon	python		
				mouse	mouth
tow	throw			boat	both

Sentences

1. I thought that her thighs were thin.
2. The thought that he was ruthless was a myth.
3. I thanked the three anesthesiologists for the ether.
4. Mr. Blythe told the truth about his health.
5. Ruth was a youthful, aesthetic theologian.
6. I think both Theda and Thad are faithful.
7. To be truthful, Bertha studied math for three years and six months.
8. Martha authored the ethereal book on Athens.
9. The Elizabethan broth was frothy and earthy.
10. When she thought of his theme and thesis, her thyroid would throb.

Tongue Twister

Theophilus Thistle, the successful thistle sifter, in sifting a sieve full of unsifted thistles, thrust 3000 thistles through the thick of his thumb. Since thousands of successful thistle sifters have sifted unsifted thistles without thrusting thistles into their thumbs, Theophilus Thistle is an unsuccessful thistle sifter indeed. We wish success to Theophilus Thistle, the faithful, if clumsy, thistle sifter.

(*th*) Diacritic   **Phonetic [ð]**

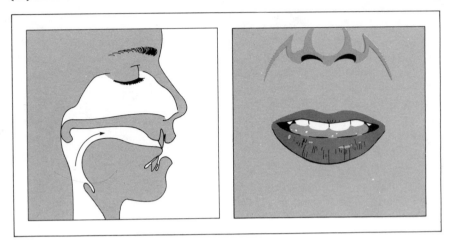

Formation

The flattened tip of the tongue is placed lightly between the edges of the upper and the lower front teeth. The soft palate is raised. The vocal folds vibrate. The air flows between the tongue and the upper teeth.

Definition

th [ð] is a tongue-to-teeth, voiced, fricative consonant sound.

Misarticulation

If the tongue does not touch the edge of the teeth properly, the v [v], d [d], or l [l] sounds replace *th* [ð]. Unvoicing the sound results in th [θ]. Some speakers place the articulators correctly, but pull the tongue back before starting the breath stream, resulting in a d [d]-like sound.

Correction

Look in a mirror. Place the forefinger of one hand across your lips, and place the other hand on your throat. Place your tongue between your teeth, as was done to produce the th [θ] sound. Breathe out as before, but add the sound of your voice (you will feel vibration on your hand). Pass the air between your upper teeth and your tongue. You will feel a vibration on the tip of your tongue. Practice the *th* [ð] sound several times. Then remove your hands from your lips and throat, and try it again. Be certain that your upper lip does not touch your tongue, or the d [d] sound will result. If you are still unable to produce the sound correctly, your professor will provide you with a model to imitate. When your sound production is approved, practice the words on the next page.

(th)

[ð]

Single Words

than	then	another	mother	lathe	smooth
the	there	bother	rhythm	lithe	teethe
their	therefore	brother	together	loathe	tithe
theirs	these	feather	whether	scathe	wreathe
them	thy	leather	wither	seethe	writhe

Word Pairs

tease	these	teasing	teething	teeth	teethe
hiss	this	dimmer	dither		
den	then	wetter	weather		
sat	that	ladder	lather		
		fodder	father		
				sued	soothe
		firmer	further		
fuss	thus	udder	other		
day	they	babes	bathes	babe	bathe
dine	thine	tiding	tithing	side	scythe
sow	thou	mouser	mouther	mouse	mouthe
dough	though	closing	clothing	close	clothe

Sentences

1. They gathered the heather together.
2. Rather than writhing, smooth your leather.
3. Bathing goes further in the southern weather.
4. Either father or mother soothes the teething baby.
5. Why bother with those breathing rhythms?
6. My brother has a tether; therefore, we can gather the feathers.
7. Although they'd rather sunbathe in southern Alaska, the weather's a bother.
8. Your breathing will bother you, the farther you run.
9. They were gathering to hear the soothing northern songs.
10. The lathe operator loathes bathing.

Tongue Twister

Whether hither or thither, the mother and father bother to tan leather for a farthing. Although their clothes are weathered with lather, they will bathe later. They writhe in unsoothed anger at their loathed employer, who pays a single farthing for the leather. They can hardly pay their tithing or buy a new scythe. Their clothing is loathsome, and their leather shoes are weathered, but they will bathe with much lather when the leather is together.

(s) Diacritic   **Phonetic [s]**

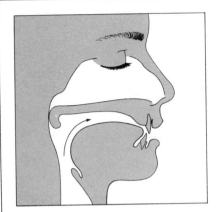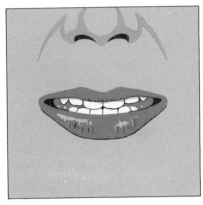

Formation

The blade of the tongue is channeled and raised toward the gum ridge, with the sides of the tongue against the upper gums and upper molars and the tongue tip behind the front teeth. The breath stream passes between the gum ridge and the tongue blade in a continuous flow. The teeth are almost closed, the lips are slightly open. The soft palate is raised. The vocal folds do not vibrate.

Definition

s [s] is a tongue-blade-to-gum-ridge, voiceless, fricative consonant.

Misarticulation

If the tongue tip contacts the gum ridge, air is allowed to pass around the sides of the tongue; this action is called a *lateral lisp*. If the tongue tip protrudes between the teeth, a sound like th [θ] is produced; this is called a *frontal lisp*. If the sound is made between the tongue and the front palate, it is given a "mushy" quality. If the s [s] sound is made with too much breath pressure, it may be noisy or whistling. The sound is sometimes incorrectly omitted at the ends of words.

Correction

Produce the sound t [t] with the blade of the tongue contacting the gum ridge and with the tongue tip pointed downward, toward the lower teeth. Repeat the sound several times, and concentrate on the feeling between the tongue and the gum ridge at the release of the sound. Keep that same feeling as you extend the air release at the end of t [t] to produce the combination ts [ts]. Repeat this several times, and concentrate on keeping the tongue tip pointed down but not touching the teeth. Now try the s [s] sound in the same position without the t [t] sound. Repeat this action several times. If you are still unable to produce the sound correctly, your professor will provide you with a model to imitate. When your sound production is approved, practice the words on the next page.

(s)   [s]

Single Words

cent	send	almost	last	across	increase
safe	serious	chest	lesson	base	miss
school	side	dancing	past	business	office
science	sleep	dust	possible	false	place
second	slip	interest	responsible	horse	yes

Word Pairs

zeal	seal	beefed	beast	leaf	lease
thin	sin	sifter	sister	myth	miss
Ted	said	getting	guessing	mesh	mess
that	sat	patting	passing	path	pass
Tod	sod	poppy	posse		
thaw	saw	mothy	mossy	laud	loss
foot	soot				
zoo	sue	looter	looser	truth	truce
fir	sir	burgher	bursar	verb	verse
thumb	some	muddle	muscle	fuzz	fuss
tale	sale	raising	racing	faith	face
thigh	sigh	prizes	prices	rise	rice
toy	soy	voiding	voicing	void	voice
how	sow	doubting	dousing	mouth	mouse
toe	so	clover	closer	clothes	close

Sentences

1. Susie fell asleep after she ate her soup.
2. The sailor sailed the salty sea.
3. Sinclair Lewis signed the lease.
4. Sam whispered his secret to Sally.
5. Sandra said she was selling seashells.
6. Many of us have strong feelings about civil rights.
7. Cesar saw the insane sapsucker and stuffed it in a sack.
8. Silly Lisa had a sister who was surly.
9. Six months later, Stan was still singing.
10. I close my eyes and sense your presence.

Tongue Twister

Sarah sat at the seashore and selected shells of several shades while she basked in the summer sun. The skipper of a schooner offshore sailed skillfully and speedily by, as he skimmed over the shimmering waters of the salty sea. Splashed by the surf from the sea, Sarah donned her diving mask, so that she could find more seashells. Suddenly, a summer storm from the south sprang up and sent Sarah skipping across the sands to safety. While ensconced in the security of the safety zone (whilst eating succotash), Sarah sat smiling at a Scottish sailor, who seemed to have seen the storm coming, as his sloop was sailing into the slip.

(z) Diacritic   **Phonetic [z]**

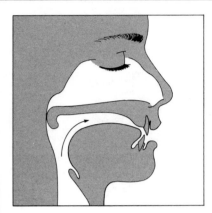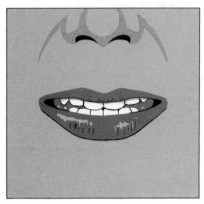

Formation

The blade of the tongue, channeled behind its front edge, is raised toward the gum ridge with the sides of the tongue against the upper gums and molars and with the tongue tip behind the front teeth. The breath stream passes between the gum ridge and the tongue blade in a continuous flow. The teeth are nearly closed. The lips are slightly parted. The soft palate is raised. The vocal folds vibrate.

Definition

z [z] is a tongue-blade-to-gum-ridge, voiced, fricative consonant.

Misarticulation

As can happen with the s [s] sound, if the tongue tip and the gum ridge are in contact, air is allowed to pass around the sides of the tongue, which creates a lateral lisp. If the tongue tip protrudes between the teeth, the th [θ] sound, or a frontal lisp, is produced. The sound is sometimes incorrectly omitted from the ends of words. Sometimes s [s] is substituted for z [z].

Correction

The z [z] sound is made with the same mouth movements as the s [s] sound is. The only difference between the two is that z [z] uses vocal vibration. First, practice the s [s] sound. Once that is correct, vocalize the sound ŭ [ʌ] with one hand on your throat. As you do that, slowly raise the tongue to the position for the s [s] sound, but continue voicing (you will feel the vibration on your hand). You will feel a vibration between your tongue and your gum ridge as the z [z] sound is produced. Repeat this action several times. Then, try z [z] alone; it sounds very much like a buzzing bee. Repeat it several times. If you are still unable to produce the sound correctly, your professor will provide you with a model to imitate. When your sound production is approved, practice the words on the next page.

(z)

[z]

Single Words

zealous	zig	amusement	exact	as	please
zebra	zinc	business	physical	because	prose
Xerox	zircon	desire	position	cheese	size
zero	xylophone	disease	prison	news	surprise
Zeus	zoom	easy	reason	noise	wise

Word Pairs

seal	zeal	eagle	easel	eat	ease
sip	zip	Billy	busy	id	is
guest	zest			said	says
sag	zag	dabble	dazzle	had	has
far	Czar	robin	rosin	card	cars
		pawning	pausing	cord	cores
sue	zoo	looses	loses	shoot	shoes
				heard	hers
		buses	buzzes	bud	buzz
sane	Zane	lady	lazy	crave	craze
		riding	rising	bide	buys
				Boyd	boys
sounds	zounds	dousing	dowsing	aloud	allows
phone	zone	clothing	closing	node	nose

Sentences

1. Busy bees buzz and buzz.
2. My cousin has some daisies.
3. His music was amazing, amusing, and pleasing.
4. Measles make Susan's eyes hazy.
5. There are zebras, monkeys, and weasels in the zoo.
6. Cesar seized the fuzzy buzzard.
7. Zeke owned a set of dazzling zircons.
8. She was full of zest and zeal when she listened to jazz.
9. The daisies she was raising were easy to seize.
10. Zachary plays jazz better than the composer.

Cortez, the bee, zigzagged lazily into the daisies. The breeze whizzed past his fuzzy face and teased his rising wings. He felt dizzy, but his cousin, Zola, seized his attention as she crazily zipped by his eyes. "Please don't whiz so zealously by me—you're twice my size," Cortez buzzed to Zola. "You're lazy and crazy, and I'll tease you until you gain zest in your life. Busy bees should buzz with ease," Zola replied.

(sh) Diacritic   **Phonetic [ʃ]**

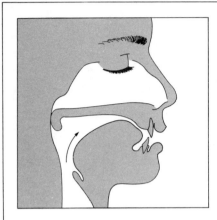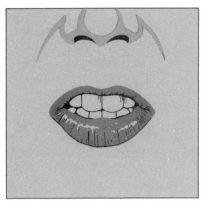

Formation

The channeled blade of the tonuge is raised, with the sides of the tongue pressing against the sides of the upper molars and with the tip pointed downward, towards the lower teeth. The breath stream passes between the tongue blade and the front section of the palate in a continuous flow. The cheeks are close to the side teeth, the lips are slightly protruded, and the soft palate is raised. The vocal folds do not vibrate.

Definition

sh [ʃ] is a tongue-blade-to-front-palate, voiceless, fricative consonant.

Misarticulation

If the tongue protrudes through the teeth, the th [θ] sound is substituted. If the tip or the blade of the tongue contacts the gum ridge or the front palate, a lateral sound results.

Correction

Production of the sh [ʃ] sound should be accomplished with attention to the wide channeling of the blade of the tongue, the nearly closed teeth, the slightly protruded lips, the flat cheeks, and a wide stream of outflowing air. Practice the contrast between s [s] and sh [ʃ]. Sometimes it helps to make the tongue thick and to draw it in from the position for the s [s] sound, so as to shift toward the position for sh [ʃ]. Look in a mirror. Produce the sound s [s], and while continuing to say it, pull the tongue back in the mouth. Keep its sides in contact with the gums and the sides of the upper teeth. Keep the cheeks close to the teeth with the lips protruded. Keep the tongue tip down. When the tongue is pulled back far enough, the sh [ʃ] sound will result. Repeat several times, then try sh [ʃ] alone. If you are still unable to produce the sound correctly, your professor will provide you a model to imitate. When your sound production is approved, practice the words on the next page.

(sh)   **[ʃ]**

shade	shop	addition	education	brush	polish
sharp	short	attention	fiction	clash	push
shelf	shut	condition	machine	crush	smash
shine	sugar	direction	special	foolish	trash
shock	sure	discussion	tension	gash	wash

see	she	leases	leashes	keep	quiche
sip	ship	willing	wishing	fit	fish
sell	shell	messed	meshed	mess	mesh
sack	shack	massing	mashing	cad	cash
sop	shop	wadding	washing	gob	gosh
tall	shawl	squalling	squashing	squab	squash
hood	should	pulling	pushing	bull	bush
sue	shoe	allusion	Aleutian		
dirt	shirt	hurdle	Herschel		
son	shun	upper	usher		
sake	shake	glazier	glacier		
sign	shine				
sour	shower				
so	show	open	ocean	goes	gauche

1. Shall we share our cash for the shrubs?
2. He was so shy that he wouldn't shave his moustache.
3. "You shall share the shrimp," the shrewish fishwife shouted.
4. "Show Sharon a shawl!" shrieked Shirley.
5. The fresh-fish shop had a shoeshine stand.
6. Cheryl pushed the trash can to the ocean.
7. The shiftless usher showed us the cash.
8. Shelley swished the fresh ocean water through the mesh.
9. The motion of the ocean made her ashen.
10. The shrapnel crashed a short distance from the glacier.

Sharon shrieked in a shrill, sharp voice, "I shall shine my shoes after I shower!" Her mother shouted back, "If you shine after you shower, you shall probably get shoe polish all over your freshly washed hands, and that would be a shame." But Sharon foolishly showered first and, sure enough, polished both her shoes and herself and had to shower again.

(zh) Diacritic   **Phonetic [ʒ]**

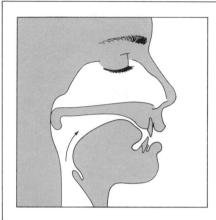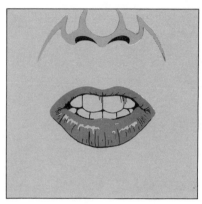

Formation

The blade of the tongue is raised with the sides of the tongue pressing against the sides of the upper molars and with the tongue tip pointed toward the lower front teeth. The breath stream passes between the tongue blade and the front palate in a continuous flow. The cheeks are close to the side teeth, the lips slightly protruded. The soft palate is raised. The vocal folds vibrate.

Definition

zh [ʒ] is a tongue-blade-to-front-palate, voiced, fricative consonant.

Misarticulation

If the tongue protrudes through the teeth, a *th* [ð] sound is substituted. This problem is similar to the misarticulation of the sh [ʃ] sound. If the tip or blade of the tongue contacts the gum ridge or the front palate, a lateral sound is produced.

Correction

Look in a mirror. This sound is produced in much the same way as the sh [ʃ] sound, except that this one is voiced. Produce the sound z [z], and while continuing to voice it, pull the tongue back in the mouth. Keep its sides in contact with the inner gums and the sides of the upper teeth. Keep the cheeks close to the teeth and the lips slightly protruded. Keep the tongue tip down. When the tongue is pulled back far enough, to point where the tongue blade is in contact with the front palate, the zh [ʒ] sound will result. Repeat this action several times. Then try the zh [ʒ] sound alone. If you are still unable to produce the sound correctly, your professor will provide you with a model to imitate. When your sound production is approved, practice the words on the next page.

(zh)

Single Words

allusion	measure	barrage	massage
artesian	pleasure	camouflage	mirage
decision	seizure	collage	persiflage
delusion	television	cortege	prestige
evasion	usual	garage	sabotage

Word Pairs

leasher	leisure	lead	liege
villain	vision		
treader	treasure		
adder	azure		

Confucian	confusion	rude	rouge
person	Persian		

glacier	glazier	bays	beige

composer	composure

Sentences

1. A mirage is confusion by illusion.
2. At her leisure, she used rouge to camouflage her features.
3. The usual red corsage was replaced by a beige scarf.
4. The barrage of illusions was unusual.
5. She made a decision to camouflage the garage.
6. The Persian got pleasure from television.
7. There is no measure of leisure time in Asia.
8. The prestige of the artesian well was an illusion.
9. His confusion from the barrage of words caused an invasion.
10. Evasion is usual in sabotage.

Tongue Twister

It was hard to measure the treasure Jack found in the beige garage. The pleasure of finding the azure sapphires gave him delusions of fabulous wealth, but their seizure by the tax agent brought confusion to his vision. His hopes were sabotaged, his composure was destroyed, and his decision to seek work as a glazier gained prestige.

(h) Diacritic   **Phonetic [h]**

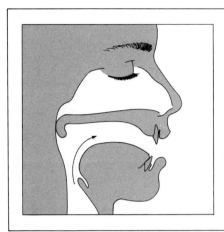
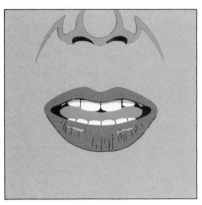

Formation

This sound is produced by a continuous flow of air through the vocal folds, the throat, and the mouth. The tongue and lips are relaxed and in position for the following vowel. The soft palate is raised, and the vocal folds do not vibrate.

Definition

h [h] is a glottal, voiceless, fricative consonant.

Misarticulation

The h [h] sound is not often mispronounced or unpronounced by native Americans. The h [h] sound is sometimes omitted in such words as *his*, *humid*, *hotel*, *human*, *huge*, and *humble*. If too much air is emitted, the h [h] sound is exaggerated.

Sometimes the back of the tongue is held near the soft palate, so that a rushing sound is heard. There is no diacritic symbol for this sound; phonetically, it is [X].

Correction

Look in a mirror. Pretend to laugh—*ha, ha, ha*. Hold a hand in front of your mouth and feel the air striking it as the h [h] sound is produced. Try *ho, ho, ho*. Feel the movement of the abdominal muscles as the h [h] sound in each syllable is produced. With a hand in front of the mouth, try the words on the following page, and concentrate on the feel of the air as you say the h [h] sound.

(h)

[h]
Single Words

hair	heart	overhear	unhallowed
hand	help	rehash	unhealthy
happy	high	rehearse	unheated
have	hope	reheated	unhook
healthy	house	rehydrate	unhurt

Word Pairs

eat	heat	repeat	reheat
is	his	in tears	inheres
Ed	head	bequest	behest
add	had	unmanned	unhand
sop	hop	cartop	carhop
all	hall	uncalled	unhauled
should	hood	uncooked	unhooked
sue	who		
sir	her	reverse	rehearse
sump	hump		
ate	hate	unfailed	unhailed
fight	height	retire	rehire
sow	how		
oh	hoe	resewed	rehoed

Sentences

1. He went to the hardware store for a heavy hose.
2. Hail to the homecoming of Henry the Hero.
3. His high, heavy heel gave him the hoped-for height.
4. Hey, Harry, hurry up and help that unhappy hunter.
5. He helped to hasten the construction of the house on the hill.
6. Harvey healed the hurting horseman.
7. How can we uphold the law on behalf of the homeowners?
8. My husband has high regard for the inhabitants of Haiti.
9. Mohair suits are prohibited in this home.
10. Grasshoppers inhabit this hillside horticultural habitat.

Tongue Twister

Horatio hurried homeward haphazardly while he hummed a hymn. He was a handsome husband and had hosted many happy occasions for his wife. Somehow, Horatio heard a hissing sound from the hill on which his house sat. Horatio stopped humming, and his heart became heavy with worry. "How can a husband who is humming hear hissing from his home on the hill?" he halfheartedly whispered. "Perhaps Hilda has harmed the hillbillies." Hurriedly, he hastened up the hill ahead, only to have his steps stopped by a hissing snake. Having a heavy harpoon in his hand, he heaved it at the hisser and hit it in the head. Happily, hoping soon to be home to Hilda, he headed up the hill again.

(ch) Diacritic   **Phonetic [tʃ]**

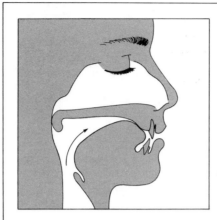

Formation

This sound is a combination of a plosive similar to t [t] and the fricative sh [ʃ]. The blade of the tongue is raised to touch the front palate lightly just behind the gum ridge. The breath stream is momentarily stopped by the tongue at the front palate. The tongue then quickly lowers slightly, allowing the breath stream to explode between it and the front palate to form the sh [ʃ] part of the sound. The soft palate is raised. The vocal folds do not vibrate.

Definition

ch [tʃ] is a tongue-blade-to-front-palate, voiceless, affricate consonant.

Misarticulation

If the tongue protrudes between the teeth, a lisped sound results. If the tongue tip or the tongue blade contacts the front palate, lateral emission of the sound results. After the plosive part of the sound, forward placement of the tongue blade can result in the substitution of a sound like ts [ts].

Correction

Look in a mirror. Produce the sh [ʃ] sound, and as you do, raise the tongue to block it. Then let it go quickly with an explosion of air. The ch [tʃ] sound will result. Alternate between sh [ʃ] and ch [tʃ]. Say the following words, and concentrate on stopping the voice after the t [t] sound and on exploding the ch [tʃ] sound— *watch, itch, catch, pitch, ditch, patch, match.* Now try the sound at the beginning of words—*chop, chase, cheese, church.* If you are still unable to produce the sound correctly, you will need help from your professor before you practice the words on the next page.

(ch)

[tʃ]

chain	chief	bachelor	picture	arch	stitch
chalk	child	digestion	question	branch	stretch
change	chin	exchange	structure	lunch	such
cheap	choose	future	suggestion	match	watch
cheese	church	natural	teaching	reach	which

Word Pairs

sheet	cheat	pieces	peaches	peace	peach
ship	chip	inning	itching	pit	pitch
jest	chest	ebbing	etching	red	retch
sat	chat	lacking	latching	cat	catch
shop	chop	water	watcher	wad	watch
talk	chalk				
				bush	Butch
shoes	choose				
perch	church	lurking	lurching		
some	chum	tugging	touching	mush	much
pace	chase				
filed	child				
voice	choice				
how	chow	crowding	crouching	pout	pouch
poke	choke	poking	poaching	coat	coach

Sentences

1. Charlie was a charming chimpanzee.
2. The child watched for each chance to chase the chickens.
3. Chester was the gum-chewing champion of Charleston.
4. Richard searched for the satchel.
5. Churches need charitable teachers.
6. The cherries she chewed made her chubby.
7. Let the child choose the chair.
8. The teacher purchased chalk for the children with a Czech check.
9. Chuck lives in Chatsworth, by the checkered church.
10. We'll exchange the cheap pitcher for a choice chalice.

Tongue Twister

Chet the chubby chipmunk filched cherries and chocolates. He chose to chomp the chocolates for lunch and exchange the cherries for natural cheese. Chet perched on a chair to reach for peaches, but couldn't stretch that much. Such a challenge was too much, and he lurched to his home in the ditch near the church.

(j) Diacritic   **Phonetic [dʒ]**

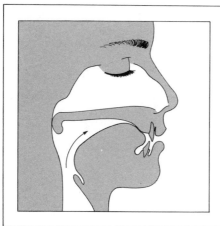

Formation

This is a combination of a stop-plosive similar to d [d] and the fricative zh [ʒ]. The blade of the tongue is raised. It lightly touches the front palate just behind the gum ridge. The breath stream is momentarily stopped by the tongue at the front palate. The tongue then quickly lowers a bit, which allows the breath stream to explode between it and the front palate to form the zh [ʒ] part of the sound. The soft palate is raised. The vocal folds vibrate.

Definition

j [dʒ] is a tongue-blade-to-front-palate, voiced, affricate consonant.

Misarticulation

If the tongue protrudes between the teeth, a *th* [ð] sound is produced. If the tongue tip or the tongue blade contacts the front palate, a lateral emission of the sound results. Forward placement of the tongue may result in the substitution of dz [dʒ]. Unvoicing sometimes occurs at the ends of words, which causes ch [tʃ] to be substituted. Sometimes y [j] is substituted for j [dʒ].

Correction

Look in a mirror. This sound is made with the same action as the ch [tʃ] sound, except that this one is voiced. Place a hand on your throat and say the sound ŭ [ʌ] as you move to the position for ch [tʃ]. Continue voicing the sound (you will feel the vibration with your hand) and explode it. The j [dʒ] will be the result. To improve the voicing of the sound at the end of words, say the following words with a hand on your throat, and concentrate on the feeling of vibration throughout this pronunciation: *edge, judge, rage, cage, badge.* If you are still having difficulty in the correct production of this sound, ask your professor for assistance before you proceed to practice the material on the next page.

(j)

[dʒ]

Single Words

general	join	adjustment	engine	carriage	orange
gentile	journey	agent	manager	charge	page
jaw	judge	danger	religion	damage	range
jelly	jump	digestion	soldier	edge	sponge
jewel	just	education	suggestion	knowledge	stage

Word Pairs

cheap	jeep	seeding	sieging	seed	siege
cheer	jeer	riches	ridges	languid	language
chest	jest	addenda	agenda	head	hedge
tab	jab	batter	badger		
yacht	jot	larder	larger	lot	lodge
yaw	jaw				
fury	jury				
youth	juice	humor	huger	hewed	huge
shirk	jerk	murder	merger	search	surge
bug	jug	budding	budging	bud	budge
Yale	jail	aiding	aging	weighed	wage
Cairo	gyro				
soy	joy				
youl	jowl	gowning	gouging	gout	gouge
yoke	joke				

Sentences

1. John jumped the hedge and nudged the cabbage.
2. Jim and Joe enjoyed watching the giraffe edging the hedge.
3. Joyce exchanged the aged jar of jam.
4. The judge and jury wanted justice for the soldier.
5. Jane knew Joe was in danger.
6. Jack joined Jim on the edge of the ledge.
7. The jalopy wouldn't budge until Jerry adjusted the engine.
8. "This joint is jumping," said John as he joined Jane in the Jungle Room.
9. Jerry was just joking with Roger.
10. Major Jeremiah Jones was jealous of General Joshua James.

Tongue Twister

The jaywalker jerked as the legion of jeeps came surging down the street. Just in time, a stranger nudged him, saying, "Jump out of the way of these jalopies. Their major joy is to make jelly of you." What a strange jargon the stranger spoke, the jaywalker thought. "Just gibberish, but genuine. If I hadn't jumped from in front of the jeeps and joined him, I would be just juice."

(hw) Diacritic   **Phonetic [ʍ]**

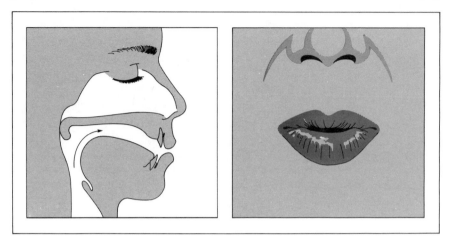

Formation

The lips are slightly rounded and protruded. The back of the tongue is raised, and its tip is behind the lower front teeth. The breath stream passes between them momentarily as the lips part, and the soft palate is raised. The vocal folds are not vibrating.

Definition

hw [ʍ] is a lip-to-lip, voiceless, glide consonant.

Misarticulation

Some people have difficulty in the production of the hw [ʍ] sound, usually because there is not enough air forced out to create the friction necessary for the sound to be formed at the lips. The w [w] sound is sometimes incorrectly substituted for the hw [ʍ] sound, particularly in English spoken as a second language and in certain American dialects.

Correction

Look in a mirror. Round the lips as if to whistle. Assume that you are blowing on hot soup in an attempt to cool it. Pretend to be blowing out candles at various distances from your lips, but do not puff out your cheeks. Now do try to blow out a candle. As you blow, allow your lips to open, and produce the vowel sound ŭ [ʌ]. Try hw [ʍ] with the sound ī [ɑɪ]. You will have said the word *why*. If you can do this successfully, put your hand in front of your mouth to feel the puff of air from the hw [ʍ] sound, and practice with the material on the next page.

(hw)   **[ʌ]**

Single Words

wheel	whip	anywhere	nowhere
when	whistle	bewhiskered	off-white
where	whit	bobwhite	overwhelming
whether	white	elsewhere	saw-whet
whine	why	everywhere	somewhere

Word Pairs

wield	wheeled		
witch	which		
wet	whet	some wear	somewhere
wax	whacks		
watt	what	some watt	somewhat

| world | whirled |

| wail | whale |
| wile | while |

Sentences

1. Meanwhile, the wheel was awhirl when the whistle blew.
2. White whales are everywhere.
3. Why wheel the whale on the wharf?
4. The bobwhite whimpered on the white whippet.
5. Whine elsewhere, or I'll whittle your whistle.
6. The whirling wheel ground the wheat.
7. Whatever Whitney whimpers, the whippoorwill whistles.
8. Which wheel was whisked out a while ago?
9. *When* and *where* and *what* and *why* and *whatever* are question words.
10. Why whisper about whiskers?

Tongue Twister

Whitman, the whimsical and bewhiskered whittler, was whisked out to sea in a wherry. When a white whale whirred by, he whistled, "What a whopper! Even wheezy white whales that whack their tails are overwhelming." While the whirling white whale whisked off somewhere, Whitman whittled and whistled as he whizzed to nowhere.

(w) Diacritic   **Phonetic [w]**

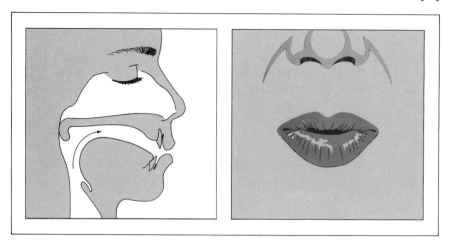

Formation

The lips are slightly rounded and protruded. The jaw is slightly open. The back of the tongue is raised toward the soft palate. The lips, tongue, and jaw then move to the position of the following vowel. The soft palate is raised, and the vocal folds vibrate.

Definition

w [w] is a lip-to-lip, voiced glide.

Misarticulation

If the vocal folds don't vibrate, the hw [ʍ] sound results. Some persons for whom English is a second language substitute v [v] for w [w].

Correction

Touch the lips. Look in a mirror. The action for the w [w] sound is the same as that for the hw [ʍ] sound, except that the former is voiced. Produce the sound o͞o [u] and blend it into the sound ŭ [ʌ]. You will have produced the syllable wu [wʌ]. Try voicing o͞o [u] and blend it into the sound ā [eɪ]. You will have pronounced the word *way*. If you think of o͞o [u] as you articulate the sound, the correct action for w [w] generally follows. Try this as you practice the material on the next page.

(w)

Single Words

walk	weight	awake	quality
wall	will	between	question
war	willow	equal	quick
watch	window	frequent	reward
water	woman	language	square

Word Pairs

wheel	we'll	sleet	sweet
whit	wit	slim	swim
where	wear	affair	aware
whacks	wax		
hollow	wallow		
vaults	Walt's		
good	wood		
food	wooed		
verse	worse		
bun	one		
whale	wail	slay	sway
while	wile	snipe	swipe

bound	wound	unbound	unwound
go	woe		

Sentences

1. You waltz very well, Willie!
2. Beware of the weirdo with the wet wig.
3. A wise woman will be wary of wily men.
4. Wendy went weeping from the wake.
5. One long walk would reward your health anyway.
6. Uncle Wiggley was a twin.
7. Does Walt know if we're going foward or backward?
8. Is anyone awake in this weirdo weather?
9. I won't swindle anyone with worthless wood.
10. The widow wished that she were wealthy.

Tongue Twister

Wee Willie Winkle was wary when he awoke. While he waited for his warm but wayward wildebeest to walk in, he swung backwards and forwards on his twin bed. He swayed upward and downward, waiting for it. Willie wondered why the wildebeest wanted to wander away from home. He wished the wild animal would wait for him before walking off. When the wildebeest walked in, Willie was the happiest waif in the world.

(y) Diacritic **Phonetic [j]**

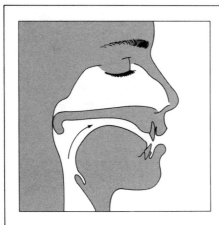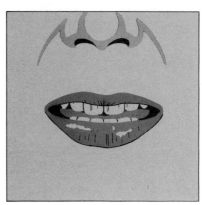

Formation

The lips are slightly spread. The jaw is slightly open. The front of the tongue is raised to the front palate. The lips, jaw, and tongue then move to the position for the following vowel. The soft palate is raised, and the vocal folds vibrate.

Definition

y [j] is a tongue-blade-to-front-palate, voiced glide.

Misarticulation

If the tongue is raised too high to the front palate, a fricative element is added to the y [j] sound. Some persons for whom English is a second language substitute j [dʒ] for y [j]

Correction

Look in a mirror. Say the ē [i] sound and blend it into the sound ä [ɑ]. Repeat several times. You will be producing the sound *yah*. Then say the ē [i] sound, and blend it into ĕs [ɛs]. Repeat several times. You will be saying the word *yes*. Now practice the material on the following page; start the y [j] sound with the ē [i] sound for each word in which it appears.

(y)　　　　　　　　　　　　　　　　　　　　　　　　**[j]**

unit	yellow	amusement	distribution
yam	yes	argument	future
yarn	yesterday	beautiful	humor
yawl	you	behavior	music
year	youth	canyon	pupil

reeled	yield		
gyp	yip		
jet	yet		
Jack	yak		
jarred	yard		
jaw	yaw	lauder	lawyer
poor	your		
juice	use		

sung	young
jail	Yale

jowl	yowl
joke	yolk

1. The yeoman on the yacht yielded to the lawyer.
2. The dog's yapping amused the youth.
3. The valiant Yankee soldier gave his opinion.
4. What is your view of the value of news and music?
5. He yearned to yell at the young man in the pavilion.
6. The stallion in your yard has unusual behavior.
7. For a beautiful future, don't abuse education in your youth.
8. Did you yell at the youngsters in the backyard?
9. The cocker spaniel was yapping at the yo-yo.
10. Yes, the yarn is brillant yellow, in my opinion.

Yale, the yellow stallion, lived with me in the Yukon. Yesterday, William, a youthful genius, used the valiant stallion like a yak in the vineyard. You must know that I yelled and yelled for William not to abuse the young yellow stallion, but he would not yield to my yelling. Yet William acquiesced to the argument of a millionaire lawyer on a yacht near the vineyard. Yale and I were reunited and the stallion pranced youthfully in the yard.

(r) Diacritic Phonetic [r]

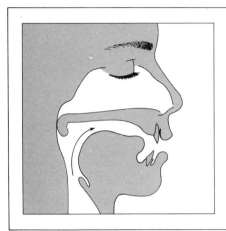

Formation

The center of the tongue is raised toward the center of the palate. The tongue tip and the tongue blade may be raised toward the palate, but they do not touch it. The lips may be slightly rounded and protruded. The jaw is slightly lowered. The soft palate is raised. The vocal folds vibrate.

Definition

r [r] is a tongue-center-to-center-palate, voiced glide.

Misarticulation

Probably no sound in the English language has more problems connected with it than the r [r] sound. The w [w] sound is sometimes incorrectly substituted for it. Those for whom English is a second language substitute a number of sounds for it. It is sometimes trilled, produced with back of the tongue close to the soft palate, and among other possibilities, replaced by the l [l] sound, called lalling. In the ending position in words, many native and nonnative speakers of English do not produce it at all.

Correction

Look in a mirror. Raise the center of the tongue toward the center of the palate and the blade of the tongue toward the front palate. Round the lips slightly and protrude them partially. Begin phonating as you then move the tongue and the lips to the position for the ē [i] sound. You will have said *ree*. Go back to the beginning action and phonate; this time say the ô [ɔ] sound. You will have said *raw*. Try the action with several other vowel sounds. Try moving into the position for r [r] from the position for ä [ɑ]. You will have said *are*. Try moving into the position for r [r] from the position for ĕ [ɛ]. You will have said *air*. If you still have difficulty, your professor will provide you with help before you move to the practice material on the next page.

(r)

[r]

Single Words

rain	respect	arm	library	are	fire
rate	reward	art	necessary	before	floor
reading	rhyme	card	theory	desire	hour
reason	write	cord	tomorrow	door	star
religion	wrong	error	very	far	store

Word Pairs

week	reek	flea	free		
witch	rich	flitter	fritter	ill	ear
led	red	bled	bread		
lack	rack	glass	grass		
lock	rock	clock	crock	calm	car
law	raw	salt	sort	fall	for
look	rook			pull	poor
loom	room	flute	fruit		

lug	rug	blush	brush		
wail	rail	play	pray		
lice	rice	climb	crime	file	fire
loyal	royal				
lout	rout	plough	prow	owl	our
load	road	bloke	broke		

Sentences

1. Arthur tried to rip the red ribbon.
2. The rain hurries the carrots' growth.
3. The aroma from the rich red rose was terrific.
4. Rearing children properly is a very real problem.
5. Rock and roll music is far out.
6. The moral of this story is rest before the race.
7. Ricky drove the Rolls Royce off the road and ruined the tires.
8. I arrived on the terrace at three.
9. Rosalind wrote recipes for radio programs.
10. Order three more pairs of trousers for Larry.

Tongue Twister

Reno is a great town for recreation. Racquetball, roulette, rugby, and rodeo are remembered as highly rated activities. When Roy and Ruth roamed the streets of the town, they rode their two-wheelers to reach the right places. After hurrying around for three days, they reeled from the merriment they had experienced and rode west toward the streets of San Francisco.

(l) Diacritic

Phonetic [l]

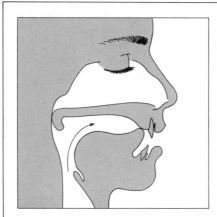

Formation

The jaw is opened fairly wide. The lips are unrounded. The broadened tip of the tongue is pressed against the upper gum ridge. The sides of the tongue allow openings between them and the side teeth for the air to flow laterally. The soft palate is raised, and the vocal folds vibrate.

Definition

l [l] is a tongue-tip-to-gum-ridge, voiced lateral.

Misarticulation

The w [w] sound is sometimes incorrectly substituted for the l [l] sound. The y [j] sound is sometimes incorrectly substituted for it. Some persons for whom English is a second language produce the sound with the tongue blade touching the front palate, which results in a "dark l" sound. Others, particularly Orientals, substitute r [r] or n [n] sounds. At word endings, the ō [oʊ] sound is sometimes incorrectly substituted.

Correction

Look in a mirror. Place the tongue tip against the gum ridge. Phonate as you move to the position for the ä [ɑ] sound. You will have produced the sound *la*. Say the ä [ɑ] sound and lift your tongue tip to the gum ridge, but do not allow your jaw to close. You will have said the sound *ahl*. Repeat *la, ahl, la, ahl* several times without allowing the jaw to close. Say the word *table*. As you produce the l [l] sound in that word, watch the mirror to be certain that your jaw does not close and that the lips do not become rounded. If you still have difficulty, check with your professor before doing the exercises on the next page.

(l)

land	little	almost	island	able	middle
language	living	building	milk	animal	nail
laugh	long	color	parallel	circle	rail
left	loose	early	public	detail	steel
letter	love	family	silver	general	table

Word Pairs

week	leak	reading	reeling	feed	feel
wit	lit	kidding	killing	hid	hill
yet	let	beds	bells	said	sell
whack	lack	shadow	shallow	pad	pal
rock	lock	sodded	solid	Don	doll
yaw	law	sort	salt	fawn	fall
rook	look	pudding	pulling	wood	wool
use (verb)	lose	spoons	spools	crude	cruel
work	lurk	girds	girls	bird	burl
rug	lug	duds	dulls	Hun	hull
wake	lake	fading	failing	wade	wail
rhyme	lime	minor	miler	I'd	I'll
royal	loyal	coining	coiling	coin	coil
wowed	loud	scouting	scowling	proud	prowl
row	low	roads	rolls	code	coal

Sentences

1. He fell into the lake and yelled for help.
2. Billy likes to blow bubbles.
3. The lake is so still that it looks almost like glass.
4. Please light the candle on the table.
5. Gail is careless with her dolls.
6. She knelt at the altar rail.
7. The lilies of the valley glow in the moonlight.
8. Jill's laughter was lilting.
9. Lisa loves Lenny and longs to call him.
10. The lad, Louis, left a little light in the hall.

Tongue Twister

Lulu Lovelace lived in the lighthouse in Lexington. The lighthouse was loaded with large electric lamps for warning sailors of the looming rocks. Lulu, in her usual ladylike manner, loved to light the lamps at twilight to allow the lolling ships to land safely at the landing. Lulu's eleven children liked to help her and never failed to tell her how lovely she looked in her lighthouse keeper's clothes.

(m) Diacritic   **Phonetic [m]**

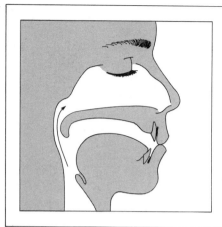

Formation

The lips are lightly closed. The soft palate is lowered to allow air to pass through and out of the nose. The tongue is relaxed and lowered, and the vocal folds vibrate.

Definition

m [m] is a lip-to-lip, voiced nasal.

Misarticulation

Sometimes, not enough air is emitted through the nose to generate a resonant m [m] sound. This can be caused by congestion from adenoids, growths in the nasal passage, allergies, or the common cold, in which case a b [b] substitution tends to result. Sometimes when it is followed by an f [f], n [n] is substituted for m [m], such as in "comfortable" and "triumphant." Some people for whom English is a second language omit the m [m] sound in the final position.

Correction

In cases in which nasal blockage is present, medical help may be required before correction can be effective. Humming the m [m] sound while you attempt to sense the vibration in the mouth, on the lips, and in the nasal passages will develop a firm m [m] sound. Flip the lips with the forefinger to confirm that there is no unnecessary tension in them. Look in a mirror as you say the word *comfort*. Confirm that you are pressing your lips lightly together on the m [m] sound before you shift to the lip-to-teeth f [f] sound. Concentrate on lip closure in cases in which the m [m] sound occurs at the ends of words in the practice lists.

(m)

Single Words

make	medical	agreement	government	autumn	rhythm
man	memory	almost	important	come	same
map	military	attempt	payment	farm	swim
married	milk	company	simmer	form	thumb
meal	minute	development	tomorrow	phlegm	warm

Word Pairs

Neil	meal	seeking	seeming	seed	seem
bill	mill	ribs	rims	lib	limb
bet	met	steps	stems	head	hem
bad	mad	cabs	cams	slab	slam
balm	mom	Bob's	bombs	cob	calm
floss	moss				
boor	moor				
boot	moot	ruby	roomy	tube	tomb
bud	mud	hubs	hums	sub	some
burr	myrrh	words	worms	furl	firm
fail	male	shaving	shaming	gave	game
buy	my	tiding	timing	dive	dime
voiced	moist				
bound	mound				
boast	most	robes	roams	lobe	loam

Sentences

1. Mother's maid is making a meal.
2. Many men remember Maude, the meed, timid mule.
3. Mabel remembers the millstream among the many elms.
4. An army must make time to muster its might.
5. Mario smiled in a macho manner.
6. It seems a shame to march a mile to Tommy's meadow.
7. The main mountian climbers maneuvered over the molehill.
8. Ms. Myers left a memorandum in the simple marble mailbox.
9. I might be in the mood for swimming tomorrow.
10. Margaret may make many mincemeat pies.

Tongue Twister

Minerva's mother, Mamie, made somber remarks about the mudpies Minerva made, but the members of the Mud-Making Merchants Committee marveled at their magnificent manufacture. They mimicked Minerva's mutterings and murmurings concerning the mercenary manners of millionaires. Minerva's marvelous mudpies, made from swamp slime and steamed loam, were meant to be mailed to millionaires, who mostly smiled and mumbled in harmony among themselves that Minerva's mudpies were the most memorable.

(n) Diacritic

Phonetic [n]

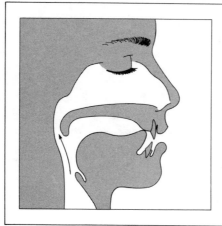

Formation

The tip of the tongue is pressed lightly against the upper gum ridge, and the sides of the tongue are in contact with the side teeth. The lips are unrounded. The air passes through the nose as the soft palate is lowered, and the vocal folds vibrate.

Definition

n [n] is a tongue-tip-to-gum-ridge, voiced nasal.

Misarticulation

If nasal blockage is present, a sound like d [d] is sometimes incorrectly substituted. The final n [n] is sometimes omitted, especially by persons for whom English is a second language. The sound is made incorrectly if the tip of the tongue touches the teeth instead of the gum ridge, so that, again, a sound like d [d] results.

Correction

If nasal blockage presents the sound from being made, medical help might be required before correction can be effective. Look in a mirror to ensure that the tip of the tongue closes with the gum ridge. Exaggerate the production of the sound. A simple exercise of opening the jaw and repeating *an, an, an* without allowing the jaw to move helps to develop flexibility of the tongue. Practice the exercises on the next page.

(n)

Single Words

knee	near	and	enough	again	discussion
knowledge	neck	answer	friend	between	plane
mnemonic	nerve	any	government	certain	religion
name	new	change	instrument	decision	then
nation	pneumonia	country	interest	dine	when

Word Pairs

deed	need	weeding	weaning	seal	seen
lip	nip	willing	winning	grill	grin
let	net	belled	bend	dead	den
dab	nab	batter	banner	pad	pan
lot	not	otter	honor	rod	Ron
law	gnaw	falling	fawning	gall	gone
look	nook				
tune	noon	cruder	crooner	sued	soon
terse	nurse	birds	burns	earl	earn
done	none	rudder	runner	gull	gun
dale	nail	waking	waning	gail	gain
light	night	miler	minor	file	fine
boys	noise	Lloyd's	loins	coil	coin
down	noun	towels	towns	crowd	crown
toes	nose	roads	roans	bowl	bone

Sentences

1. Nancy's narrow neck needed a necklace.
2. None of the lawn under that bunch of ferns gets any sun.
3. Nick's nervous niece knew a nurse.
4. Nellie doesn't know that her nose is running.
5. News reporters never need uniforms.
6. The panel of neurologists was seen in the dining commons.
7. Norman Norton nudged his nephew, Nicholas.
8. Clean the nickels until they're nice and shiny.
9. Needless to say, canned noodles are nauseating.
10. The wind, the rain, and the thunder are natural phenomena.

Tongue Twister

Neurotic Nanette had experienced nightmares, but now her mind was gaining. The nurse was sunning Nanette on the sanitorium grounds, near the sunroom. The reflection from the lawn in the window reminded the nurse to run around the corner and snatch a handful of nice, new orange and brown pansies for the sunny woman. Now Nanette knows how nice the nurse was to notice her needs.

(ng) Diacritic Phonetic [ŋ]

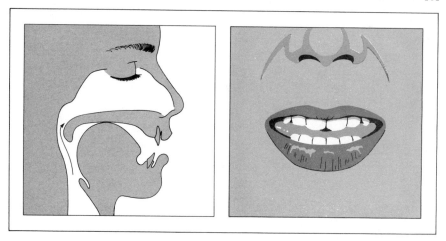

Formation

The lips are unrounded. The jaw is slightly open. The back of the tongue is raised against the soft palate, so that the exit of air from the mouth is completely prevented. The tip of the tongue rests low behind the lower front teeth. The soft palate is lowered, allowing the air to pass through the nasal passage. The vocal folds vibrate.

Definition

ng [ŋ] is a back-of-tongue-to-soft-palate, voiced nasal.

Misarticulation

If nasal blockage is present, the sound g [g] is sometimes substituted for the ng [ŋ]. Some persons for whom English is a second language and speakers of some dialects of American English add a g [g] or a k [k] sound after the ng [ŋ]. The sound n [n] is sometimes substituted for the ng [ŋ] sound at the end of words.

Correction

Look in a mirror. With the mouth open, raise the back of the tongue, so that it contacts the soft palate. Phonate through the nose. Stop the phonation before you lower the tongue. You will have made the ng [ŋ] sound. Now say the vowel ô [ɔ]; then move the back of the tongue up to the position for the ng [ŋ] sound, and allow the air to escape through the nose. Stop phonating before you lower your tongue. You will have said the sound *ong*. Repeat it several times; make certain that you do not produce the g [g] or the k [k] sound at the end. Try repeating the pattern *ding-dong, ding-dong* several times, and be sure that the g [g] and the k [k] sounds do not occur. Try the practice lists on the next page. Be especially careful of ng [ŋ] sounds at the end of words.

(ng)   **[ŋ]**

Single Words

angle	length	among	reading
angry	ringing	feeling	strong
hanging	singing	learning	thing
ink	strength	meeting	wing
language	tongues	morning	wrong

Word Pairs

sinner	singer	brig	bring
clanned	clanged ⁻	ran	rang
logging	longing	sawn	song
runs	rungs	sun	sung

Sentences

1. Sing a song that brings longing.
2. Wong Wong rang the gong in Hong Kong.
3. "Younger Than Springtime" is a singer's song.
4. She's thinking of improving your language.
5. Some singers elongate diphthongs into triphthongal glides.
6. The angry monkey was reaching for the ripening mangoes.
7. Bing Crosby was a singer among singers.
8. Mr. Cunningham is bringing over the rings to the ladder.
9. I long for the clanging of the dining bell.
10. My tongue hung out of my mouth when I heard the slang he used.

Tongue Twister

There's not a single standard for judging all kings. They have to be young and strong with kingly singing voices. Picking the winning king from among so many who are working and longing for the title is a long, anguishing task. One's hair is too long, and his slang is all wrong. Strings are hanging from this one's shirt. And that one belongs to a gang! Too many rings . . . , laughing too long . . . , an arm in a sling. How can I bring myself to choose the king?

SUMMARY

At this point, you have learned to accurately produce the sounds of standard American English. The next step is to put them together in various combinations to form the words of our language.

9

Pronunciation

Earlier, we emphasized articulation, which refers to, among other things, the exactness of the production of sound. Now, we will focus on *pronunciation*, the production of the correct sounds in the correct sequence with the correct stress. Misarticulation within a word occurs when one or more of its sounds are not produced accurately. Mispronunciation, however, occurs when we leave out appropriate sounds, add inappropriate ones, substitute sounds, reverse them in sequence, or stress the wrong syllable.

Most listeners will tolerate some errors in articulation, but few will ignore mispronunciation. Nothing can identify your ethnic, cultural, and educational background or your social and occupational level as readily as the accuracy of your pronunciation.

With your knowledge of either diacritic symbols or the International Phonetic Alphabet, and with a good modern dictionary, you can determine the current pronunciation of every word you wish to use. Knowledge of these makes it possible to pronounce all English words in the same manner as that of most educated speakers in your community.

English is a living language, however, and is in a constant state of change. New words are invented every day, especially in such fields as space exploration, computer technology, and transportation. We talk about astronauts instead of drovers, jets instead of stagecoaches, laser beams instead of gaslights, trailer hitches instead of singletrees, disc-drive computers instead of adding machines, and uranium instead of coal oil.

Meanings of words change: *uncouth* once meant *unknown*, and a *wench* at one time was a *child*. In the seventeenth century, *amusing* meant *amazing* and *awful* meant *awe inspiring*.

Pronunciations also change with time. *Laboratory* was once pronounced (lə-bô′ rə-tô-rē) [lə'bɔ-rə-tɔ-rɪ] (it still is in England), *author* was (ô′ tər) ['ɔ-təʳ], and *abdomen* was (ăb-dō′ mən) [æb′doʊ-mən].

We know that American English words are not pronounced the same way everywhere but vary from place to place and from person to person. Nevertheless, standard, acceptable pronunciations are included in any reputable, modern dictionary. Sometimes two or more options are listed. In most cases, the first pronunciation noted is the one used by the majority of educated speakers. In some cases, however, the second pronunciation is more accepted in a particular area. For example, Bostonians pronounce *either* (ī´ thər) [aɪ-ðɚ]. Los Angeleans say (ē´ thər) [iːðɚ]. Both are right.

Frequently, we are asked, "Who determines how a word should be pronounced?" The question implies that the dictionary writers impose their will on the rest of us and require that their personal choices be used. In some countries, this is essentially true. In France, for example, this is done by the French Academy, a group of language experts who set linguistic standards in an attempt to keep the French language "pure." In the People's Republic of China, a commission has been established to simplify the spelling of that ideographic language and decide how words will be pronounced. In the United States, however, the people determine what is standard. The dictionary writers periodically survey the way we pronounce words and then reflect the combined results in each new edition.

Language is a social institution. Dictionary writers record how educated American society is currently saying words. You can take advantage of the editor's work by getting a good dictionary, learning how to use it, and then referring to it frequently.

Consider this: Standard American English is rarely judged odd by speakers of other dialects, but nonstandard pronunciation will likely be noted by speakers of Standard American English. The dictionary is your key to Standard American pronunciation. Pronunciation is nonstandard if the way you speak is noticed more than what you say.

TYPES OF MISPRONUNCIATION

Five types of pronunciation errors that occur frequently are the following.

1. Omission of sounds.
2. Addition of sounds.
3. Substitution of sounds.
4. Reversal of sounds.
5. Misplacement of stress.

Omission of Sounds

Omission of sounds, or leaving sounds out of words, is the most common type of mispronunciation. It usually results either from lack of awareness of the need to include certain speech sounds or from incomplete articulation of consonants in the middle and or at the end of a word.

Read aloud the following words and give special attention to the underlined sounds; use a rising inflection and sustain them more than you do in normal conversation. Say these words.

almost (ôl´mōst) ['ɔl-most] not (ôl´mōs) ['ɔ-mos]
battery (bă´tə-rē) ['bæ-tə-ri] not (băt´rē) ['bæ-tri]
captain (kăp´tən) ['kæp-tən] not (kap´ən) ['kæp-ən]
cold (kōld) [koʊld] not (kōl) [koʊl]
conditioner (kən-dĭsh´ə-nər) [kən'dɪʃənɚ] not (kən-dĭsh´nər) [kən-'dɪʃnɚ]
different (dĭ´fə-rənt) ['dɪ-fə-rənt] not (dĭf´rənt) ['dɪf-rənt]
don't (dōnt) [doʊnt] not (dōn) [doʊn]
grocery (grō´sə-rē) ['gro-sərɪ] not (grō´srē) ['gro-srɪ]
library (lī´brě-rē) ['laɪ-brɛ-ri] not (lī´bě-rē) ['laɪ-bɛ-ri]
little (lĭ´təl) ['lɪ-təl] not (lĭl) [lɪl]
ninety (nīn´tē) ['naɪn-ti] not (nī´nē) ['naɪ-ni]
orange (ôr´ĭnj) ['ɔrɪndʒ] not (ôrnj) [ɔrndʒ]
past (păst) [pæst] not (păs) [pæs]
prominent (prŏm´ə-nənt) ['prɒm-ə-nənt] not (prŏm´nənt) ['prɒm-nənt]
recognize (rěk´əg-nīz) ['rək-əg-naɪz] not (rěk´ə-nīz) ['rək-ə-naɪz]
remnant (rěm´nənt) ['rem-nənt] not (rěm´ə-nənt) ['rem-ə-nənt]
restaurant (rěs´tər ənt) ['res-tə-rənt] not (rěst´rənt) ['rest-rənt]
violent (vī´ə-lənt) ['vaɪ-ə-lənt] not (vī´lənt) ['vaɪ-lənt]

Addition of Sounds

Addition involves the introduction of extra sounds into words. For example, many persons pronounce the word *athlete* as (ăth´ ə-lēt) ['æθ-ə-lit] or *burglar* as (bûrg´ ə-lər) ['bɝg-ə-lɚ]. They add the sound ə [ə] in the middle of the word. Some say *idear* for *idea*. Sometimes addition is caused by spelling that does not represent pronunciation. For example, *calm* looks like the *l* should be pronounced, but it should not. *Forehead* includes the letter *h*, but it is not pronounced, and *subtle* has the letter *b*, which should not be sounded. Practice these words.

arithmetic (ə-rĭth´mə-tĭk) [ə'rɪθ mə ˌtɪk] not (ə-rĭ´thə-mətĭk) [ə'rɪθə mə ˌtɪk]
brethren (brě´thrĭn) ['brɛ ðrɪn] not (brě´thə-ə-rĭn) ['brɛ ðə rɪn]
draw (drô) [drɔ] not (drôr) [drɔr]
entrance (ĕn´trəns) ['ɛn-trəns] not (ĕn´tə-rəns) ['ɛn-tə-rəns]
epistle (ĭ-pĭs´əl) [ɪ'pɪsl̩] not (ĭ-pĭs´təl) [ɪ'pɪs təl]
girl (gûrl) [gɝl] not (gûr´rəl) ['gɝ-rəl]
inertia (ĭn-ûr´shə) [ɪn ˈɝ ʃə] not (ĭn-ûr´shē-ə) [ɪn ˈɝ ʃiə]
irascible (ĭ-răs´ə-bəl) [ɪ'rasəbl̩] not (ĭ-răs´kə bəl) [ɪ-´raskəbl̩]
once (wŭns) [wʌns] not (wŭnst) [wʌnst]
parliament (pär´lə-mənt) ['par-lə-mənt] not (pär´lĭ-ə-mənt) ['par-lɪ-ə-mənt]
prodigious (prə-dĭj´əs) [prə'dɪdʒəs] not (prə-dĭ´jē-əs) [prə'dɪdʒiəs]
remembrance (rĭ-měm´brəns) [rɪ'mɛm-brəns] not (rĭ-měm´bə-rəns)
   [rɪ'mɛm-bə-rəns]
salmon (să´mən) ['sæ-mən] not (săl´mən) ['sæl-mən]
similar (sĭm´ə lər) ['sɪməlɚ] not (sĭm´yə lɚ) ['sɪmjəlɚ]

singer (sĭng´ər) [ˈsɪŋ-ɚ] not (sĭng´gər) [ˈsɪŋ-gɚ]
statistics (stə-tĭs´tĭks) [stəˈtɪs-tɪks] not (stə-stĭs-tĭks) [stəˈstɪs-tɪks]
umbrella (əm-brĕ´lə) [əmˈbrɛ-lə] not (əm-bə-rĕ´lə) [əm-bəˈrɛ-lə]
wash (wäsh) [waʃ/wɔʃ] not (wärsh) [warʃ/wrɔʃ]

Substitution of Sounds

The substitution of another sound in place of the correct one is a most noticeable pronunciation problem. For this reason, the word lists that follow emphasize words in which this type of error is likely to occur. As you develop independence and self-assurance in articulation, you will say:

bath (băth) [bæθ] not (băf) [bæf]
butter (bŭ´tər) [ˈbʌ-tɚ] not (bŭ´dər) [ˈbʌ-dɚ]
deaf (dĕf) [dɛf] not (dēf) [dif]
experiment (ĕk-spĕr´ə-mənt) [ɪkˈspɛrəmənt] not (ĕk-spĭr´ə-mənt)
  [ɪkˈspɪrəmənt]
get (gĕt) [gɛt] not (gĭt) [gɪt]
going (gō´ĭng) [ˈgou-ɪŋ] not (gō´ĭn) [ˈgou-ɪn]
just (jŭst) [dʒʌst] not (jĭst) [dʒɪst]
length (lĕngkth) [lɛŋkθ] not (lĭnth) [lɪnθ]
little (lĭt´əl) [ˈlɪt-əl] not (lĭl) [lɪl]
novice (nŏ´vĭs) [ˈnɒvɪs] not (nô´vĭs) [ˈnɔ vɪs]
pumice (pŭm´ĭs) [ˈpʌmɪs] not (pyoo´mĭs) [ˈpjumɪs]
soláce (sŏl´ĭs) [ˈsalɪs] not (sōl´ĭs) [ˈsou lɪs]
sherbet (shŭr´bĭt) [ˈʃɚbɪt] not (shŭr´bərt) [ˈʃɚ bərt]
sure (shoor) [ʃʊr] not (shûr) [ʃɚ]
tedious (tēd´ē-əs) [ˈtid-i-əs] not (tē´jəs) [ˈti-dʒəs]
theater (thē´ə-tər) [ˈθi-ə-tɚ] not (thē-ā´tər) [θi-ˈeɪ-tɚ]
tyranny (tĭr´ə-nē) [ˈtɪrənɪ] not (tīr´ə nē) [ˈtaɪrənɪ]
where (hwâr) [hwɛr] not (wâr) [wɛr]

Reversal of Sounds

Some words are likely to be mispronounced because it is easy to reverse the sequence of sounds within them. Errors of this type are quite obvious, but fortunately, the number of words whose pronunciations are affected by this problem is small. For practice, say:

ask (ăsk) [æsk] not (ăks) [æks]
asterisk (ăs´tə-rĭsk´) [ˈæs tə, rɪsk] not (ăs´tə riks´) [ˈæs tə, rɪks]
children (chĭl´drən) [ˈtʃɪl-drən] not (chĭl´dərn) [ˈtʃɪl-dɚn]
equanimity (ē´kwə-nĭm´ə-tē) [ˌi kwəˈnɪmətɪ] not (ē´ kwə-mĭn´ə-tē)
  [ˌi kwəˈmɪnətɪ]
hospital (hŏs´pə-təl) [ˈhɒspɪtl̩] not (hŏp´sə-təl) [ˈhɒp sɪtl̩]
hundred (hŭn´drəd) [ˈhʌn-drəd] not (hŭn´dərd) [ˈhʌn-dɚd]
introduce (ĭn-trə-doos´) [ɪn-trəˈdus] not (ĭn-tər-doos´) [ɪn-tɚˈdus]
larynx (lăr´ĭngks) [ˈlær-ɪŋks] not (lăr´nĭks) [ˈlæar-nɪks]

modern (mŏd´ərn) ['mɒd-ɚn] not (mŏd´rən) ['mɒd-rən]
officer (ô´fĭ-sər) ['ɔ-fɪ-sɚ] not (ô´sĭ-fər) ['ɔ-sɪ-fɚ]
perform (pər-fôrm´) [pər'fɔrm] not (prē fôrm´) [prɪ 'fɔrm]
prerequisite (prē-rek´wa-zĭt) [pri'rɛkwəzɪt] not (pə-rĕk´wə-zĭt) [pə'rɛkwəzɪt]
prescribe (prĭ-skrīb´) [prɪ'skraɪb] not (pûr-skrīb´) [pɝ'skraɪb]
prescription (prĭ-skrĭp´shən) [prɪ'skrɪp-ʃən] not (pər-skrĭp´shən) [pɚ'skrɪp-ʃən]
professor (prə-fĕs´ər) [prə'fɛs-ɚ] not (pər-fĕs´ər) [pɚ'fɛs-ɚ]
relevant (rĕl´ə-vənt) ['rɛl-ə-vənt] not (rĕv´ə-lənt) ['rɛv-ə-lənt]
solemnity (sə-lĕm´nə-tē) [sə'lɛmnətɪ] not (sələn´mə-tē) [sə'lɛnmətɪ]
spaghetti (spə-gĕt´ē) [spə'gɛtɪ] not (ps-gĕt´ē) [ps'gɛtɪ]

Misplacement of Stress

American English is dependent on stress to distinguish some words from others.
The stressed, or accented, syllable normally has (1) more loudness, (2) higher pitch,
and (3) longer duration. Following are some words that are often mispronounced
because the stress is placed on the wrong syllable. Say:

cement (sĭ-mĕnt´) [sɪ'mɛnt] not (sē´mĕnt) ['si:-mɛnt]
chaparral (shăp´-ə-răl´) [ˌtʃæpə'ræl] not (shăp´ə-ral´) [ˌtʃæpəræl]
clandestine (klăn-dĕs´tĭn) [klæn'dɛstɪn] not (klăn-des-tīn´) [klæn dɛs'taɪn]
decline (dĭ-klīn´) [dɪ'klaɪn] not (dē´klīn) ['diklaɪn]
habitable (hăb´-tə-bəl) ['hæbɪtəbl̩] not (ha-bĭt´-ə-bəl) [hə'bɪtəbl̩]
horizon (hə-rī´zən) [hə'raɪzən] not (hô´rĭ-zən) ['hɔrɪzən]
ignominy (ĭg´nə-mĭn-ē) ['ɪgnəˌmɪnɪ] not (ĭg-nə-mĭn´ē) [ɪgnə'mɪnɪ]
indicative (ĭn-dĭ´kə-təv) [ɪn'dɪ-kə-təv] not (ĭn-də-kā´tĭv) [ɪn-də'keɪ-tɪv]
industry (ĭn´də-strē) ['ɪn-də-stri] not (ĭn-dŭ´strē) [ɪn'dʌ-stri]
irrevocable (î-rĕv´ə-kə-bəl) [ɪ'rɛv-ə-kə-bəl] not (î-rĭ-vō´kə-bəl)
    [ɪ-rɪ'voʊ-kə-bəl]
libertine (lĭb´ər-tēn) ['lɪbɚtin] not (lĭ-bər-tēn´) [lɪbɚ'tin]
obdurate (ŏb´dyōō-rĭt) ['abdjʊrɪt] not (əb-dyōō´rĭt) [əb'djʊrɪt]
orchestra (ôr´kĭ-strə) ['ɔr kɪstrə] not (ôr-kĕ´strə) [ɔr'kɛɪstrə]
ordeal (ôr-dēl´) [ɔr'dil] not (ôr´dēl) ['ɔrdil]
prestige (prĕ-stēzh´) [prɛ'stizh] not (prĕ´stēzh) ['prɛ stizh]
prevalence (prĕv´ə-ləns) ['prɛv-ə-ləns] not (prĭ-vā´ləns) [prɪ'veɪ-ləns]
superfluous (soo-pûr´flōō-əs) [sʊ'pɝfluəs] not (sōō pər'flōō´əs) [ˌsupər'fluəs]
theater (thē´ə-tər) ['θi:-ə-tɚ] not (thĭ-ā´tər) [θɪ'eɪ-tɚ]
vehement (vē´ə-mənt) ['viəmənt] not (vĭ-hē´mənt) [vɪ'himənt]

Stress can determine meaning, as, for example, in:

per´fect or *per fect´*
pres´ent or *pre sent´*

Quite often a change in the accepted pronunciation of a word depends on a
change in stress. For example, you may have grown up saying,

preced´ence instead of *prec´edence*
re spite´ instead of *res´pite*
superflu´ous instead of *super´fluous*
u´nited instead of *unit´ed*

When you are trying to place the stress correctly in an unfamiliar word, say the stressed syllable first, repeat with the following syllable, and then say the entire word. For example, for the word *environment*,

say   (vī) [vaɪ]
then say (vī´rən) ['vaɪ-rən]
then say (vī´rən-mənt) ['vaɪ-rən-mənt]
then say (ĕn-vī´rən-mənt] [ɛn'vaɪ-rən-mənt]

The more you check pronunciations in your dictionary, the more you will control syllable stress and the more accurate you will be in pronunciation.

SUMMARY

In this chapter, we have discussed the five major types of mispronunciation (omission, addition, substitution, reversal, and misplacement of accent) and presented examples of each. Practice material has been provided in the Appendix B to assist you in learning the correct forms of frequently mispronounced words.

10

Vocal Variety and Expression

The ability to create interest, excitement, and high and low emotions in the voice is called *vocal expression*. It involves the addition of variety in pitch, volume, and timing to the clear voice and distinct articulation that you have already developed. Vocal variations will be discussed separately in the following sections. Appropriate exercises are provided for the development of these necessary characteristics in your speech.

PITCH VARIETY

In Chapter 3, we defined pitch as one of the vocal characteristics, explained what optimal pitch is, and indicated how to acquire it. If you spoke at the level of optimal pitch all the time, however, your voice would be monotonous, and obviously, you would sound rather dull and uninteresting.

Two classes of pitch changes are used in spoken language—*inflections*, or changes within words, and *step shifts*, or changes between words.

Inflection

There are four types of changes you can make in pitch within words.

1. Inflection up ⌒
2. Inflection down ⌒
3. Inflection up and down or down and up ⌒ ⌣
4. Noninflection →

Inflection up is the raising of the pitch within a word. We pick up the telephone and say:

Hello ⌒

Inflection down is the lowering of the pitch within a word. We meet someone we dislike and say:

Hello ⬎

Inflection up and down or down and up combines these. We feel happy and almost flirtatious when we meet a friend and say:

Hello ⌢ or ⌣

Noninflection is the maintenance of a constant pitch level. We meet someone when we are feeling tired and preoccupied and say:

Hello ⟶

Practice the following words and sentences. Change the pitch as indicated. As you become more aware of the variety of ways in which inflection can enliven your voice, you should incorporate these expressions into your everyday speaking. Since most inexperienced readers do not use enough inflection *up* on important words or at the end of sentences, given special attention to this shift.

Yes ⬈	No ⬈
Yes ⬊	No ⬊
Yes ⌢	No ⌢
Yes ⟶	No ⟶
Who ⬈	Where ⬈
Who ⬊	Where ⬊
Who ⌣	Where ⌣
Who ⟶	Where ⟶
Maybe ⬈	How ⬈
Maybe ⬊	How ⬊
Maybe ⌢	How ⌢
Maybe ⟶	How ⟶

Some days are bright, ⬈   others gloomy. ⬊

I wish I knew ⬈   what to do. ⬊

Don't go south, ⬈   go north. ⬊

I'll have the soup, ⬈   salad, ⬈   and steak. ⌢

Should I buy a dog, ⬈   a cat, ⬈   or a lion? ⬊

Consider the various types of inflection as you say the sentence *I like peanut butter.*

1. Say it as though you really do like peanut butter.
2. Say it as though you are not sure that you like peanut butter.
3. Say it as though peanut butter is the most important thing in the world to you.
4. Say it as though you are disgusted by peanut butter.

Step Shifts

Step shifts are changes in pitch, either down or up, between words in phrases and sentences. The following sentences indicate various types of such changes.

Rising Pitch

```
                here.
        up
1. Come
```

```
            much?
2. How
```

Falling Pitch

```
1. That's
            dumb.
```

```
2. Hit
        the
            ball.
```

Rising and Falling Pitch

```
1. You
        may
            pick
        it              drop
            up,    don't    it.
                but
```

```
                game,
            the        but
        loved          I am
2. I                       very
                            tired.
```

```
3. The plan
            of
                attack,                          last
                    because                  the
                        of the            at
                            obstacles  changed
                                was            moment.
```

```
                                                        here
                                              are,        is
                                        you                    the
  4. If                                        of                    proof.
        you                        some
            are              suspect
                doubtful,      I
                    and
```

These sentences can be read with different patterns. Try each variation.

```
                              sight?
                    beautiful
                a
            that
  1. Isn't
            that
                a
                    beautiful
                        sight?
```

```
                                    money.
                              of
                        meaning
                    the
                know
            doesn't
  2. He
            doesn't
                know
                    the
                        meaning
                            of
                                money.
```

```
                everything.
            tried
        have
  3. I
        have
            tried
                everything.
```

                              mean?
                    you
              what
          that
4. Is
          that
                 what
                       you
                            mean?

                                        moment!
                                    a
                            for
                        it
                 doubted
          never
5. I've
          never
                 doubted
                          it
                        for
                    a
                       moment!

                                 that?
                            to
                      say
                  you
              do
          what
6. Now,
          what
                do
                    you
                        say
                            to
                               that?

```
                    this?
               do
           you
       do
7.  How
       do
           you
               do
                   this?
```

```
                            beach.
                        the
                    of
                end
            the
        to
8.  Drive
        to
            the
                end
                    of
                        the
                            beach.
```

```
                    it.
               believe
           won't
9.  He
        won't
            believe
                it.
```

Now, try combining step shifts and inflection.

```
                                        mo
            love    lend              ney,          broke. ⟍
                        you
1.  I would      to          the          but I'm
```

```
                                    going
        want    go                  go. ⟶
2.  I        to      and I'm      to
```

3. When we get to Grand ma's, ⟋ ask her for can dy.

4. I just can't be- lieve ⟋ she's wearing the same dress that I am. ⟋

5. Young man ⟍ I hope you don't do that again! ⟋

6. Oh, you want to go to the movies do you? ⟋

7. We thought you might have a problem; we told you that you would. ⟋

8. I thought you bought a new car; what did you say you paid for it? ⟋

TIME VARIETY

Time variety is a combination of changes in rate (number of words per minute), changes in duration within words, and changes in the length of pauses between words.

Rate Variety

Rate variety concerns how fast or slowly we talk. It is the number of words or syllables per minute. One hundred words per minute is slow. Two hundred words per minute is very fast. The optimum ranges of interesting and understandable speech are 150–185 words per minute for reading and 135–185 words per minute for speaking.

The following section contains exactly 220 words. Read it aloud and time yourself. There is a diagonal line after each 50 words.

/Have you walked up and down upon the earth lately? I have; and I have examined Man's wonderful inventions. And I tell you that in the arts of life man invents nothing; but in the arts of death he outdoes Nature herself, and produces by chemistry and machinery all the / slaughter of plague, pestilence, and famine. The peasant I tempt today eats and drinks what was eaten and drunk by the peasants of ten thousand years ago; and the house he lives in has not altered as much in a thousand centuries as the fashion of a lady's bonnet in / a score of weeks. But when he goes out to slay, he carries a marvel of mechanism that lets loose at the touch of his finger all the hidden molecular energies, and leaves the javelin, the arrow, the blowpipe of his fathers far behind. In the arts of peace Man / is a bungler. I have seen his cotton factories and the like, with machinery that a greedy dog could have invented if it had wanted money instead of food. I know his clumsy typewriters and bungling locomotives and tedious bicycles: they are toys compared to the Maxim gun, the submarine / torpedo boat. There is nothing in Man's industrial machinery but his greed and sloth: his heart is in his weapons.

Bernard Shaw, *Man and Superman*

Did you find that you were at or beyond the extreme limits of reading? Practice the selection as many times as necessary to obtain a rate within the set boundaries, and then use it in several selections to establish that rate habitually.

Not all selections should be read at the same rate, however. Some must be produced more rapidly than others to obtain the effect you desire. For example, read the lyrics to the "Nightmare Song," from a Gilbert and Sullivan operetta. Here the rate should be rather fast.

When you're lying awake with a dismal headache, and repose it taboo'd by
     anxiety,
I conceive you may use any language you choose to indulge in, without
     impropriety,
For your brain is on fire—the bedclothes conspire of usual slumber to plun-
     der you:
First your counterpane goes, and uncovers your toes, and your sheet slips
     demurely from under you;
Then the blanketing tickles—you feel like mixed pickles—so terribly sharp
     is the pricking,
And you're hot, and you're cross, and you tumble and toll till there's noth-
     ing 'twixt you and the ticking;
Then your bedclothes all creep to the ground in a heap, and you pick 'em up
     all in a tangle;
Next your pillow resigns and politely declines to remain at its usual angle!
Well, you get some repose in the form of a doze, with hot eye-balls and
     head ever aching;
But your slumbering teems with such horrible dreams that you'd very much
     better be waking, . . .

You're a regular wreck, with a crick in your neck, and no wonder you snore,
    for your head's on the floor, and you've needles and pins from your
    soles to your shins, and your flesh is a-creep, for your left leg's
    asleep, . . . and some fluff in your lung, and a feverish tongue, and a
    thirst that's intense, and a general sense that you haven't been sleeping
    in clover;
But the darkness has passed, and it's daylight at last, and the night has been
    long—ditto ditto my song—and thank goodness they're both of them
    over!

                       W.S. Gilbert, *Iolanthe*

Now, in contrast, try this selection. It should be read with a much slower rate than the previous one.

Tomorrow, and tomorrow, and tomorrow,
Creeps in this petty pace from day to day
To the last syllable of recorded time;
And all our yesterdays have lighted fools
The way to dusty death. Out, out, brief candle!
Life's but a walking shadow, a poor player
That struts and frets his hour upon the stage
And then is heard no more. It is a tale
Told by an idiot, full of sound and fury.
Signifying nothing.
          William Shakespeare, *Macbeth*

Duration Variety

Duration refers to the amount of time it takes to say a word. Primarily, it is governed by the length of time given to stressed vowel and diphthong sounds. In one reading situation, we many want to say a particular word quickly, while in another we may wish to stretch it out. This variety adds meaning and importance to some words and makes others trivial.

Read aloud the following material, and experiment with different durations of vowel and diphthong sounds.

1. On, on, on it came; at first slowly; then faster, faster and faster!

2. Crack, lightning, blow, bugle; answer, echoes, dying, dying, dying.

3. If at first you don't succeed, try, try again.

4. Wait, let me concentrate for one minute.

Now use duration variety as you read aloud this sonnet.

How do I love thee? Let me count the ways.
I love thee to the depth and breadth and height
My soul can reach, when feeling out of sight
For the ends of Being and ideal Grace.

I love thee to the level of everyday's
Most quiet need, by sun and candle-light.
I love thee freely, as men strive for Right;
I love thee purely, as they turn from Praise.
I love thee with the passion put to use
In my old griefs, and with my childhood's faith.
I love thee with a love I seemed to lose
With my lost saints,—I love thee with the breath,
Smiles, tears, of all my life!—and, if God choose,
I shall but love thee better after death.

Elizabeth Barrett Browning, "How Do I Love Thee?"

Pause Variety

Pause is the period of silence between words and phrases. Such silence is effective in separating ideas and in holding attention. We enjoy listening to a reader or a speaker who gives us time to assimilate each idea or group of thoughts.

To develop the ability to use pause, first collect your thoughts in groups and then practice allowing periods of silence between words and phrases that express complete ideas.

Use these exercises to practice different pause placements for different meanings.

1. Advice to the lean: don't eat fast.
   Advice to the fat: don't eat, fast.

2. I don't know Joe.
   I don't know, Joe.

3. It was there for the first time.
   It was, therefore, the first time.

4. To be, or not to be, that is the question. (William Shakespeare)

5. The only thing we have to fear is fear itself. (Franklin D. Roosevelt)

6. Be always sure you're right, then go ahead. (David Crockett)

7. Law grinds the poor, and rich men rule the law. (Oliver Goldsmith)

8. Beware of all enterprises that require new clothes. (Henry David Thoreau)

9. Every man desires to live long, but no man would be old. (Jonathan Swift)

10. Love is strong as death; jealousy is cruel as the grave. (Song of Solomon 8:6)

11. Experience keeps a dear school, but fools will learn in no other. (Ben Franklin)

12. A sharp tongue is the only tool that grows keener with constant use. (Washington Irving)

13. A university should be a place of light, of liberty, and of learning. (Benjamin Disraeli)

14. I swear to the Lord I still can't see why Democracy means everybody but me. (Langston Hughes)

15. For of all sad words of tongue or pen,
    The saddest are these: "It might have been!" (John Greenleaf Whittier)

16. A prophet is not without honor, save in his own country, and in his own house. (Matthew 13:57)

17. I shall endeavor to enliven morality with wit, and to temper wit with morality. (Joseph Addison)

18. Though I speak with the tongues of men and of angels, and have not charity, I am become as sounding brass, or a tinkling cymbal. (I Corinthians 13:1)

19. Vice is a monster of so frightful mien, as to be hated needs but to be seen; yet seen too oft, familiar with her face, we first endure, then pity, then embrace. (Alexander Pope)

20. If liberty and equality, as is thought by some, are chiefly to be found in democracy, they will be best attained when all persons alike share in the government to the utmost. (Aristotle)

21. I went to the woods because I wished to live deliberately, to front only the essential facts of life, and see if I could not learn what it had to teach, and not, when I came to die, discover that I had not lived. (Henry David Thoreau)

22. Required in every good lover . . . the whole alphabet . . . Agreeable, Bountiful, Constant, Dutiful, Easy, Faithful, Gallant, Honorable, Ingenious, Kind, Loyal, Mild, Noble, Officious, Prudent, Quiet, Rich, Secret, True, Valiant, Wise . . . Young and Zealous. (Miguel de Cervantes)

23. Appearances to the mind are of four kinds. Things either are what they appear to be; or they neither are, nor appear to be; or they are, and do not appear to be; or they are not, and yet appear to be. Rightly to aim in all these cases is the wise man's task. (Epictetus)

24. Grant us brotherhood, not only for this day but for all our years—a brotherhood not of words but of acts and deeds. We are all of us children of earth—grant us that simple knowledge. If our brothers are oppressed, then we are oppressed. If they hunger, we hunger. If their freedom is taken away our freedom is not secure. (Stephen Vincent Benet)

25. During the whole of a dull—dark—and soundless day in the autumn of the year—when the clouds hung oppressively low in the heavens—I had been passing alone—on horseback—through a singularly dreary tract of country—and at length found myself—as the shades of the evening drew on—within view of the melancholy House of Usher——I know not how it was—but—with the first glimpse of the building—a sense of insufferable gloom pervaded my spirit—I say insufferable—for the feeling was unrelieved by any of that half-pleasurable—because poetic—sentiment with which the mind usually receives even the sternest—natural image of the desolate—or terrible——I look upon the scene before me—upon the mere house—and the simple landscape features of the domain—upon the bleak walls—upon the vacant eye-like windows—upon a few rank hedges—and upon a few white trunks of

decayed trees—with an utter depression of soul—which I can compare to no earthly sensation more properly—than to the after-dream of the reveller upon opium—the bitter lapse into every-day life—the hideous dropping off of the veil (Edgar Allan Poe, *The Fall of the House of Usher*).

LOUDNESS VARIETY

Loudness is the level of sound heard by the listener. Although it can be measured with a sound-level meter, most people can informally sense whether a speaker is loud enough.

In this section, we are concerned not so much with the adequecy of your habitual loudness level as with the variations in loudness you use. All of your speaking should be intelligible, but if you wish to be interesting, some should be loud and some should be soft.

The following are some simple exercises to give you a sense of loudness variety. Remember to use abdominal respiration.

1. Count from one to ten, increasing the loudness from *one* to *five* and then decreasing it from *six* to *ten*.

2. Say *ah*. Begin at a soft volume and increase the loudness as long as it is comfortable.

3. Now say *ah*, but begin at a loud volume and reduce the sound to nothing.

4. Read aloud the following material. Before starting, go through and underline the words and phrases that you feel should be spoken with either an increase or a decrease in volume.

> Was it possible they heard not? Almighty God!—no, no! They heard!—they suspected!—they knew!—they were making mockery of my horror!—this I thought, and this I think. But anything was better than this agony! Anything was more tolerable than this derision! I could bear those hypocritical smiles no longer! I felt that I must scream or die!—and now—again!—hark! louder! louder! louder! louder!—
>
> "Villains!" I shrieked, "dissemble no more! I admit the deed!—tear up the planks!—here, here!—it is the beating of his hideous heart!"
>
> Edgar Allan Poe, *The Tell-Tale Heart*

WORD EMPHASIS

Some readers give almost the same amount of emphasis to every word. They seem to be reading as they did when they first learned to read—only one word at a time. Effective word emphasis prevents such monotony and generates listener interest.

It may help if you sense what types of words should usually be stressed and what types are usually unstressed. Content words are usually stressed.

1. Verbs: swim, write, speak, drive (auxiliary verbs are usually unstressed).

2. Nouns: Alice, Los Angeles, cat, speech.

3. Adjectives: big, most, red, above.

4. Adverbs: happily, lamely, coldly, finally.

5. Demonstratives: this, that, these, those.

6. Interrogatives: who, when, what, why.

Function words are usually unstressed.

1. Articles: a, an, the.

2. Prepositions: to, of, in, out, above.

3. Personal pronouns: I, me, he, she, it.

4. Possessive adjectives: my, his, your, hers.

5. Relative pronouns: who, that, which.

6. Conjunctions: and, but, that, if.

7. Auxiliary verbs: be, have, will, shall, could, can, may, might.

Incorrect stressing is particulary noticeable with the words *the* and *a*. Use these rules: *The* is pronounced *thē* [ði] prior to a vowel sound, for example: *the easy, the olympic, the actual. The* is pronounced thə [ðə] prior to a consonant sound, for example: *the cat, the man, the school. A* is almost always pronounced ə [ə].
Practice the words in these sentences.

1. The man is sitting in the easy chair with a cat.

2. The ambassador will give the closing speech at a banquet.

3. The runner is competing in the Olympics on a lark.

4. The evenings at the beach are the best on a Friday.

5. A word to the wise: the elevator to success is seldom running; try the stairs.

Materials for Practicing Unstressed Words

Articles.

a: A way to pay is a dollar a day.
an: An old man and an eager boy had an interesting conversation.
the: The first of the month is the time to pay the bills.

Prepositions.

at: They met at the bank at First and Main at noon.
for: Here's one for you, one for me, and one for the coffee pot.
from: They came from here, from there, and from everywhere.
into: He got into his pajamas, went into the bedroom, and got into bed.
of: Of the three of these, this is the best of the bunch.
to: To get from here to there, go to the corner and turn to the right.

Conjunctions.

and: The dog and the cat and the parrot ate the bone and the fish and the seeds.
as: As often as not I can only work as fast as this.
but: I won't, but I might if I could, but I can't.
or: Either you or I or someone must do this or that or fail.
than: Rather than walk, than run, than drive, I would fly.

Auxiliary Verbs.

am: I am hungry, so I am going to eat; then I am leaving.
are: We are busy, because some are reading, some are writing and some are speaking.
can: She can command, she can can, and she can can-can.
could: He could run, and he could pass, and he could kick.
do: How do you feel, and what do you think?
does: He does not want to go, he does not want to stay, and he does not want to decide.
had: We had gone; we had seen; we had laughed.
has: He has found the theme he has written and has gotten an "A."
have: You have tried; you have worked. You have succeeded!
must: We must learn that we must be who we must be.
shall: She shall sell sea shells that she shall find and shall sing by the sea.
should: If they should train and they should practice, they should win.
was: I was dreaming as I was driving and was soon lost.
were: We were hoping that you were coming and were sad when you were late.
will: She will wish and he will hope that they will soon be wed.
would: I would hope that you would want what we would need.

Linking Verb Forms.

am: I am sure that I am right as often as I am wrong.
are: The athletes are tired but they are finished.
was: It was time that he was ready, but he was not.
were: They were early so they were prepared.

Pronouns.

he: He forgot, but he knows he knew.
her: Her face, her bed and her mind were always made up.
him: To know him is to love him.
his: He is known by his walk, his talk, and his looks.
she: She said she saw what she thought was insipid.
some: If I had some ham, I'd have some ham and eggs, if I had some eggs.
that: That dog is after that cat which is chasing that rat.
them: I like them, but my doctor won't let me eat them.
us: You know us, so take us as you find us.
you: Did you ever have the feeling that you wanted to do what you couldn't?
your: Your shift and your tie are your choice.

VOCAL INTEGRATION

As you gain control of each vocal variable, combine these abilities into an integrated whole. One way this talent can be practiced and used is in emphasizing words appropriately. One word can be stressed by a louder volume, another by a raise in pitch, still a third by a longer duration, and a fourth by a combination of several actions (e.g., it may be soft, high, and long).

Practice using all elements of variety in the following sentences.

1. He crept up behind her and yelled, "Boo!"
2. You could hear the banging of the drum grow stronger and stronger.
3. Aren't you driving too fast? Look out for that car!
4. As he neared the goal line, the crowd roared, "Touchdown!"
5. The crash of thunder echoed through the forest, booming at first and then fading until there was no sound at all.
6. She's just come in. Don't let her overhear you.

After you have practiced the words and phrases in this chapter, choose selections from Chapter 11 and read them aloud with the appropriate emphasis and de-emphasis. Use all your talents to speak these selections with accurate articulation, proper pronunciation, and expressive vocal variety.

SUMMARY

Vocal expression is accomplished by variations in the timing, the pitch, and the loudness of your reading and speaking voice. You can practice in conversation, in classroom situations, and in prepared readings.

We have explored together the various characteristics of your speech abilities. We have looked at how you breathe, phonate, resonate, articulate, and pronounce. We have discussed the improvement of your vocal expression. Now you have the opportunity to put it all together and use the ideas and techniques you have learned to speak clearly and understandably wherever you may be.

11

Reading Selections

The following selections of prose and poetry were chosen to give you a variety of reading experiences. Some were selected for their content and interest. Some provide the opportunity to practice specific speech skills: voice and articulation, pronunciation and pitch, time and loudness variety. We have identified the speech skills of each selection.

IN AN ATELIER   (Articulation and Vocal Variety)

I pray you, do not turn your head;
And let your hands lie folded, so.
It was a dress like this, wine-red,
That troubled Dante, long ago.
You don't know Dante? Never mind.
He loved a lady wondrous fair—
His model? Something of the kind.
I wonder if she had your hair!

I wonder if she looked so meek,
And was not meek at all (my dear,
I want that side light on your cheek).
He loved her, it is very clear,
And painted her, as I paint you,
But rather better, on the whole
(Depress your chin; yes, that will do):
He was a painter of the soul!

(And painted portraits, too, I think,
In the *Inferno*—devilish good!
I'd make some certain critics blink
Had I his method and his mood.)
Her name was (Fanny, let your glance
Rest there, by that majolica tray)—
Was Beatrice; they met by chance—
They met by chance, the usual way.

(As you and I met, months ago,
Do you remember? How your feet
Went crinkle-crinkle on the snow
Along the bleak gas-lighted street!
An instant in the drug-store's glare
You stood as in a golden frame,
And then I swore it, then and there,
To hand your sweetness down to fame.)

They met, and loved, and never wed
(All this was long before our time),
And though they died, they are not dead—
Such endless youth gives mortal rhyme!
Still walks the earth, with haughty mien,
Pale Dante, in his soul's distress;
And still the lovely Florentine
Goes lovely in her wine-red dress.

You do not understand at all?
He was a poet; on his page
He drew her; and, though kingdoms fall,
This lady lives from age to age.
A poet—that means painter too,
For words are colors, rightly laid;
And they outlast our brightest hue,
For varnish cracks and crimsons fade.

The poets—they are lucky ones!
When *we* are thrust upon the shelves,
Our works turn into skeletons
Almost as quickly as ourselves;
For our poor canvas peels at length,
At length is prized—when all is bare:
"What grace!" the critics cry, "what strength!"
When neither strength nor grace is there.

Ah, Fanny, I am sick at heart,
It is so little one can do;
We talk our jargon—live for Art!
I'd much prefer to live for you.
How dull and lifeless colors are!
You smile, and all my picture lies:
I wish that I could crush a star
To make a pigment for your eyes.

Yes, child, I know, I'm out of tune;
The light is bad; the sky is gray:
I paint no more this afternoon,
So lay your royal gear away.
Besides, you're moody—chin on hand—

I know not what—not in the vein—
Not like Anne Bullen, sweet and bland:
You sit there smiling in disdain.

Not like the Tudor's radiant Queen,
Unconscious of the coming woe,
But rather as she might have been.
Preparing for the headsman's blow.
So, I have put you in a miff—
Sitting bolt-upright, wrist on wrist.
How *should* you look? Why, dear, as if—
Somehow—as if you'd just been kissed!

Thomas Bailey Aldrich

ON WOMEN'S RIGHT OF SUFFRAGE (1873)   (Articulation)

Friends and fellow-citizens: I stand before you tonight under indictment for the alleged crime of having voted at the last Presidential election, without having a lawful right to vote. It shall be my work this evening to prove to you that in thus voting, I not only committed no crime, but, instead simply exercised my citizen's rights, guaranteed to me and all United States citizens by the National Constitution, beyond the power of any State to deny.

The preamble of the Federal Constitution says:

> We, the people of the United States, in order to form a more perfect union, establish justice, insure domestic tranquility, provide for the common defense, promote the general welfare, and secure the blessings of liberty to ourselves and our posterity, do ordain and establish this Constitution for the United States of America.

It was we, the people; not we, the white male citizens; nor yet we, the male citizens; but we, the whole people, who formed the Union. And we formed it, not to give the blessings of liberty, but to secure them; not to the half of ourselves and the half of our posterity, but to the whole people—women as well as men. And it is a downright mockery to talk to women of their enjoyment of the blessings of liberty while they are denied the use of the only means of securing them provided by this democratic-republican government—the ballot. . . .

Webster, Worcester and Bouvier all define a citizen to be a person in the United States, entitled to vote and hold office.

The only question left to be settled now is: Are women persons? And I hardly believe any of our opponents will have the hardihood to say they are not. Being persons, then, women are citizens; and no State has a right to make any law, or to enforce any old law, that shall abridge their privileges or immunities. Hence, every discrimination against women in the constitutions and laws of the several States is today null and void, precisely as is every one against Negroes.

Susan B. Anthony

DOVER BEACH   (Time Variety)

The sea is calm to-night,
The tide is full, the moon lies fair
Upon the Straits;—on the French coast, the light
Gleams, and is gone; the cliffs of England stand,
Glimmering and vast, out in the tranquil bay.
Come to the window, sweet is the night air!
Only, from the long line of spray
Where the ebb meets the moon-blanch'd sand,
Listen! you hear the grating roar
Of pebbles which the waves suck back, and fling,
At their return, up the high strand,
Begin, and cease, and then again begin,
With tremulous cadence slow, and bring
The eternal note of sadness in.
    Sophocles long ago
Heard it on the Aegaean, and it brought
Into his mind the turbid ebb and flow
Of human misery; we
Find also in the sound a thought,
Hearing it by this distant northern sea.

The sea of faith
Was once, too, at the full, and round earth's shore
Lay like the folds of a bright girdle furl'd;
But now I only hear
Its melancholy, long, withdrawing roar,
Retreating to the breath
Of the night-wind down the vast edges drear
And naked shingles of the world.

Ah, love, let us be true
To one another! for the world, which seems
To lie before us like a land of dreams,
So various, so beautiful, so new,
Hath really neither joy, nor love, nor light,
Nor certitude, nor peace, nor help for pain;
And we are here as on a darkling plain
Swept with confused alarms of struggle and flight,
Where ignorant armies clash by night.

Matthew Arnold

from FOR THE TIME BEING, A CHRISTMAS ORATORIO
(Articulation and Vocal Variety)

Well, so that is that. Now we must dismantle the tree,
Putting the decorations back into their cardboard boxes—
Some have got broken—and carrying them up into the attic.
The holly and the mistletoe must be taken down and burnt,

And the children got ready for school. There are enough
Left-overs to do, warmed-up, for the rest of the week—
Not that we have much appetite, having drunk such a lot,
Stayed up so late, attempted—quite unsuccessfully—
To love all of our relatives, and in general
Grossly overestimated our powers. Once again
As in previous years we have seen the actual Vision and failed
To do more than entertain it as an agreeable
Possibility, once again we have sent Him away,
Begging though to remain His disobedient servant,
The promising child who cannot keep His word for long.
The Christmas Feast is already a fading memory,
And already the mind begins to be vaguely aware
Of an unpleasant whiff of apprehension at the thought
Of Lent and Good Friday which cannot, after all, now
Be very far off. . . .

                           . . . In the meantime
There are bills to be paid, machines to keep in repair,
Irregular verbs to learn, the Time Being to redeem
From insignificance. . . .

W. H. Auden

from JONATHAN LIVINGSTON SEAGULL   (Time Variety)

There in the night, a hundred feet in the air, Jonathan Livingston Seagull—blinked.
His pain, his resolutions, vanished.

Short wings. *A falcon's short wings!*

That's the answer! What a fool I've been! All I need is a tiny little wing, all I need is
to fold most of my wings and fly on just the tips alone! *Short wings!*

He climbed two thousand feet above the black sea, and without a moment for thought
of failure and death, he brought his forewings tightly in to his body, left only the narrow
swept daggers of his wingtips extended into the wind, and fell into a vertical dive.

The wind was a monster roar at his head. Seventy miles per hour, ninety, a hundred
and twenty and faster still. The wing-strain now at a hundred and forty miles per hour wasn't
nearly as hard as it had been before at seventy, and with the faintest twist of his wingtips
he eased out of the dive and shot above the waves, a gray cannonball under the moon.

He closed his eyes to slits against the wind and rejoiced. A hundred forty miles per
hour! And under control! If I dive from five thousand feet instead of two thousand, I wonder
how fast . . .

He was alive, trembling ever so slightly with delight, proud that his fear was under
control. Then without ceremony he hugged in his forewings, extended his short, angled
wingtips, and plunged directly toward the sea. By the time he passed four thousand feet he
had reached terminal velocity, the wind was a solid beating wall of sound against which he
could move no faster. He was flying now straight down, at two hundred fourteen miles per
hour. He swallowed, knowing that if his wings unfolded at that speed he'd be blown into
a million tiny shreds of seagull. But the speed was power, and the speed was joy, and the
speed was pure beauty.

He began his pullout at a thousand feet, wingtips thudding and blurring in that gigantic wind, the boat and the crowd of gulls tilting and growing meteor-fast, directly in his path.

He couldn't stop; he didn't know yet even how to turn at that speed.

Collision would be instant death.

And so he shut his eyes.

It happened that morning, then, just after sunrise, that Jonathan Livingston Seagull fired directly through the center of Breakfast Flock, ticking off two hundred twelve miles per hour, eyes closed, in a great roaring shriek of wind and feathers. The Gull of Fortune smiled upon him this once, and no one was killed.

Richard Bach

from GO TELL IT ON THE MOUNTAIN   (Time Variety)

Then I buckled up my shoes,
And I started.

He knew, without knowing how it had happened, that he lay on the floor, in the dusty space before the altar which he and Elisha had cleaned; and knew that above him burned the yellow light which he had himself switched on. Dust was in his nostrils, sharp and terrible, and the feet of the saints, shaking the floor beneath him, raised small clouds of dust that filmed his mouth. He heard their cries, so far, so high above him—he could never rise that far. He was like a rock, a dead man's body, a dying bird, fallen from an awful height; something that had no power of itself, any more, to turn.

And something moved in John's body which was not John. He was invaded, set at naught, possessed. This power had struck John, in the head or in the heart; and, in a moment, wholly, filling him with an anguish that he could never in his life have imagined, that he surely could not endure, that even now he could not believe, had opened him up; had cracked him open, as wood beneath the axe cracks down the middle, as rocks break up; had ripped him and felled him in a moment, so that John had not felt the wound, but only the agony, had not felt the fall, but only the fear; and lay here, now helpless, screaming, at the very bottom of darkness.

He wanted to rise—a malicious, ironic voice insisted that he rise—and, at once, to leave this temple and go out into the world.

He wanted to obey the voice, which was the only voice that spoke to him; he tried to assure the voice that he would do his best to rise; he would only lie here a moment, after his dreadful fall, and catch his breath. It was at this moment, precisely, that he found he could not rise; something had happened to his arms, his legs, his feet—ah, something had happened to John! And he began to scream again in his great, bewildered terror, and felt himself, indeed, begin to move—not upward, toward the light, but down again, a sickness in his bowels, a tightening in his loin-strings; he felt himself turning, again and again, across the dusty floor, as though God's toe had touched him lightly. And the dust made him cough and retch; in his turning the center of the whole earth shifted, making of space a sheer void and a mockery of order, and balance, and time. Nothing remained: all was swallowed up in chaos.

James Baldwin

from JAWS   (Time Variety)

The woman continued to swim away from the beach, stopping now and then to check her position by the lights shining from the house. The tide was slack, so she had not moved up or down the beach. But she was tiring, so she rested for a moment, treading water, and then started for shore.

The vibrations were stronger now, and the fish recognized prey. The sweeps of its tail quickened, thrusting the giant body forward with a speed that agitated the tiny phosphorescent animals in the water and caused them to glow, casting a mantle of sparks over the fish.

The fish closed on the woman and hurtled past, a dozen feet to the side and six feet below the surface. The woman felt only a wave of pressure that seemed to lift her up in the water and ease her down again. She stopped swimming and held her breath. Feeling nothing further, she resumed her lurching stroke.

The fish smelled her now, and the vibrations—erratic and sharp—signaled distress. The fish began to circle close to the surface. Its dorsal fin broke water, and its tail, thrashing back and forth, cut the glassy surface with a hiss. A series of tremors shook its body.

For the first time, the woman felt fear, though she did not know why. Adrenaline shot through her trunk and her limbs, generating a tingling heat and urging her to swim faster. She guessed that she was fifty yards from shore. She could see the line of white foam where the waves broke on the beach. She saw the lights in the house, and for a comforting moment she thought she saw someone pass by one of the windows.

The fish was about forty feet away from the woman, off to the side, when it turned suddenly to the left, dropped entirely below the surface, and, with two quick thrusts of its tail, was upon her.

At first, the woman thought she had snagged her leg on a rock or a piece of floating wood. There was no initial pain, only one violent tug on her right leg. She reached down to touch her foot, treading water with her left leg to keep her head up, feeling in the blackness with her left hand. She could not find her foot. She reached higher on her leg, and then she was overcome by a rush of nausea and dizziness. Her groping fingers had found a nub of bone and tattered flesh. She knew that the warm, pulsing flow over her fingers in the chill water was her own blood.

Pain and panic struck together. The woman threw her head back and screamed a guttural cry of terror.

Peter Benchley

from JOHN BROWN'S BODY   (Articulation)

Lincoln, six feet one in his stocking feet,
The lank man, knotty and tough as a hickory rail,
Whose hands were always too big for white-kid gloves,
Whose wit was a coonskin sack of dry, tall tales,
Whose weathered face was homely as a plowed field—
Abraham Lincoln, who padded up and down
The sacred White House in nightshirt and carpet-slippers,
And yet could strike young hero-worshipping Hay
As dignified past any neat, balanced, fine

Plutarchan sentences carved in a Latin bronze;
The low clown out of the prairies, the ape-buffoon,
The small-town lawyer, the crude small-time politician,
State-character but comparative failure at forty
In spite of ambition enough for twenty Caesars,
Honesty rare as a man without self-pity,
Kindness as large and plain as a prairie wind,
And a self-confidence like an iron bar: . . .

Stephen Vincent Benét

THE BILL OF RIGHTS   (Pronunciation)

For my own part, I believe that our Constitution, with its absolute guarantees of individual rights, is the best hope for the aspirations of freedom which men share everywhere. I cannot agree with those who think of the Bill of Rights as an 18th Century straitjacket, unsuited for this age. It is old but not all old things are bad. The evils it guards against are not only old, they are with us now, they exist today. Almost any morning you open your daily paper you can see where some person somewhere in the world is on trial or has just been convicted of supposed disloyalty to a new group controlling the government which has set out to purge its suspected enemies and all those who had dared to be against its successful march to power. Nearly always you see that these political heretics are being tried by military tribunals or some other summary and sure method for disposition of the accused. Now and then we even see the convicted victims as they march to their execution.

Experience all over the world has demonstrated, I fear, that the distance between stable, orderly government and one that has been taken over by force is not so great as we have assumed. Our own free system to live and progress has to have intelligent citizens, citizens who cannot only think and speak and write to influence people, but citizens who are free to do that without fear of governmental censorship or reprisal.

The provisions of the Bill of Rights that safeguard fair legal procedures came about largely to protect the weak and the oppressed from punishment by the strong and the powerful who wanted to stifle the voices of discontent raised in protest against oppression and injustice in public affairs. Nothing that I have read in the Congressional debates on the Bill of Rights indicates that there was any belief that the First Amendment contained any qualifications. The only arguments that tended to look in this direction at all were those that said "that all paper barriers against the power of the community are too weak to be worthy of attention." Suggestions were also made in and out of Congress that a Bill of Rights would be a futile gesture since there would be no way to enforce the safeguards for freedom it provided. Mr. Madison answered this argument in these words:

> If they [the Bill of Rights amendments] are incorporated into the Constitution, independent tribunals of justice will consider themselves in a peculiar manner the guardians of those rights; they will be an impenetrable bulwark against any assumption of power in the Legislative or Executive; they will be naturally led to resist every encroachment upon rights expressly stipulated for in the Constitution by the declaration of rights.

I fail to see how courts can escape this sacred trust.

Hugo L. Black

FAREWELL TO BLACK HAWK   (Time Variety)

You have taken me prisoner, with all my warriors. I am much grieved; for I expected, if I did not defeat you, to hold out much longer, and give you more trouble, before I surrendered. I tried hard to bring you into ambush, but your last general understood Indian fighting. I determined to rush on you, and fight you face to face. I fought hard. But your guns were well aimed. The bullets flew like birds in the air, and whizzed by our ears like the wind through the trees in winter. My warriors fell around me; it began to look dismal.

I saw my evil day at hand. The sun rose dim on us in the morning, and at night it sank in a dark cloud, and looked like a ball of fire. That was the last sun that shone on Black Hawk. His heart is dead, and no longer beats quick in his bosom. He is now a prisoner of the white men; they will do with him as they wish. But he can stand torture, and is not afraid of death. He is no coward. Black Hawk is an Indian. He has done nothing for which an Indian ought to be ashamed. He has fought for his countrymen, against white men, who came, year after year, to cheat them and take way their lands. . . .

The spirits of our fathers arose, and spoke to us to avenge our wrongs or die. We set up the war-whoop, and dug up the tomahawk; our knives were ready and the heart of Black Hawk swelled high in his bosom, when he led his warriors to battle. He is satisfied. He will go to the world of spirits contented. He has done his duty. His father will meet him there and commend him.

Black Hawk is a true Indian, and disdains to cry like a woman. He feels for his wife, his children, and his friends. But he does not care for himself. He cares for the Nation and the Indians. They will suffer. He laments their fate. Farewell, my Nation! Black Hawk tried to save you, and avenge your wrongs. He drank the blood of some of the whites. He has been taken prisoner, and his plans are crushed. He can do no more. He is near his end. His sun is setting and he will rise no more. Farewell to Black Hawk.

Black Hawk

HOW DO I LOVE THEE?   (Pitch Variety)

How do I love thee? Let me count the ways.
I love thee to the depth and breadth and height
My soul can reach, when feeling out of sight
For the ends of Being and ideal Grace.
I love thee to the level of everyday's
Most quiet need, by sun and candle-light.
I love thee freely, as men strive for Right;
I love thee purely, as they turn from Praise.
I love thee with the passion put to use
In my old griefs, and with my childhood's faith.
I love thee with a love I seemed to lose
With my lost saints,—I love thee with the breath,
Smiles, tears, of all my life!—and, if God choose,
I shall but love thee better after death.

Elizabeth Barrett Browning

MY LAST DUCHESS   (Time Variety)

That's my last Duchess painted on the wall,
Looking as if she were alive. I call
That piece a wonder, now: Frà Pandolf's hands
Worked busily a day, and there she stands.
Will't please you sit and look at her? I said
"Frà Pandolf" by design, for never read
Strangers like you that pictured countenance,
The depth and passion of its earnest glance,
But to myself they turned (since none puts by
The curtain I have drawn for you, but I)
And seemed as they would ask me, if they durst,
How such a glance came there; so, not the first
Are you to turn and ask thus. Sir, 'twas not
Her husband's presence only, called that spot
Of joy into the Duchess' cheek: perhaps
Frà Pandolf chanced to say, "Her mantle laps
Over my lady's wrist too much," or "Paint
Must never hope to reproduce the faint
Half-flush that dies along her throat:" such stuff
Was courtesy, she thought, and cause enough
For calling up that spot of joy. She had
A heart—how shall I say?—too soon made glad,
Too easily impressed: she liked whate'er
She looked on, and her looks went everywhere.
Sir, 'twas all one! My favor at her breast,
The dropping of the daylight in the West,
The bough of cherries some officious fool
Broke in the orchard for her, the white mule
She rode with round the terrace—all and each
Would draw from her alike the approving speech,
Or blush, at least. She thanked men,—good! but thanked
Somehow—I know not how—as if she ranked
My gift of a nine-hundred-years-old name
With anybody's gift. Who'd stoop to blame
This sort of trifling? Even had you skill
In speech—(which I have not)—to make your will
Quite clear to such an one, and say, "Just this
Or that in you disgusts me; here you miss,
Or there exceed the mark"—and if she let
Herself be lessoned so, nor plainly set
Her wits to yours, forsooth, and made excuse,
—E'en then would be some stooping; and I choose
Never to stoop. Oh sir, she smiled, no doubt,
Whene'er I passed her; but who passed without
Much the same smile? This grew; I gave commands;
Then all smiles stopped together. There she stands

As if alive. Will't please you rise? We'll meet
The company below, then. I repeat,
The Count your master's known munificence
Is ample warrant that no just pretence
Of mine for dowry will be disallowed;
Though this fair daughter's self, as I avowed
At starting, is my object. Nay, we'll go
Together down, sir. Notice Neptune, though,
Taming a sea-horse, thought a rarity,
Which Claus of Innsbruck cast in bronze for me!

Robert Browning

PROSPICE   (Loudness Variety)

Fear death?—to feel the fog in my throat,
    The mist in my face,
When the snows begin, and the blasts denote
    I am nearing the place,
The power of the night, the press of the storm,
    The post of the foe;
Where he stands, the Arch Fear in a visible form,
    Yet the strong man must go:
For the journey is done and the summit attained,
    And the barriers fall,
Though a battle's to fight ere the guerdon be gained,
    The reward of it all.
I was ever a fighter, so—one fight more,
    The best and the last!
I would hate that death bandaged my eyes, and forbore,
    And bade me creep past.
No! let me taste the whole of it, fare like my peers
    The heroes of old,
Bear the brunt, in a minute pay glad life's arrears
    Of pain, darkness and cold.
For sudden the worst turns the best to the brave,
    The black minute's at end,
And the elements' rage, the fiend-voices that rave,
    Shall dwindle, shall blend,
Shall change, shall become first a peace out of pain,
    Then a light, then thy breast,
O thou soul of my soul! I shall clasp thee again,
    And with God be the rest!

Robert Browning

from UP AT A VILLA—DOWN IN THE CITY   (Time Variety)

Had I but plenty of money, money enough and to spare,
The house for me, no doubt, were a house in the city-square;
Ah, such a life, such a life, as one leads at the window there!

Something to see, by Bacchus, something to hear, at least!
There, the whole day long, one's life is a perfect feast;
While up at a villa one lives, I maintain it, no more than
    a beast.

Well now, look at our villa! stuck like the horn of a bull
Just on a mountain-edge as bare as the creature's skull,
Save a mere shag of a bush with hardly a leaf to pull!
—I scratch my own, sometimes, to see if the hair's turned
    wool.

But the city, oh the city—the square with the houses! Why?
They are stone-faced, white as a curd, there's something to
    take the eye!
Houses in four straight lines, not a single front awry;
You watch who crosses and gossips, who saunters, who
    hurries by;
Green blinds, as a matter of course, to draw when the sun
    gets high;
And the shops with fanciful signs which are painted properly.

What of a villa? Though winter be over in March by rights,
'Tis May perhaps ere the snow shall have withered well off
    the heights:
You've the brown ploughed land before, where the oxen
    steam and wheeze,
And the hills over-smoked behind by the faint gray olive-trees.

Robert Browning

JABBERWOCKY   (Articulation)

'Twas brillig and the slithy toves
    Did gyre and gimble in the wabe:
All mimsy were the borogroves,
    And the mome raths outgrabe.

"Beware the Jabberwock, my son!
    The jaws that bite, the claws that catch!
Beware the Jubjub bird, and shun
    The frumious Bandersnatch!"

He took his vorpal sword in hand:
    Long time the manxome foe he sought—
So rested he by the Tumtum tree,
    And stood awhile in thought.

And as in uffish thought he stood,
    The Jabberwock, with eyes of flame,
Came whiffling through the tulgey wood,
    And burbled as it came!

One, two! One, two! And through and through
    The vorpal blade went snicker-snack!
He left it dead, and with its head
    He went galumphing back.

"And hast thou slain the Jabberwock?
    Come to my arms, my beamish boy!
O frabjous day! Callooh! Callay!"
    He chortled in his joy.

'Twas brillig and the slithy toves
    Did gyre and gimble in the wabe:
All mimsy were the borogroves,
    And the mome raths outgrabe.

Lewis Carroll

YOU ARE OLD, FATHER WILLIAM   (Pitch Variety)

"You are old, Father William," the young man said,
    "And your hair has become very white;
And yet you incessantly stand on your head—
    Do you think, at your age, it is right?"

"In my youth," Father William replied to his son,
    "I feared it might injure the brain;
But, now that I'm perfectly sure I have none,
    Why, I do it again and again."

"You are old," said the youth, "as I mentioned before,
    And have grown most uncommonly fat;
Yet you turned a back somersault in at the door—
    Pray, what is the reason for that?"

"In my youth," said the sage, as he shook his grey locks.
    "I kept all my limbs very supple
By use of this ointment—one shilling the box—
    Allow me to sell you a couple?"

"You are old," said the youth, "and your jaws are too weak
    For anything stronger than suet;
Yet you finished the goose, with the bones and the beak—
    Pray, how did you manage to do it?"

"In my youth," said his father, "I took to the law,
    And argued each case with my wife;
And the muscular strength, which it gave to my jaw,
    Has lasted the rest of my life."

"You are old," said the youth, "one would hardly suppose
    That your eye was as steady as ever;
Yet you balanced an eel on the end of your nose—
    What made you so awfully clever?"

"I have answered three questions, and that is enough,"
    Said his father. "Don't give yourself airs!
Do you think I can listen all day to such stuff?
    Be off, or I'll kick you down-stairs!"

Lewis Carroll

from A SPEECH IN THE HOUSE OF COMMONS JUNE 18, 1940   (Resonance)

The whole fury and might of the enemy must very soon be turned on us. Hitler knows that he will have to break us in this island or lose the war. If we can stand up to him, all Europe may be free and the life of the world may move forward into broad, sunlit uplands. But if we fail, then the whole world, including the United States, including all that we have known and cared for, will sink into the abyss of a new dark age made more sinister, and perhaps more protracted, by the lights of perverted science. Let us therefore brace ourselves to out duties, and so bear ourselves that, if the British Empire and its Commonwealth last for a thousand years, men will still say, "This was their finest hour."

Winston S. Churchill

from THE RED BADGE OF COURAGE   (Resonance)

The youth tried to observe everything. He did not use care to avoid trees and branches, and his forgotten feet were constantly knocking against stones or getting entangled in briers. He was aware that these battalions with their commotions were woven red and startling into the gentle fabric of softened greens and browns. It looked to be a wrong place for a battlefield.

The skirmishers in advance fascinated him. Their shots into thickets and at distant prominent trees spoke to him of tragedies—hidden, mysterious, solemn.

Once the line encountered the body of a dead soldier. He lay upon his back staring at the sky. He was dressed in an awkward suit of yellowish brown. The youth could see that the soles of his shoes had been worn to the thinness of writing paper, and from a great rent in one the dead foot projected piteously. And it was as if fate had betrayed the soldier. In death it exposed to his enemies that poverty which in life he had perhaps concealed from his friends.

Stephen Crane

WAR IS KIND   (Loudness Variety)

Do not weep, maiden, for war is kind.
Because your lover threw wild hands toward the sky
And the affrighted steed ran on alone,
Do not weep.
War is kind.

Hoarse, booming drums of the regiment,
Little souls who thirst for fight,
These men were born to drill and die.
The unexplained glory flies above them,
Great is the battle-god, great, and his kingdom—
A field where a thousand corpses lie.

Do not weep, babe, for war is kind.
Because your father tumbled in the yellow trenches,
Raged at his breast, gulped and died,
Do not weep.
War is kind.

Swift blazing flag of the regiment,
Eagle with crest of red and gold,
These men were born to drill and die.
Point for them the virtue of slaughter,
Make plain to them the excellence of killing
And a field where a thousand corpses lie.

Mother whose heart hung humble as a button
On the bright splendid shroud of your son,
Do not weep.
War is kind.

Stephen Crane

THE PUBLIC DUTY OF EDUCATED MEN   (Pronunciation)

This was the discharge of a public duty by an educated man. It illustrated an indispensable condition of a progressive republic, the active, practical interest in politics of the most intelligent citizens. Civil and religious liberty in this country can be preserved only through the agency of our political institutions. But those institutions alone will not suffice. It is not the ship so much as the skilful sailing that assures the prosperous voyage. American institutions presuppose not only general honesty and intelligence in the people, but their constant and direct application to public affairs. Our system rests upon all the people, not upon a part of them, and the citizen who evades his share of the burden betrays his fellows. Our safety lies not in our institutions, but in ourselves. It was under the forms of the republic that Julius Caesar made himself emperor of Rome. It was while professing reverence for the national traditions that James II. was destroying religious liberty in England. To labor, said the old monks, is to pray. What we earnestly desire we earnestly toil for. That she may be prized more truly, heaven-eyed Justice flies from us, like the Tartar maid from her lovers, and she yields her embrace at last only to the swiftest and most daring of her pursuers.

By the words public duty I do not necessarily mean official duty, although it may include that. I mean simply that constant and active practical participation in the details of politics without which, upon the part of the most intelligent citizens, the conduct of public affairs falls under the control of selfish and ignorant, or crafty and venal men. I mean that personal attention—which, as it must be incessant, is often wearisome and even repulsive—to the details of politics, attendance at meetings, service upon committees, care and trouble and expense of many kinds, patient endurance of rebuffs, chagrins, ridicules, disappointments, defeats—in a word, all those duties and services which, when selfishly and meanly performed, stigmatize a man as a mere politician; but whose constant, honorable, intelligent, and vigilant performance is the gradual building, stone by stone and layer by layer, of that great temple of self-restrained liberty which all generous souls mean that our government shall be.

George William Curtis

from A TALE OF TWO CITIES   (Pitch and Time Variety)

It was the best of times, it was the worst of times, it was the age of wisdom, it was the age of foolishness, it was the epoch of belief, it was the epoch of incredulity, it was the season of Light, it was the season of Darkness, it was the spring of hope, it was the winter of despair, we had everything before us, we had nothing before us, we were all going direct to Heaven, we were all going direct the other way.

Charles Dickens

from MANHATTAN TRANSFER   (Articulation and Loudness Variety)

Three gulls wheel above the broken boxes, orangerinds, spoiled cabbage heads that heave between the splintered plank walls, the green waves spume under the round bow as the ferry, skidding on the tide, crashes, gulps the broken water, slides, settles slowly into the slip. Handwinches whirl with jingle of chains. Gates fold upwards, feet step out across the crack, men and women press through the manuresmelling wooden tunnel of the ferry-house, crushed and jostling like apples fed down a chute into a press. . . .

Dusk gently smooths crispangled streets. Dark presses tight the steaming asphalt city, crushes the fretwork of windows and lettered signs and chimneys and watertanks and ventilators and fire-escapes and moldings and patterns and corrugations and eyes and hands and neckties into blue chunks, into black enormous blocks. Under the rolling heavier heavier pressure windows blurt light. Night crushes bright milk out of arclights, squeezes the sullen blocks until they drip red, yellow, green into streets resounding with feet. All the asphalt oozes light. Light spurts from lettering on roofs, mills dizzily among wheels, stains rolling tons of sky. . . .

They pair off hurriedly. STANDING UP IN CARS STRICTLY FORBIDDEN. The climbing chain grates, grips the cogs; jerkily the car climbs the incline out of the whirring lights, out of the smell of crowds and steamed corn and peanuts, up jerkily grating up through the tall night of September meteors.

Sea, marshsmell, the lights of an Iron Steamboat leaving the dock. Across wide violet indigo a lighthouse blinks. Then the swoop. The sea does a flipflop, the lights soar. Her hair in his mouth, his hand in his ribs, thighs grind together.

The wind of their falling has snatched their yells, they jerk rattling upwards through the tangled girderstructure. Swoop. Soar. Bubbling lights in a sandwich of darkness and sea. Swoop. KEEP YOUR SEATS FOR THE NEXT RIDE. . . .

Glowworm trains shuttle in the gloaming through the foggy looms of spiderweb bridges, elevators soar and drop in their shafts, harbor lights wink.

Like sap at the first frost at five o'clock men and women begin to drain gradually out of the tall buildings downtown, grayfaced throngs flood subways and tubes, vanish underground.

All night the great buildings stand quiet and empty, their million windows dark. Drooling light the ferries chew tracks across the lacquered harbor. At midnight the fourfunneled express steamers slide into the dark out of their glary berths. Bankers blearyeyed from secret conferences hear the hooting of the tugs as they are let out of side doors by lightningbug watchmen; they settle grunting into the back seats of limousines, and are whisked uptown into the Forties, clinking streets of gin-white whiskey-yellow ciderfizzling lights. . . .

Seeping in red twilight out of the Gulf Stream fog, throbbing brassthroat that howls through the stiff-fingered streets, prying open glazed eyes of skyscrapers, splashing red lead on the girdered thighs of the five bridges, teasing caterwauling tugboats into heat under the toppling smoketrees of the harbor.

Spring puckering our mouths, spring giving us gooseflesh grows gigantic out of the droning of sirens, crashes with enormous scaring din through the halted traffic, between attentive frozen tiptoe blocks.

John Dos Passos

THE HUNTERS   (Articulation and Pronunciation)

He had traversed plow-furrowed fields when silence, imminent with violence, weighted him down like a pack. He had traversed shell-pelted fields when fear tangled his legs like a barricade. He had seen his enemy and his comrades sprawled grotesque and cold in the neutrality of death, as impersonal as the cows among them, angling stiff legs to the sky. He had thrown grenades at hidden men; and once, staring into wide, stark eyes down the bead of his aim, he had sighed out his breath toward a union more intimate than love—and more treacherous than its denial. He had seen a dog, tethered at the gate, howl at the noise of destruction and die in terror; had seen bees swarm from their hives at the ground of a cannon and hang in the air, directionless. He had seen Frenchmen return to their villages to gesticulate the glory of victory and, sobering, to peer from behind a silly grin at the rubbish that had been their homes. But these things had not touched him. He had left himself somewhere, and the farther he walked the terrain of war, the farther he went from himself.

He heard the spasmodic eruptions of war. He listened to silence hissing like the quick fuse of a bomb. Yet he felt nothing—unless it was weariness. He walked under the high fire of artillery as though it were a canopy against the rain. At first he had been unhappy and afraid; and perhaps, in the static musing, in the constant but unapprehended memory that was himself, he was yet unhappy and afraid.

Harris Downey

from THE PIRATES OF PENZANCE   (Articulation)

I am the very model of a modern Major-General,
I've information vegetable, animal, and mineral,
I know the kings of England, and I quote the fights historical,
From Marathon to Waterloo, in order categorical;
I'm very well acquainted too with matters mathematical,
I understand equations, both the simple and quadratical,
About binomial theorem I'm teeming with a lot o' news—
With many cheerful facts about the square of the hypothenuse.
. . . .
I'm very good at integral and differential calculus,
I know the scientific names of beings animalculous;
In short, in matters vegetable, animal, and mineral,
I am the very model of a modern Major-General.

W. S. Gilbert

from TRIAL BY JURY   (Time Variety)

When I, good friends, was called to the bar,
    I'd an appetite fresh and hearty,
But I was, as many young barristers are,
    An impecunious party.

I'd a swallow-tail coat of a beautiful blue—
    A brief which I bought of a booby—
A couple of shirts and a collar or two,
    And a ring that looked like a ruby!
. . . .
In Westminster Hall I danced a dance,
    Like a semi-despondent fury;
For I thought I should never hit on a chance
    Of addressing a British Jury—
But I soon got tired of third-class journeys,
    And dinners of bread and water;
So I fell in love with a rich attorney's
    Elderly, ugly daughter.
. . . .
The rich attorney, he jumped with joy,
    And replied to my fond professions:
"You shall reap the reward of your pluck, my boy
    At the Bailey and Middlesex Sessions.
You'll soon get used to her looks," said he,
    "And a very nice girl you'll find her!
She may very well pass for forty-three
    In the dusk, with a light behind her!"

W. S. Gilbert

from THE FEMALE EUNUCH   (Articulation)

Maybe I don't have a pretty smile, good teeth, long legs, a cheeky arse, a sexy voice. Maybe I don't know how to handle men and increase my market value, so that the rewards due to the feminine will accrue to me. Then, again, maybe I'm sick of the masquerade. I'm sick of pretending eternal youth. I'm sick of belying my own intelligence, my own will, my own sex. I'm sick of peering at the world through false eyelashes, so everything I see is mixed with a shadow of bought hairs; I'm sick of weighting my head with a dead mane, unable to move my neck freely, terrified of rain, of wind, of dancing too vigorously in case I sweat into my lacquered curls. I'm sick of the Powder Room. I'm sick of pretending that some male's self-important pronouncements are the objects of my undivided attention. I'm sick of going to films and plays when someone else wants to, and sick of having no opinions of my own about either. I'm sick of being a transvestite. I refuse to be a female impersonator. I am a woman.

Germaine Greer

from CATCH-22   (Articulation and Pronunciation)

Colonel Cathcart was a slick, successful, slipshod, unhappy man of thirty-six who lumbered when he walked and wanted to be a general. He was dashing and dejected, poised and chagrined. He was complacent and insecure, daring in the administrative stratagems he employed to bring himself to the attention of his superiors and craven in his concern that his schemes might all backfire. He was handsome and unattractive, a swashbuckling, beefy, conceited man who was putting on fat and was tormented chronically by prolonged seizures of apprehension. Colonel Cathcart was conceited because he was a full colonel with a combat command at the age of only thirty-six; and Colonel Cathcart was dejected because although he was already thirty-six he was still only a full colonel.

Colonel Cathcart was impervious to absolutes. He could measure his own progress only in relationship to others, and his idea of excellence was to do something at least as well as all the men his own age who were doing the same thing even better. The fact that there were thousands of men his own age and older who had not even attained the rank of major enlivened him with foppish delight in his own remarkable worth; on the other hand, the fact that there were men of his own age and younger who were already generals contaminated him with an agonizing sense of failure and made him gnaw at his fingernails with an unappeasable anxiety.

Joseph Heller

WHITE DARKNESS   (Loudness Variety)

Antarctica is the land of White Darkness.

Day after day the landscape is veiled in a thick, downy whiteness in which visibility is at times non-existent. Strange things happen, such as the sudden disappearance before the eyes of moving objects.

Two men, dressed in white, may be walking across the snow side by side. They are in a world of complete whiteness. The air is white; earth and sky are white; the wind in the face is white with clouds of snow. Suddenly one man becomes conscious that the other no longer is walking beside him. He has disappeared, as though the thin, white air has dissolved him. Yet he continues to talk as if nothing has happened, unaware that he has become a substanceless phantom. His voice is unchanged; it seems to come from the same direction and the same distance. A moment later he reappears—perhaps floating in the air a few feet ahead and at about eye-level. Still he talks as if he were walking beside the other man. He has no awareness of his own preternatural levitation. . . .

In white darkness there are no shadows; these are seen only when the sun is high in a cloudless sky. As a result Antarctica most of the time is a shadowless land. On a cloudy day the illumination of the landscape is so diffuse that there is no perspective by which one can estimate the contours, size, or distance of white objects. The feet cannot find the snow underfoot. One staggers and stumbles like a drunken man. Walking becomes extremely difficult and tiresome. Sledge and tractor drivers cannot move for days at a time until shadows reappear by which they can detect the parallel ridges which indicate the presence of crevasses. Otherwise they might well stumble blindfolded into the area crisscrossed with thousand-foot-deep rifts in the ice which are the death traps of polar explorers.

Elsewhere, perhaps, shadows do not play an important part in life. But in the infinity of whiteness black images on the snow provide a pattern by which the human mind can function. Without them the difficulties of finding one's way are enormously multiplied. They may mean the difference between reason and utter confusion—in extreme cases between life and death. Where all reality is white it vanishes in whiteness, and the world is left empty of substance.

Thomas R. Henry

from THE DEATH PENALTY   (Loudness Variety)

A man, a convict, a sentenced wretch, is dragged, on a certain morning, to one of our public squares. There he finds the scaffold! He shudders, he struggles, he refuses to die. He is young yet—only twenty-nine. Ah! I know what you will say,—"He is a murderer!" But hear me. Two officers seize him. His hands, his feet, are tied. He throws off the two officers. A frightful struggle ensues. His feet, bound as they are, become entangled in the ladder. He uses the scaffold against the scaffold! The struggle is prolonged. Horror seizes on the crowd. The officers,—sweat and shame on their brows,—pale, panting, terrified, despairing,—despairing with I know not what horrible despair,—skrinking under that public reprobation which ought to have visited the penalty, and spared the passive instrument, the executioner,—the officers strive savagely. The victim clings to the scaffold, and shrieks for pardon. His clothes are torn,—his shoulders bloody,—still he resists. At length, after three-quarters of an hour of this monstrous effort, of this spectacle without a name, of this agony,—agony for all, be it understood,—agony for the assembled spectators as well as for the condemned man—after this age of anguish, Gentlemen of the Jury, they take back the poor wretch to his prison.

The People breathe again. The People, naturally merciful, hope that the man will be spared. But no,—the guillotine, though vanquished, remains standing. There it frowns all day, in the midst of a sickened population. And at night, the officers, reinforced, drag forth the wretch again, so bound that he is but an inert weight,—they drag him forth, haggard, bloody, weeping, pleading, howling for life—calling upon God, calling upon his father and mother,—for like a very child had this man become in the prospect of death—they drag him forth to execution. He is hoisted on the scaffold, and his head falls!—And then through every conscience runs a shudder.

Victor Hugo

from KNICKERBOCKER'S HISTORY OF NEW YORK   (Articulation)

These were the honest days in which every woman staid at home, read the Bible, and wore pockets,—ay, and that too of a goodly size, fashioned with patchwork into many curious devices, and ostentatiously worn on the outside. These, in fact, were convenient receptacles, where all good housewives carefully stored away such things as they wished to have at hand; by which means they often came to be incredibly crammed; and I remember there was a story current, when I was a boy, that the lady of Wouter Van Twiller once had occasion to empty her right pocket in search of a wooden ladle, when the contents filled a couple of corn-baskets, and the utensil was discovered lying among some rubbish in one corner;—but we must not give too much faith to all these stories, the anecdotes of those remote periods being very subject to exaggeration.

Besides these notable pockets, they likewise wore scissors and pin-cushions suspended from their girdles by red ribands, or, among the more opulent and showy classes, by brass, and even silver chains,—indubitable tokens of thrifty housewives and industrious spinsters. I cannot say much in vindication of the shortness of the petticoats; it doubtless was introduced for the purpose of giving the stockings a chance to be seen, which were generally of blue worsted, with magnificent red clocks,—or, perhaps, to display a well-turned ankle, and a neat, though serviceable foot, set off by a high-heeled leathern shoe, with a large and splendid silver buckle. Thus we find that the gentle sex in all ages have shown the same disposition to infringe a little upon the laws of decorum, in order to betray a lurking beauty, or gratify an innocent love of finery.

From the sketch here given, it will be seen that our good grandmothers differed considerably in their ideas of a fine figure from their scantily dressed descendents of the present day. A fine lady, in those times, waddled under more clothes, even on a fair summer's day, than would have clad the whole bevy of a modern ball-room. Nor were they the less admired by the gentlemen in consequence thereof. On the contrary, the greatness of a lover's passion seemed to increase in proportion to the magnitude of its object,—and a voluminous damsel, arrayed in a dozen petticoats, was declared by a Low-Dutch sonneteer of the province to be radiant as a sunflower, and luxuriant as a full-blown cabbage. Certain it is, that in those days the heart of a lover could not contain more than one lady at a time; whereas the heart of a modern gallant has often room enough to accommodate half a dozen. The reason of which I conclude to be, that either the hearts of the gentlemen have grown larger, or the persons of the ladies smaller: this, however, is a question for physiologists to determine.

Washington Irving

WISDOM   (Resonance)

But where shall wisdom be found? and where is the place of understanding?
Man knoweth not the price thereof; neither is it found in the land of the living.
The depth saith, It is not in me: and the sea saith, It is not with me.
It cannot be gotten for gold, neither shall silver be weighed for the price thereof.
It cannot be valued with the gold of Ophir, with the precious onyx, or the sapphire.
The gold and the crystal cannot equal it: and the exchange of it shall not be for
    jewels of fine gold.
No mention shall be made of coral, or of pearls: for the price of wisdom is above
    rubies.
The topaz of Ethiopia shall not equal it, neither shall it be valued with pure gold.
Whence then cometh wisdom? and where is the place of understanding?

Job 28:12–20

ON FIRST LOOKING INTO CHAPMAN'S HOMER   (Articulation)

Much have I travell'd in the realms of gold,
    And many goodly states and kingdoms seen;
    Round many western islands have I been
Which bards in fealty to Apollo hold.
Oft of one wide expanse had I been told.
    That deep-brow'd Homer ruled as his demesne;
    Yet did I never breathe its pure serene
Till I heard Chapman speak out loud and bold:
Then felt I like some watcher of the skies
    When a new planet swims into his ken;
Or like stout Cortez when with eagle eyes
    He star'd at the Pacific—and all his men
Look'd at each other with a wild surmise—
    Silent, upon a peak in Darien.

John Keats

from THE PRESIDENT'S MESSAGE ON EDUCATION
TO CONGRESS, JANUARY 29, 1963   (Pronounciation)

Education is the keystone in the arch of freedom and progress. Nothing has contributed more to the enlargement of this nation's strength and opportunities than our traditional system of free, universal elementary and secondary education, coupled with widespread availability of college education.

For the individual, the doors to the schoolhouse, to the library and to the college lead to the richest treasures of our open society: to the power of knowledge—to the training and skills necessary for productive employment—to the wisdom, the ideals, and the culture which enrich life—and to the creative, self-disciplined understanding of society needed for good citizenship in today's changing and challenging world.

For the nation, increasing the quality and availability of education is vital to both our national security and our domestic well-being. A free Nation can rise no higher than the standard of excellence set in its schools and colleges. Ignorance and illiteracy, unskilled workers and school dropouts—these and other failures of our educational system breed failures in our social and economic system: delinquency, unemployment, chronic dependence, a waste of human resources, a loss of productive power and purchasing power and an increase in tax-supported benefits. The loss of only one year's income due to unemployment is more than the total cost of twelve years of education through high school. Failure to improve educational performance is thus not only poor social policy, it is poor economics.

At the turn of the century, only 10 percent of our adults had a high school or college education. Today such an education has become a requirement for an increasing number of jobs. Yet nearly 40 percent of our youths are dropping out before graduating from high school; only 43 percent of our adults have completed high school; only 8 percent of our adults have completed college; and only 16 percent of our young people are presently completing college. As my Science Advisory Committee has reported, one of our most serious manpower shortages is the lack of Ph.D.'s in engineering, science and mathematics; only about one half of 1 percent of our school age generation is achieving Ph.D. degrees in all fields.

This nation is committed to greater investment in economic growth; and recent research has shown that one of the most beneficial of all such investments is education, accounting for some 40 percent of the nation's growth and productivity in recent years. It is an investment which yields a substantial return in the higher wages and purchasing power of trained workers, in the new products and techniques which come from skilled minds and in the constant expansion of this nation's storehouse of useful knowledge.

In the new age of science and space, improved education is essential to give new meaning to our national purpose and power. In the last 20 years, mankind has acquired more scientific information than in all of previous history. Ninety percent of all the scientists that ever lived are alive and working today. Vast stretches of the unknown are being explored every day for military, medical, commercial and other reasons. And finally, the twisting course of the cold war requires a citizenry that understands our principles and problems. It requires skilled manpower and brainpower to match the power of totalitarian discipline. It requires a scientific effort which demonstrates the superiority of freedom. And it requires an electorate in every state with sufficiently broad horizons and sufficient maturity and judgment to guide this nation safely through whatever lies ahead.

John F. Kennedy

from I HAVE A DREAM   (Pitch, Loudness, and Time Variety)

I am not unmindful that some of you have come here out of great trials and tribulations. Some of you have come fresh from narrow jail cells. Some of you have come from areas where your quest for freedom left you battered by the storms of persecution and staggered by the winds of police brutality. . . .

Go back to Mississippi, go back to Alabama, go back to South Carolina, go back to Georgia, go back to Louisiana, go back to the slums and ghettos of our Northern cities, knowing that somehow this situation can and will be changed. Let us not wallow in the valley of despair.

I say to you today, my friends, that in spite of the difficulties and frustrations of the moment I still have a dream. It is a dream deeply rooted in the American dream.

I have a dream that one day this nation will rise up and live out the true meaning of its creed: "We hold these truths to be self-evident; that all men are created equal." . . .

I have a dream that my four little children will one day live in a nation where they will not be judged by the color of their skin but by the content of their character.

I have a dream today. . . .

I have a dream that one day every valley shall be exalted, every hill and mountain shall be made low, the rough places will be made plains, and the crooked places will be made straight, and the glory of the Lord shall be revealed, and all flesh shall see it together.

This is our hope. This is the faith with which I return to the South. With this faith we will be able to hew out of the mountain of despair a stone of hope. With this faith we will be able to transform the jangling discords of our nation into a beautiful symphony of brotherhood.

With this faith we will be able to work together, to pray together, to struggle together, to go to jail together, to stand up for freedom together, knowing that we will be free one day.

This will be the day when all of God's children will be able to sing with new meaning, "My country 'tis of thee, sweet land of liberty, of thee I sing. Land where my fathers died, land of the Pilgrims' pride, from every mountainside, let freedom ring."

And if America is to be a great nation, this must become true. So let freedom ring from the prodigious hilltops of New Hampshire. Let freedom ring from the mighty mountains of New York. Let freedom ring from the heightening Alleghenies of Pennsylvania!

Let freedom ring from the snowcapped Rockies of Colorado! Let freedom ring from the curvaceous peaks of California! But not only that; let freedom ring from Stone Mountain of Georgia! Let freedom ring from Lookout Mountain of Tennessee!

Let freedom ring from every hill and molehill of Mississippi. From every mountainside, let freedom ring.

When we let freedom ring, when we let it ring from every village and every hamlet, from every state and every city, we will be able to speed up that day when all of God's children, black men and white men, Jews and Gentiles, Protestants and Catholics, will be able to join hands and sing in the words of the old Negro spiritual, "Free at last! Free at last! Thank God Almighty, we are free at last!"

Martin Luther King, Jr.

from A SEPARATE PEACE   (Loudness Variety)

A little fog hung over the river so that as I neared it I felt myself becoming isolated from everything except the river and the few trees beside it. The wind was blowing more steadily here, and I was beginning to feel cold. I never wore a hat, and had forgotten gloves. There were several trees bleakly reaching into the fog. Any one of them might have been the one I was looking for. Unbelievable that there were other trees which looked like it here. It had loomed in my memory as a huge lone spike dominating the riverbank, forbidding as an artillery piece, high as the beanstalk. Yet here was a scattered grove of trees, none of them of any particular grandeur.

John Knowles

TO A MOTHER ON THE DEATH OF HER SONS   (Time Variety)

Executive Mansion,
Washington, Nov. 21, 1864.

Dear Madam,—

I have been shown in the files of the war Department a statement of the Adjutant General of Massachusetts, that you are the mother of five sons who have died gloriously on the field of battle.

I feel how weak and fruitless must be any word of mine which should attempt to beguile you from the grief of a loss so overwhelming. But I cannot refrain from tendering to you the consolation that may be found in the thanks of the Republic they died to save.

I pray that our Heavenly Father may assuage the anguish of your bereavement, and leave you only the cherished memory of the loved and lost, and the solemn pride that must be yours, to have laid so costly a sacrifice upon the altar of Freedom.

Yours, very sincerely and respectively,
A. Lincoln

Abraham Lincoln

from OLD SOLDIERS NEVER DIE   (Time Variety)

The Japanese people since the war have undergone the greatest reformation recorded in modern history. With a commendable will, eagerness to learn, and marked capacity to understand, they have, from the ashes left in war's wake, erected in Japan an edifice dedicated to the primacy of individual liberty and personal dignity, and in the ensuing process there has been created a truly representative government committed to the advance of political morality, freedom of economic enterprise, and social justice. Politically, economically and socially Japan is now abreast of many free nations of the earth and will not again fail the universal trust. That it may be counted upon to wield a profoundly beneficial influence over the course of events in Asia is attested by the magnificent manner in which the Japanese people have met the recent challenge of war, unrest, and confusion surrounding them from the outside, and checked communism within their own frontiers without the slightest slackening in their forward progress . . . I know of no nation more serene, orderly, and industrious—nor in which higher hopes can be entertained for future constructive service in the advance of the human race.

Of our former wards, the Philippines, we can look forward in confidence that the existing unrest will be corrected and a strong healthy nation will grow in the longer aftermath of war's terrible destructiveness. We must be patient and understanding and never fail them, as in our hour of need they did not fail us.

Douglas MacArthur

from MOBY DICK   (Time Variety)

Call me Ishmael. Some years ago—never mind how long precisely—having little or no money in my purse, and nothing particular to interest me on shore, I thought I would sail about a little and see the watery part of the world. It is a way I have of driving off the spleen, and regulating the circulation. Whenever I find myself growing grim about the mouth; whenever it is a damp, drizzly November in my soul; whenever I find myself involuntarily pausing before coffin warehouses, and bringing up the rear of every funeral I meet; and especially whenever my hypos get such an upper hand of me, that it requires a strong moral principle to prevent me from deliberately stepping into the street, and methodically knocking people's hats off—then, I account it high time to get to sea as soon as I can. This is my substitute for pistol and ball. With a philosophical flourish Cato throws himself upon his sword; I quietly take to the ship. There is nothing surprising in this. If they but knew it, almost all men in their degree, some time or other, cherish very nearly the same feelings towards the ocean with me.

Herman Melville

CULTURE AND COMMUNICATION   (Articulation)

I recall very well a scene of some years ago, just as daylight was breaking, on the island of Wake, in the mid-Pacific. The commercial passenger plane on which I was flying from Tokyo to San Francisco had put down to refuel, and we passengers were shepherded into the restaurant at the terminal building to have breakfast. All of us were sleepy, disheveled, and tired after a night-long flight. As a consequence, we did not feel particulary sociable.

I took my seat at a small table along with two other American men, who appeared to be businessmen, and a middle-aged Japanese, who proved to be a college professor barely able to speak a few words of English.

None of us paid any attention to any of the others until I noticed that the Japanese was regarding his American companions with rather obvious distaste. Then I smiled at him, and handed him the salt cellar for his eggs, holding it toward him in my right hand, with the fingers of the left hand lightly touching the base of my right hand palm—a typical Japanese gesture of respect. For a moment he looked unbelievingly at the unexpected behavior of this strange foreigner. Then his face broke into a broad smile of sheer relief and I could almost hear him say to himself, "Perhaps they are not barbarians, after all." It was quite a lot to accomplish by so simple a device as knowing how to hold one's hands.

Robert T. Oliver

from 1984   (Resonance)

Outside, even through the shut window pane, the world looked cold. Down in the street little eddies of wind were whirling dust and torn paper into spirals, and though the sun was shining and the sky a harsh blue, there seemed to be no color in anything except the posters that were plastered everywhere. The black-mustachio'd face gazed down from every commanding corner. There was one on the house front immediately opposite. BIG BROTHER IS WATCHING YOU, the caption said, while dark eyes looked deep into Winston's own. Down at street level another poster, torn at one corner, flapped fitfully in the wind, alternately covering and uncovering the single word INGSOC. In the far distance a helicopter skimmed down between the roofs, hovered for an instant like a bluebottle, and darted away again with a curving flight. It was the Police Patrol, snooping into people's windows. The patrols did not matter, however. Only the Thought Police mattered.

George Orwell

ODE   (Time Variety)

We are the music makers,
    And we are the dreamers of dreams,
Wandering by lone sea-breakers,
    And sitting by desolate streams;—
World-losers and world-forsakers,
    On whom the pale moon gleams;
Yet we are the movers and shakers
    Of the world for ever, it seems.

With wonderful deathless ditties
We build up the world's great cities,
    And out of a fabulous story
    We fashion an empire's glory:
One man with a dream, at pleasure,
    Shall go forth and conquer a crown;
And three with a new song's measure
    Can trample a kingdom down.

We, in the ages lying
    In the buried past of the earth,
Built Nineveh with our sighing,
    And Babel itself in our mirth;
And o'erthrew them with prophesying
    To the old of the new world's worth;
For each age is a dream that is dying,
    Or one that is coming to birth.

Arthur O'Shaughnessy

from THE PREMATURE BURIAL   (Loudness Variety)

I remained without motion. . . . I could not summon courage to move. I dared not make the effort which was to satisfy me of my fate—and yet there was something at my heart which whispered me *it was sure*. Despair—such as no other species of wretchedness ever calls into being—despair alone urged me, after long irresolution, to uplight the heavy lids of my eyes. I uplifted them. It was dark—all dark. I knew that the fit was over. I knew that the crisis of my disorder had long passed. I knew that I had now fully recovered the use of my visual faculties—and yet it was dark—all dark—the intense and utter raylessness of the Night that endureth for evermore.

I endeavored to shriek; and my lips and my parched tongue moved convulsively together in the attempt—but no voice issued from the cavernous lungs, which, oppressed as if by the weight of some incumbent mountain, gasped and palpitated, with the heart, at every elaborate and struggling inspiration.

The movement of the jaws, in this effort to cry aloud, showed me that they were bound up, as is usual with the dead. I felt, too, that I lay upon some hard substance; and by something similar my sides were, also, closely compressed. So far, I had not ventured to stir any of my limbs—but now I violently threw up my arms, which had been lying at length, with the wrists crossed. They struck a solid wooden substance, which extended above my person at an elevation of not more than six inches from my face. I could no longer doubt that I reposed within a coffin at last. . . .

As this awful conviction forced itself, thus, into the innermost chambers of my soul, I once again struggled to cry aloud. And in this second endeavor I succeeded. A long, wild, and continuous shriek, or yell, of agony, resounded through the realms of the subterranean Night.

Edgar Allan Poe

from THE TELL-TALE HEART   (Time Variety)

It is impossible to say how first the idea entered my brain; but once conceived, it haunted me day and night. Object there was none. Passion there was none. I loved the old man. He had never wronged me. He had never given me insult. For his gold I had no desire. I think it was his eye! yes, it was this! One of his eyes resembled that of a vulture—a pale blue eye, with a film over it. Whenever it fell upon me, my blood ran cold; and so by degrees—very gradually—I made up my mind to take the life of the old man, and thus rid myself of the eye for ever.

Now this is the point. You fancy me mad. Madmen know nothing. But you should have seen *me*. You should have seen how wisely I proceeded—with what caution—with what foresight—with what dissimulation I went to work! I was never kinder to the old man than during the whole week before I killed him. And every night, about midnight, I turned the latch of his door and opened it—oh, so gently! And then, when I had made an opening sufficient for my head, I put in a dark lantern, all closed, closed, so that no light shone out, and then I thrust in my head. Oh, you would have laughed to see how cunningly I thrust it in! I moved it slowly—very, very slowly, so that I might not disturb the old man's sleep. It took me an hour to place my whole head within the opening so far that I could see him as he lay upon his bed. Ha!—would a madman have been so wise as this? An then, when my head was well in the room, I undid the lantern cautiously—oh, so cautiously—cautiously (for the hinges creaked)—I undid it just so much that a single thin ray fell upon the vulture eye. And this I did for seven long nights—every night just at midnight—but I found the eye always closed; and so it was impossible to do the work; for it was not the old man who vexed me, but his Evil Eye. . . .

Upon the eighth night I was more than usually cautious in opening the door. A watch's minute hand moves more quickly than did mine. Never before that night had I *felt* the extent of my own powers—of my sagacity. I could scarcely contain my feelings of triumph. To think that there I was, opening the door, little by little, and he not even to dream of my secret deeds or thoughts. I fairly chuckled at the idea; and perhaps he heard me; for he moved on the bed suddenly, as if startled. Now you may think that I drew back—but no. His room was as black as pitch with the thick darkness (for the shutters were close fastened, through fear of robbers), and so I knew that he could not see the opening of the door, and I kept pushing it on steadily, steadily.

I had my head in, and was about to open the lantern, when my thumb slipped upon the tin fastening, and the old man sprang up in bed, crying out—"Who's there?"

Edgar Allan Poe

from A SPEECH BY A NATIVE AMERICAN   (Resonance)

Friend and Brother:—It was the will of the Great Spirit that we should meet together this day. He orders all things and has given us a fine day for our council. He has taken His garment from before the sun and caused it to shine with brightness upon us. Our eyes are open that we see clearly; our ears are unstopped that we have been able to hear distinctly the words you have spoken. . . .

Brother, you say there is but one way to worship and serve the Great Spirit. If there is but one religion, why do you white people differ so much about it? . . .

Brother, we do not understand these things. We are told that your religion was given to your forefathers and has been handed down from father to son. We also have a religion which was given to our forefathers and has been handed down to us, their children. We worship in that way. It teaches us to be thankful for all the favors we receive, to love each other, and to be united. We never quarrel about religion.

Brother, the Great Spirit has made us all, but He has made a great difference between His white and His red children. He has given us different complexions and different customs. To you He has given the arts. To these He has not opened our eyes. We know these things to be true. Since He has made so great a difference between us in other things, why may we not conclude that He has given us a different religion according to our understanding? The Great Spirit does right. He knows what is best for His children; we are satisfied.

Brother, we do not wish to destroy your religion of take it from you. We only want to enjoy our own.

Red Jacket

RICHARD CORY   (Time Variety)

Whenever Richard Cory went down town,
We people on the pavement looked at him:
He was a gentleman from sole to crown,
Clean favored, and imperially slim.

And he was always quietly arrayed,
And he was always human when he talked;
But still he fluttered pulses when he said,
"Good-morning," and he glittered when he walked.

And he was rich—yes, richer than a king—
And admirably schooled in every grace:
In fine, we thought that he was everything
To make us wish that we were in his place.

So on we worked, and waited for the light,
And went without the meat, and cursed the bread;
And Richard Cory, one calm summer night,
Went home and put a bullet through his head.

Edwin Arlington Robinson

from HAMLET, ACT 3, SCENE 1   (Articulation)

HAMLET. To be, or not to be—that is the question.
Whether 'tis nobler in the mind to suffer
The slings and arrows of outrageous fortune,
Or to take arms against a sea of troubles
And by opposing end them. To die, to sleep—
No more, and by a sleep to say we end
The heartache and the thousand natural shocks
That flesh is heir to. 'Tis a consummation
Devoutly to be wished. To die, to sleep,
To sleep—perchance to dream. Aye, there's the rub,
For in that sleep of death what dreams may come
When we have shuffled off this mortal coil
Must give us pause. There's the respect
That makes calamity of so long life.
For who would bear the whips and scorns of time,
The oppressor's wrong, the proud man's contumely,
The pangs of déspised love, the law's delay,
The insolence of office and the spurns
That patient merit of the unworthy takes,
When he himself might his quietus make
With a bare bodkin? Who would fardels bear,
To grunt and sweat under a weary life,
But that the dread of something after death,

The undiscovered country from whose bourn
No traveler returns, puzzles the will,
And makes us rather bear those ills we have
Than fly to others that we know not of?
Thus conscience does make cowards of us all,
And thus the native hue of resolution
Is sicklied o'er with the pale cast of thought,
And enterprises of great pitch and moment
With this regard their currents turn awry
And lose the name of action. . . .

William Shakespeare

from HAMLET, ACT 3, SCENE 2   (Articulation)

HAMLET. Speak the speech, I pray you, as I pronounced it to you, trippingly on the tongue. But if you mouth it, as many of your players do, I had as lief the town crier spoke my lines. Nor do not saw the air too much with your hand, thus, but use all gently. For in the very torrent, tempest, and, as I may say, whirlwind of passion, you must acquire and beget a temperance that may give it smoothness. . . .

Be not too tame neither, but let your own discretion be your tutor. Suit the action to the word, the word to the action, with this special observance, that you o'erstep not the modesty of nature. For anything so overdone is from the purpose of playing, whose end, both at the first and now, was and is to hold as 'twere the mirror up to Nature—to show Virture her own feature, scorn her own image, and the very age and body of the time his form and pressure. Now this overdone or come tardy off, though it make the unskillful laugh, cannot but make the judicious grieve, the censure of the which one must in your allowance o'erweigh a whole theater of others.

William Shakespeare

from JULIUS CAESAR, ACT 1, SCENE 2   (Loudness and Time Variety)

CASSIUS. . . . Honor is the subject of my story.
I cannot tell what you and other men
Think of this life, but for my single self
I had as lief not be as live to be
In awe of such a thing as I myself.
I was born free as Caesar; so were you.
We both have fed as well, and we can both
Endure the winter's cold as well as he.
For once, upon a raw and gusty day,
The troubled Tiber chafing with her shores,
Caesar said to me "Darest thou, Cassius, now
Leap in with me to this angry flood
And swim to yonder point?" Upon the word,
Accoutered as I was, I plungèd in
And bade him follow. So indeed he did.

The torrent roared, and we did buffet it
With lusty sinews, throwing it aside
And stemming it with hearts of controversy.
But ere we could arrive the point proposed.
Caesar cried, "Help me, Cassius, or I sink!"
I, as Aeneas our great ancestor
Did from the flames of Troy upon his shoulder
The old Anchises bear, so from the waves of Tiber
Did I the tired Caesar—and this man
Is now become a god, and Cassius is
A wretched creature, and must bend his body
If Caesar carelessly but nod on him.
He had a fever when he was in Spain,
And when the fit was on him, I did mark
How he did shake. 'Tis true, this god did shake.
His coward lips did from their color fly,
And that same eye whose bend doth awe the world
Did lose his luster. I did hear him groan.
Aye, and that tongue of his that bade the Romans
Mark him and write his speeches in their books,
Alas, it cried, "Give me some drink, Titinius,"
As a sick girl. Ye gods, it doth amaze me,
A man of such a feeble temper should
So get the start of the majestic world,
And bear the palm alone.

. . . .

Why, man, he doth bestride the narrow world
Like a Colossus; and we petty men
Walk about under his huge legs, and peep about
To find ourselves dishonorable graves.
Mean at some time are masters of their fates:
The fault, dear Brutus, is not in our stars,
But in ourselves, that we are underlings.

William Shakespeare

from MACBETH, ACT 2, SCENE 1   (Pitch Variety)

MACBETH. Is this a dagger which I see before me,
The handle toward my hand? Come, let me clutch thee.
I have thee not, and yet I see thee still.
Art thou not, fatal vision, sensible
To feeling as to sight? Or art thou but
A dagger of the mind, a false creation,
Proceeding from the heat-oppressèd brain?

I see thee yet, in form as palpable
As this which now I draw.
Thou marshal'st me the way that I was going,
And such an instrument I was to use.
Mine eyes are made the fools o' the other senses,
Or else worth all the rest. I see thee still,
And on thy blade and dudgeon gouts of blood,
Which was not so before. There's no such thing.
It is the bloody business which informs
Thus to mine eyes. . . .

William Shakespeare

from THE MERCHANT OF VENICE, ACT 3, SCENE 2   (Loudness Variety)

BASSANIO. So may the outward shows be least themselves.
The world is still deceived with ornament.
In law, what plea so tainted and corrupt
But, being seasoned with a gracious voice,
Obscures the show of evil? In religion,
What damnèd error but some sober brow
Will bless it, and approve it with a text,
Hiding the grossness with fair ornament?
There is no vice so simple but assumes
Some mark of virtue on his outward parts.
How many cowards whose hearts are all as false
As stairs of sand wear yet upon their chins
The beards of Hercules and frowning Mars,
Who, inward searched, have livers white as milk.
And these assume but valor's excrement
To render them redoubted! Look on beauty
And you shall see 'tis purchased by the weight,
Which therein works a miracle in nature,
Making them lightest that wear most of it.
So are those crispèd snaky golden locks
Which make such wanton gambols with the wind
Upon supposèd fairness, often known
To be the dowry of a second head,
The skull that bred them in the sepulcher.
Thus ornament is but the guilèd shore
To a most dangerous sea, the beauteous scarf
Veiling an Indian beauty—in a word,
The seeming truth which cunning times put on
To entrap the wisest. . . .

William Shakespeare

from THE CATARACT OF LODORE   (Articulation and Pitch Variety)

"How does the water
Come down at Lodore?"
My little boy asked me
Thus, once on a time;
And moreover he tasked me
To tell him in rhyme.
Anon, at the word,
There first came one daughter,
And then came another,
To second and third
The request of their brother,
And to hear how the water
Comes down at Lodore,
With its rush and its roar,
As many a time
They had seen it before.
So I told them in rhyme,
For of rhymes I had store;
And 'twas in my vocation
For their recreation
That so I should sing;
Because I was Laureate
To them and the King.

From its sources which well
In the tarn on the fell;
From its fountains
In the mountains,
Its rills and its gills;
Through moss and through brake,
It runs and it creeps
For a while, till it sleeps
In its own little lake.
And thence at departing,
Awakening and starting,
It runs through the reeds,
And away it proceeds,
Through meadow and glade,
In sun and in shade,
And through the wood-shelter,
Among crags in its flurry,
Helter-skelter,
Hurry-skurry.
Here it comes sparkling,
And there it lies darkling;
Now smoking and frothing
Its tumult and wrath in,

Till, in this rapid race
On which it is bent,
It reaches the place
Of its steep descent.

The cataract strong
Then plunges along,
Striking and raging
As if a war raging
Its caverns and rocks among;
Rising and leaping,
Sinking and creeping,
Swelling and sweeping,
Showering and springing,
Flying and flinging,
Writhing and ringing,
Eddying and whisking,
Spouting and frisking,
Turning and twisting,
Around and around
With endless rebound:
Smiting and fighting,
A sight to delight in;
Confounding, astounding
Dizzying and deafening the ear with its sound.

Dividing and gliding and sliding,
And falling and brawling and sprawling,
And driving and riving and striving,
And sprinkling and twinkling and wrinkling,
And sounding and bounding and rounding,
And bubbling and troubling and doubling,
And grumbling and rumbling and tumbling,
And clattering and battering and shattering;
Retreating and beating and meeting and sheeting,
Delaying and straying and playing and spraying,
Advancing and prancing and glancing and dancing,
Recoiling, turmoiling and toiling and boiling,
And gleaming and streaming and steaming and beaming,
And rushing and flushing and brushing and gushing,
And flapping and rapping and clapping and slapping,
And curling and whirling and purling and twirling,
And thumping and plumping and bumping and jumping,
And dashing and flashing and splashing and clashing;
And so never ending, but always descending,
Sounds and motions for ever and ever are blending
All at once and all o'er, with a mighty uproar,—
And this way the water comes down at Lodore.

                                                    Robert Southey

from THE GRAPES OF WRATH   (Time Variety)

The owners of the land came onto the land, or more often a spokesman for the owners came. They came in closed cars, they felt the dry earth with their fingers, and sometimes they drove big earth augers into the ground for soil tests. The tenants, from their sun-beaten dooryards, watched uneasily when the closed cars drove along the fields. And at last the owner men drove into the dooryards and sat in their cars to talk out of the windows. The tenant men stood beside the cars for a while, and then squatted on their hams and found sticks with which to mark the dust.

In the open doors the women stood looking out, and behind them the children—corn-headed children, with wide eyes, one bare foot on top of the other bare foot, and the toes working. The women and the children watched their men talking to the owner men. They were silent.

Some of the owner men were kind because they hated what they had to do, and some of them were angry because they hated to be cruel, and some of them were cold because they had long ago found that one could not be an owner unless one were cold. And all of them were caught in something larger than themselves. Some of them hated the mathematics that drove them, and some were afraid, and some worshiped the mathematics because it provided a refuge from thought and from feeling. If a bank or a finance company owned the land, the owner man said, The Bank—or the Company—needs —wants—insists—must have—as though the Bank or the Company were a monster, with thought and feeling, which had ensnared them. These last would take no responsibility for the banks or the companies because they were men and slaves, while the banks were machines and masters all at the same time. Some of the owner men were a little proud to be slaves to such cold and powerful masters. The owner men sat in the cars and explained. You know the land is poor. You've scrabbled at it long enough, God knows.

The squatting tenant men nodded and wondered and drew figures in the dust, and yes, they knew, God knows. If the dust only wouldn't fly. If the top would only stay on the soil, it might not be so bad.

The owner men went on leading to their point: You know the land's getting poorer. You know what cotton does to the land; robs it, sucks all the blood out of it.

The squatters nodded—they knew, God knew. If they could only rotate the crops they might pump blood back into the land.

Well, it's too late. And the owner men explained the workings and thinkings of the monster that was stronger than they were. A man can hold land if he can just eat and pay taxes; he can do that.

Yes, he can do that until his crops fail one day and he has to borrow money from the bank.

But—you see, a bank or a company can't do that, because those creatures don't breathe air, don't eat side-meat. They breathe profits; they eat the interest on money. If they don't get it, they die the way you die without air, without side-meat. It is a sad thing, but it is so. It is just so.

The squatting men raised their eyes to understand. Can't we just hang on? Maybe the next year will be a good year. God knows how much cotton next year. And with all the wars—God knows what price cotton will bring. Don't they make explosives out of cotton? And uniforms? Get enough wars and cotton'll hit the ceiling. Next year, maybe. They look up questioningly.

We can't depend on it. The bank—the monster has to have profits all the time. It can't wait. It'll die. No, taxes go on. When the monster stops growing, it dies. It can't stay one size.

Soft fingers began to tap the sill of the car window, and hard fingers tightened on the restless drawing sticks. In the doorways of the sun-beaten tenant houses, women sighed and then shifted feet so that the one that had been down was now on top, and the toes working. Dogs came sniffing near the owner cars and wetted on all four tires one after another. And chickens lay in the sunny dust and fluffed their feathers to get the cleansing dust down to the skin. In the little sties the pigs grunted inquiringly over the muddy remnants of the slops.

The squatting men looked down again. What do you want us to do? We can't take less share of the crop—we're half starved now. The kids are hungry all the time. We got no clothes, torn an' ragged. If all the neighbors weren't the same, we'd be ashamed to go to meeting.

And at last the owner men came to the point. The tenant system won't work any more. One man on a tractor can take the place of twelve or fourteen families. Pay him a wage and take all the crop. We have to do it. We don't like to do it. But the monster's sick. Something's happened to the monster.

John Steinbeck

from THE LADY OF SHALOTT   (Loudness Variety)

Lying, robed in snowy white
That loosely flew to left and right—
The leaves upon her falling light—
Through the noises of the night
    She floated down to Camelot;
And as the boat-head wound along
The willowy hills and fields among,
They heard her singing her last song,
    The Lady of Shalott.

Alfred, Lord Tennyson

THE OWL WHO WAS GOD   (Time Variety)

Once upon a starless midnight there was an owl who sat on the branch of an oak tree. Two ground moles tried to slip quietly by, unnoticed. "You!" said the owl. "Who?" they quavered, in fear and astonishment, for they could not believe it was possible for anyone to see them in that thick darkness. "You two!" said the owl. The moles hurried away and told the other creatures of the field and forest that the owl was the greatest and wisest of all animals because he could see in the dark and because he could answer any question. "I'll see about that," said a secretary bird, and he called on the owl one night when it was again very dark. "How many claws am I holding up?" said the secretary bird. "Two," said the owl, and that was right. "Can you give me another expression for 'that is to say,' or 'namely'?" asked the secretary bird. "To wit," said the owl. "Why does a lover call on his love?" asked the secretary bird. "To woo," said the owl.

The secretary bird hastened back to the other creatures and reported that the owl was indeed the greatest and wisest animal in the world because he could see in the dark and because he could answer any question. "Can he see in the daytime too?" asked a red fox. "Yes," echoed a dormouse and a French poodle. "Can he see in the daytime too?" All the other creatures laughed loudly at this silly question, and they set upon the red fox and his friends and drove them out of the region. Then they sent a messenger to the owl and asked him to be their leader.

When the owl appeared among the animals it was high noon and the sun was shining brightly. He walked very slowly, which gave him an appearance of great dignity, and he peered about him with large, staring eyes, which gave him an air of tremendous importance. "He's God!" screamed a Plymouth Rock hen. And others took up the cry. "He's God!" So they followed him wherever he went and when he began to bump into things they began to bump into things, too. Finally he came to a concrete highway and he started up the middle of it and all the other creatures followed him. Presently, a hawk, who was acting as outrider, observed a truck coming toward them at fifty miles an hour, and he reported to the secretary bird and the secretary bird reported to the owl. "There's danger ahead," said the secretary bird. "To wit?" said the owl. The secretary bird told him. "Aren't you afraid?" he asked. "Who?" said the owl calmly, for he could not see the truck. "He's God!" cried all the creatures again, and they were still crying "He's God!" when the truck hit them and ran them down. Some of the animals were merely injured, but most of them, including the owl, were killed.

Moral: You can fool too many of the people too much of the time.

James Thurber

UNIVERSITY DAYS   (Loudness Variety)

I passed all the other courses that I took at my university, but I could never pass botany. This was because all botany students had to spend several hours a week in a laboratory looking through a microscope at plants cells, and I could never see through a microscope. I never once saw a cell through a microscope. This used to enrage my instructor. He would wander around the laboratory pleased with the progress all the students were making in drawing the involved and, so I am told, interesting structure of flower cells, until he came to me. I would just be standing there. "I can't see anything," I would say. He would begin patiently enough, explaining how anybody can see through a microscope, but he would always end up in a fury, claiming, that I could *too* see through a microscope but just pretended that I couldn't. "It takes away from the beauty of flowers anyway," I used to tell him. "We are not concerned with beauty in this course," he would say. "We are concerned solely with what I may call the *mechanics* of flars." "Well," I'd say, "I can't see anything." "Try it just once again," he'd say, and I would put my eye to the microscope and see nothing at all, except now and again, nebulous milky substance—a phenomenon of maladjustment. You were supposed to see a vivid, restless clockwork of sharply defined plant cells. "I see what looks like a lot of milk," I would tell him. This, he claimed, was the result of my not having adjusted the microscope properly; so he would readjust it for me, or rather, for himself. And I would look again and see milk.

I finally took a deferred pass, as they called it, and waited a year and tried again. (You had to pass one of the explain cell-structure again to his classes. "Well," he said to me, cheerily, when we met in the first laboratory hour of the semester, "we're going to see cells this time, aren't we?" "Yes, sir," I said. Students to right of me and to left of me and in front of me were seeing cells; what's more, they were quietly drawing pictures of them in their notebooks. Of course, I didn't see anything.

"We'll try it," the professor said to me grimly, "with every adjustment of the microscope known to man. As God is my witness, I'll arrange this glass so that you see cells through it or I'll give up teaching. In twenty-two years of botany, I—" He cut off abruptly for he was beginning to quiver all over, like Lionel Barrymore, and he genuinely wished to hold onto his temper; his scenes with me had taken a great deal out of him.

So we tried it with every adjustment of the microscope known to man. With only one of them did I see anything but blackness or the familiar lacteal opacity, and that time I saw, to my pleasure and amazement, a variegated constellation of flecks, specks, and dots. These I hastily drew. The instructor, noting my activity, came back from an adjoining desk, a smile on his lips, and his eyebrows high in hope. He looked at my cell drawing. "What's that?" he demanded, with a hint of a squeal in his voice. "That's what I saw," I said. "You didn't, you didn't, you *did*n't!" he screamed, losing control of his temper instantly, and he bent over and squinted into the microscope. His head snapped up. "That's your eye!" he shouted. "You've fixed the lens so that it reflects! You've drawn your eye!"

James Thurber

from THE ADVENTURES OF HUCKLEBERRY FINN   (Articulation)

It was a real bully circus. It was the splendidest sight that ever was when they all come riding in, two and two, gentleman and lady, side by side, the men just in their drawers and undershirts, and no shoes nor stirrups, and resting their hands on their thighs easy and comfortable—there must 'a' been twenty of them—and every lady with a lovely complexion, and perfectly beautiful, and looking just like a gang of real sure-enough queens, and dressed in clothes that cost millions of dollars, and just littered with diamonds. It was a powerful fine sight; I never see anything so lovely. And then one by one they got up and stood, and went a-weaving around the ring so gentle and wavy and graceful, the men looking ever so tall and airy and straight, with their heads bobbing and skimming along, away up there under the tent-roof, and every lady's rose-leafy dress flapping soft and silky around her hips, and she looking like the most loveliest parasol.

And then faster and faster they went, all of them dancing, first one foot out in the air and then the other, the horses leaning more and more, and the ringmaster going round and round the center pole, cracking his whip and shouting "Hi!—hi!" and the clown cracking jokes behind him; and by and by all hands dropped the reins, and every lady put her knuckles on her hips and every gentleman folded his arms, and then how the horses did lean over and hump themselves! And so one after the other they all skipped off into the ring, and made the sweetest bow I ever see, and then scampered out, and everybody clapped their hands and went just about wild.

Mark Twain

from THE AUTOBIOGRAPHY OF MARK TWAIN   (Loudness and Time Variety)

I can see the farm yet, with perfect clearness. I can see all its belongings, all its details; the family room of the house, with a "trundle" bed in one corner and a spinning-wheel in another—a wheel whose rising and falling wail, heard from a distance, was the mournfulest of all sounds to me and made me homesick and low spirited and filled my atmosphere with the wandering spirits of the dead; the vast fireplace, piled high on winter nights with flaming hickory logs from whose ends a sugary sap bubbled out but did not go to waste, for we scraped it off and ate it; the lazy cat spread out on the rough hearthstones; the drowsy dogs braced against the jambs and blinking; my aunt in one chimney corner, knitting; my uncle in the other, smoking his corn-cob pipe; the slick and carpetless oak floor faintly mirroring the dancing flame tongues and freckled with black indentations where fire coals had popped out and died a leisurely death; half a dozen children romping in the background twilight; "split"-bottomed chairs here and there, some with rockers; a cradle—out of service but waiting with confidence; in the early cold mornings a snuggle of children in shirts and chemises, occupying the hearthstone and procrastinating—they could not bear to leave that comfortable place and go out on the wind-swept floor space between the house and kitchen where the general tin basin stood, and wash.

Along outside of the front fence ran the country road, dusty in the summertime and a good place for snakes—they liked to lie in it and sun themselves; when they were rattlesnakes or puff adders we killed them; when they were black snakes or racers or belonged to the fabled "hoop" breed we fled without shame; when they were "house snakes" or "garters" we carried them home and put them in Aunt Patsy's work basket for a surprise; for she was prejudiced against snakes, and always when she took the basket in her lap and they began to climb out of it it disordered her mind. She never could seem to get used to them.

Mark Twain

from LIFE ON THE MISSISSIPPI   (Loudness Variety)

I had myself called with the four-o'clock watch, mornings, for one cannot see too many summer sunrises on the Mississippi. They are enchanting. First, there is the eloquence of silence; for a deep hush broods everywhere. Next, there is the haunting sense of loneliness, isolation, remoteness from the worry and bustle of the world. The dawn creeps in stealthily; the solid walls of black forest soften to gray, and vast stretches of the river open up and reveal themselves; the water is glass-smooth, gives off spectral little wreaths of white-mist, there is not the faintest breath of wind, nor stir of leaf; the tranquillity is profound and infinitely satisfying. Then a bird pipes up, another follows, and soon the pipings develop into a jubilant riot of music. You see none of the birds; you simply move through an atmosphere of song which seems to sing itself. When the light has become a little stronger, you have one of the fairest and softest pictures imaginable. You have the intense green of the massed and crowded foliage near by; you see it paling shade by shade in front of you; upon the next projecting cape, a mile off or more, the tint has lightened to the tender young green of spring; the cape beyond that one has almost lost color, and the furthest one, miles away under the horizon, sleeps upon the water a mere dim vapor, and hardly separable from the sky above it and about it. And all this stretch of river is a mirror, and you have the shadowy reflections of the leafage and the curving shores and the receding capes pictured in it. Well, that is all beautiful; soft and rich and beautiful; and when the sun gets well up, and distributes a pink flush here and a powder of gold yonder and a purple haze where it will yield the best effect, you grant that you have seen something that is worth remembering.

Mark Twain

BEAT! BEAT! DRUMS!   (Loudness and Time Variety)

Beat! beat! drums!—blow! bugles! blow!
Through the windows—through doors—burst like a ruthless force,
Into the solemn church, and scatter the congregation,
Into the school where the scholar is studying;
Leave not the bridegroom quiet—no happiness must he have now with his bride,
Nor the peaceful farmer any peace, plowing his field or gathering his grain,
So fierce your whirr and pound you drums—so shrill you bugles blow.

Beat! beat! drums!—blow! bugles! blow!
Over the traffic of cities—over the rumble of wheels in the streets;
Are beds prepared for sleepers at night in the houses? no sleepers must sleep in those
    beds,
No bargainers' bargins by day—no brokers or speculators—would they continue?
Would the talkers be talking? would the singer attempt to sing?
Would the lawyer rise in the court to state his case before the judge?
Then rattle quicker, heavier drums—you bugles wilder blow.

Beat! beat! drums!—blow! bugles! blow!
Make no parley—stop for no expostulation,
Mind not the timid—mind not the weeper or prayer,
Mind not the old man beseeching the young man,
Let not the child's voice be heard, nor the mother's entreaties,
Make even the trestles to shake the dead where they lie awaiting the hearses,
So strong you thump O terrible drums—so loud you bugles blow.

Walt Whitman

THE TORCH   (Pitch Variety)

On my Northwest coast in the midst of the night a fishermen's group stands
    watching.
Out on the lake that expands before them, others are spearing salmon,
The canoe, a dim shadowy thing, moves across the black water,
Bearing a torch ablaze at the prow.

Walt Whitman

THE WORLD IS TOO MUCH WITH US   (Loudness Variety)

The world is too much with us; late and soon,
Getting and spending, we lay waste our powers;
Little we see in Nature that is ours;
We have given our hearts away, a sordid boon!
The sea that bares her bosom to the moon;
The winds that will be howling at all hours,
And are up-gathered now like sleeping flowers;
For this, for everything, we are out of tune;
It moves us not.—Great God! I'd rather be
A Pagan suckled in a creed outworn;
So might I, standing on this pleasant lea,
Have glimpses that would make me less forlorn;
Have sight of Proteus rising from the sea;
Or hear old Triton blow his wreathéd horn.

William Wordsworth

READING SELECTION CREDITS

Voice Analysis and Articulation Analysis

The selection below, entitled *Evening Classes*, contains all the sounds of Standard American English presented in the same order as arranged in the text and on the Articulation Analysis Sheet. The other selections contain all of the sounds of Standard American English. Your professor may have you record these, or others, to analyze your speech production.

Evening Classes

Each evening, interesting lessons and classes are held at this college. Probably all of them are good, but a few are certainly surprising. Some classes, of course, are just fair, but only one or two are really weird.

These days, we find educational enjoyment without going far from home. The people who begin to study can go on, finish, and have growth. Though the subjects some choose are foolish, most are usually hard and challenging. When students have worked for a couple of years religiously, many notice that their study is satisfying.

Virginia Theater

It is usually rather easy to reach the Virginia Theater. Board the car number 56 somewhere along Churchill Street and ride to the highway. Transfer there to the Mississippi bus. When you arrive at Judge Avenue, begin walking toward the business zone. You will pass a gift shop, displaying little children's playthings, which often look so clever that you will wish yourself young again. There are such things as books and toys and, behind the counter, a playroom with an elegant red rug and smooth, shining mirrors. Beyond this shop are the National Bank and the Globe Garage. Turn south at the next corner and you will find that the theater is to your left.

My Grandfather

You wished to know all about my grandfather. Well, he is nearly 93 years old; he dresses himself in an ancient, black frock coat, usually minus several buttons, yet he still thinks as swiftly as ever. A long, flowing beard clings to his chin, giving those who observe him a pronounced feeling of the utmost respect. When he speaks, his voice is just a bit cracked and quivers a trifle.

Twice each day, he plays skillfully, and with zest, upon our small organ. Except in the winter, when the ooze or snow or ice prevents, he slowly takes a short walk in the open air each day. We have often urged him to walk more and smoke less, but he always answers, "Banana oil!" Grandfather likes to be modern in his language.

The Mouse and the Lion

A mouse went into a lion's cave by mistake, and before he knew what he was doing, he ran over the nose of the sleeping lion. The lion reached out his paw and caught the mouse and was about to eat him when the mouse said, "Forgive me, King of Beasts, I did not know where I was. I should never have been so proud as to come into this cave if I had known it was yours."

The lion smiled at the poor frightened little mouse and let him go. Not long after this, the lion fell into a rope net left for him by some hunters, and his roars filled the forest. The mouse recognized the voice and ran to see if he could help him. He set to work nibbling the ropes, and soon the lion was free.

Aesop

Analysis Sheets

On the following pages, we have provided analysis sheets to allow a comparison of your voice and articulation at the beginning of the term and at the end. On the voice analysis form, the ideal voice would receive checks on the right-hand side. The articulation analysis form may help your professor to identify flaws in the initial, middle, or final position of words for the various sounds (some sounds do not occur in each position). We feel sure that if these analysis sheets are used as development guides, you will make significant progress in achieving clear speech.

VOICE ANALYSIS

Use this page to indicate particular strengths and weaknesses in your voice production. The chapter numbers indicate passages in which corrective exercises can be found.

Respiration (Chapter 2)

Placement   upper chest _____ abdominal

Control

     Inhalation   shallow _____ sufficient

     Exhalation   inefficient _____ efficient

Phonation (Chapter 3)

Vocal pitch   too high _____ optimal

      too low _____ optimal

Vocal loudness   too loud _____ adequate

      too soft _____ adequate

Vocal tract dimension   constricted _____ open

Vocal fold vibrancy   breathy _____ fully voiced

Vocal tract focus   unbalanced _____ balanced

Vocal fold contact   rough _____ smooth

Vocal effort   much _____ little

Vocal fold mode   light _____ optimal

      pulsated _____ optimal

Resonation (Chapter 4)

Jaw closure   tight _____ flexible

Tongue retraction   back _____ forward

Nasality   nasal _____ optimal

      denasal _____ optimal

Vocal Variety (Chapter 10)

Pitch variety   monopitch _____ optimal

      excessive _____ optimal

Loudness variety   none ————————————————————————— optimal

                          excessive ——————————————————————— optimal

Rate variety   too slow ———————————————————————— optimal

                          too fast ————————————————————————— optimal

ARTICULATION ANALYSIS

The following sentences can be used to determine articulation skills. Each sentence contains its indicated sound in the position in which it normally occurs as the initial (I), middle (M), or final (F) sound of a word. This sheet can be used to indicate errors of articulation at the beginning of the term and progress at its end. (The vowel sounds ā [e] and ō [o] are rarely misarticulated and therefore are not included in this analysis. See Chapter 6.)

Vowels

Front

			Start of Term I	M	F	End of Term I	M	F	
1	ē [i]	Each meeting is at three.							1
2	ĭ [ɪ]	It is in the middle of the room.		▓				▓	2
3	ĕ [ɛ]	The entrance has a red door.		▓				▓	3
4	ă [æ]	The actor sat on the hat.		▓				▓	4

Back

			Start of Term I	M	F	End of Term I	M	F	
5a	ä [ɑ]	My honest father runs a spa.							5a
5b	ŏ [ɒ]	The opposite of cold is hot.					▓		5b
6	ô [ɔ]	In August, I bought a saw.							6
7	o͝o [ʊ]	Please put the book on the table.	▓		▓	▓			7
8	o͞o [u]	Here are oodles of shoes for you.							8

Central

			Start of Term I	M	F	End of Term I	M	F	
9	ûr [ɝ]	We earn money working for her.							9
10	ər [ɚ]	We will survive the winter.	▓			▓			10
11	ŭ [ʌ]	Under the table was some money.		▓				▓	11
12	ə [ə]	About six, I purchased a pizza.							12

			Start of Term			End of Term			
			I	M	F	I	M	F	

Diphthongs

13	ā [eɪ]	The eight kids played ball all day.							13
14	ī [aɪ]	I like apple pie.							14
15	oi [ɔɪ]	The oysters were enjoyed by a boy.							15
16	ou [aʊ]	An hour ago, he found the cow.							16
17	ō [oʊ]	The old man knows where to go.							17

Consonants

Stop-Plosives

18	p [p]	The piece of paper was on the top.							18
19	b [b]	The boy put the baby into the tub.							19
20	t [t]	Tell the senator to have a seat.							20
21	d [d]	The dog ran under the bed.							21
22	k [k]	The king is taking a walk.							22
23	g [g]	I will give you a bigger bag.							23

Fricatives

24	f [f]	My friend offered to save my life.							24
25	v [v]	The visitors will never leave.							25
26	th [θ]	I think I know nothing about math.							26
27	*th* [ð]	That leather is very smooth.							27
28	s [s]	I sent a message to the class.							28
29	z [z]	The zoo has dozens of animals.							29
30	sh [ʃ]	She paid for a washer with cash.							30
31	zh [ʒ]	Measure the length of the garage.							31
32	h [h]	It's hard to keep ahead.							32

	Start of Term			End of Term			
	I	M	F	I	M	F	

Affricates

33 ch [tʃ]   The champ is watching the match.   33

34 j [dʒ]   Jokes are enjoyed at any age.   34

Glides

35 hw [ʍ]   He whistled everywhere he went.   35

36 w [w]   I went away for a month.   36

37 y [j]   You must buy the onions.   37

38 r [r]   Let's ride around in the car.   38

Lateral semivowel

39 l [l]   She lost her only doll.   39

Nasals

40 m [m]   Mother brought the lemons home.   40

41 n [n]   No one took enough money to town.   41

42 ng [ŋ]   The singers were practicing.   42

Pronunciation Lists

The following pages contain lists of words that are often mispronounced. As mentioned in Chapter 9, there are five types of mispronunciation: omission of sounds, addition of sounds, substitution of sounds, reversal of sounds, and misplacement of stress.

On these lists, write the pronunciation symbols and a short definition for each word. Practice sounding each word from the symbols, and then use the word aloud in a sentence. Although many words have more than one acceptable pronunciation, use the first one listed in the dictionary unless your professor directs otherwise.

PRONUNCIATION LIST A (OMISSION)

Spelling	Diacritic/IPA Meaning
1. accelerate	
2. accessory	
3. accuracy	
4. adjective	
5. Antarctic	
6. asphyxiate	
7. attacked	
8. barbiturate	
9. calculus	
10. candidate	
11. casualty	
12. champion	
13. correct	
14. cumulus	
15. definite	
16. environment	
17. facsimile	
18. February	
19. forte (loudly)	
20. genuflect	
21. geography	
22. government	
23. guarantee	
24. individual	
25. ineffectual	

PRONUNCIATION LIST B (OMISSION)

Spelling	**Diacritic/IPA Meaning**
1. kept	_____
2. length	_____
3. library	_____
4. mutual	_____
5. nucleus	_____
6. particular	_____
7. picture	_____
8. poem	_____
9. probably	_____
10. quixotic	_____
11. realize	_____
12. recognize	_____
13. ridiculous	_____
14. regular	_____
15. scrupulous	_____
16. slept	_____
17. succinct	_____
18. suggest	_____
19. superintendent	_____
20. temperature	_____
21. twenty	_____
22. ubiquitous	_____
23. veterinarian	_____
24. violence	_____
25. winter	_____

PRONUNCIATION LIST C (ADDITION)

Spelling	Diacritic/IPA Meaning
1. accompanist	
2. across	
3. aluminum	
4. almond	
5. aperture	
6. athlete	
7. athletics	
8. balk	
9. balmy	
10. Bethlehem	
11. burglar	
12. business	
13. calm	
14. chasten	
15. chimney	
16. column	
17. comptroller	
18. corps	
19. disastrous	
20. drowned	
21. epistle	
22. escape	
23. evening	
24. film	
25. forehead	

PRONUNCIATION LIST D (ADDITION)

Spelling	Diacritic/IPA	Meaning
1. forte (strong point)		
2. garrulous		
3. grievous		
4. harangue		
5. height		
6. hindrance		
7. hurricane		
8. idea		
9. judicious		
10. lightning		
11. mischievous		
12. monstrous		
13. often		
14. pedantic		
15. preventive		
16. psalm		
17. remembrance		
18. righteous		
19. scintillate		
20. scion		
21. singing		
22. statistics		
23. subtle		
24. toward		
25. Worcestershire		

PRONUNCIATION LIST E (SUBSTITUTION)

Spelling	Diacritic/IPA Meaning
1. agile	
2. ambidextrous	
3. anesthetist	
4. architect	
5. attaché	
6. bade	
7. badinage	
8. baste	
9. bathe	
10. Beethoven	
11. beige	
12. bestial	
13. blasé	
14. blatant	
15. boatswain	
16. brevity	
17. brochure	
18. bury	
19. cache	
20. caste	
21. catch	
22. celestial	
23. censure	
24. chameleon	
25. charlatan	

PRONUNCIATION LIST F (SUBSTITUTION)

Spelling   **Diacritic/IPA   Meaning**

1. chasm _____

2. chassis _____

3. chef _____

4. chic _____

5. chiropodist _____

6. coiffure _____

7. coma _____

8. comely _____

9. congratulate _____

10. conjecture _____

11. connoisseur _____

12. copious _____

13. crescendo _____

14. crux _____

15. cuisine _____

16. deaf _____

17. debauched _____

18. demise _____

19. deprecate _____

20. derisive _____

21. dichotomy _____

22. dictionary _____

23. diphtheria _____

24. diphthong _____

25. discretion _____

PRONUNCIATION LIST G (SUBSTITUTION)

Spelling	Diacritic/IPA	Meaning
1. docile		
2. echelon		
3. education		
4. elite		
5. ensemble		
6. err		
7. escape		
8. esoteric		
9. et cetera		
10. exactly		
11. examine		
12. exemplary		
13. facade		
14. facile		
15. faux pas		
16. fission		
17. forbade		
18. fusion		
19. futile		
20. genuine		
21. gesture		
22. handkerchief		
23. height		
24. heinous		
25. heir		

PRONUNCIATION LIST H (SUBSTITUTION)

Spelling	Diacritic/IPA	Meaning
1. heroism		
2. hiatus		
3. histamine		
4. homage		
5. hover		
6. hysteria		
7. illusion		
8. indict		
9. in vitro		
10. Italian		
11. just		
12. kibbutz		
13. laconic		
14. laissez faire		
15. latent		
16. lesion		
17. loath		
18. longevity		
19. lozenge		
20. luxury		
21. masochist		
22. medieval		
23. memento		
24. microscopic		
25. negligee		

PRONUNCIATION LIST I (SUBSTITUTION)

Spelling   **Diacritic/IPA   Meaning**

  1. niche   _____

  2. novice   _____

  3. obesity   _____

  4. official   _____

  5. oil   _____

  6. orgy   _____

  7. pantomime   _____

  8. particular   _____

  9. partner   _____

10. pathos   _____

11. phenomenon   _____

12. pique   _____

13. pitcher   _____

14. plagiarism   _____

15. poignant   _____

16. portentous   _____

17. posthumous   _____

18. preclude   _____

19. precocious   _____

20. pronunciation   _____

21. propitiate   _____

22. pugilist   _____

23. pumice   _____

24. querulous   _____

25. rabid   _____

PRONUNCIATION LIST J (SUBSTITUTION)

Spelling	**Diacritic/IPA Meaning**
1. radiator	
2. recalcitrant	
3. ribald	
4. rudiment	
5. ruthless	
6. sagacious	
7. salient	
8. saline	
9. salon	
10. short-lived	
11. slovenly	
12. solace	
13. strength	
14. suave	
15. tacit	
16. tedious	
17. titular	
18. transient	
19. unscathed	
20. vagrant	
21. verbatim	
22. visa	
23. worsted	
24. zealous	
25. zoology	

PRONUNCIATION LIST K (REVERSAL)

Spelling	Diacritic/IPA Meaning
1. ask	
2. causal	
3. cavalry	
4. children	
5. fraternity	
6. hundred	
7. introduce	
8. introduction	
9. irrelevant	
10. jewelry	
11. larynx	
12. modern	
13. nuclear	
14. officer	
15. perform	
16. perspiration	
17. pharynx	
18. prescription	
19. professor	
20. provide	
21. realtor	
22. relevant	
23. secretary	
24. tragedy	
25. voluminous	

PRONUNCIATION LIST L (MISPLACED STRESS)

Spelling   **Diacritic/IPA   Meaning**

1. abdomen _____

2. absurd _____

3. abyss _____

4. acclimate _____

5. acumen _____

6. address (verb) _____

7. admirable _____

8. adult _____

9. aggravate _____

10. alias _____

11. alienate _____

12. ally (noun) _____

13. amicable _____

14. animosity _____

15. applicable _____

16. aspirant _____

17. assimilation _____

18. atrophy _____

19. authoritative _____

20. autopsy _____

21. baptize _____

22. barbarous _____

23. beneficent _____

24. blasphemy _____

25. bravado _____

PRONUNCIATION LIST M (MISPLACED STRESS)

Spelling	Diacritic/IPA Meaning
1. combatant	
2. comparable	
3. confidence	
4. contrite	
5. coupon	
6. decadent	
7. decorous	
8. degradation	
9. deluge	
10. demoniacal	
11. demonstration	
12. despicable	
13. diminutive	
14. electoral	
15. epitome	
16. equanimity	
17. equivalent	
18. exemplary	
19. exigency	
20. exquisite	
21. financier	
22. formidable	
23. fortuitous	
24. frivolity	
25. gamut	

PRONUNCIATION LIST N (MISPLACED STRESS)

Spelling   **Diacritic/IPA   Meaning**

1. impious   _____

2. impotence   _____

3. incomparable   _____

4. incongruous   _____

5. indolence   _____

6. industry   _____

7. infamous   _____

8. inquiry   _____

9. integral   _____

10. interested   _____

11. irreparable   _____

12. lamentable   _____

13. magnanimous   _____

14. maintenance   _____

15. mischievous   _____

16. obdurate   _____

17. omnipotent   _____

18. perseverance   _____

19. pianist   _____

20. police   _____

21. precedent   _____

22. preferable   _____

23. quintuplets   _____

24. respite   _____

25. resources   _____

APPENDIX C

Dialects and
Accents for Actors

INTRODUCTION

The student of acting will often use Standard American English in the roles he/she will play, but not all. Frequently, you will be called upon to assume a dialect or accent in a production. This section will provide you with material for learning several of these and practice material for each.

Three dialects and three accents are presented: the Eastern American, Southern American, and British English dialects, and the Spanish, French, and Japanese accents. Each of these dialects and accents, however, is not shown in its entirety. Enough characteristics are presented so that you will be able to play the role without losing understandability.

New Symbols

Though many of the sounds you will need to learn to use a new accent or dialect are substitutions of those you know in Standard American English, you will have to learn a few new ones as well. For example, in French and Spanish, the sound (i)-[ɪ] is often not used. Substituting (ē)-[i] will be sufficient to indicate the change. In Spanish, however, there is no (th)-[θ] sound. Substituting a simple (t)-[t] for it will not quite sound Spanish, however, for the Spanish (t)-[t] is also different. A new form is needed, one in which the tongue touches the teeth, not the gum ridge.

Most of the new sounds have no counterpart in the American Heritage Diacritic system. In some cases, a symbol has been modified to make the new one. In other cases, the phonetic symbol is used for both. Note the following new sounds and their symbols:

(à)-[a] This is a sound produced with the tongue midway between (ă)-[æ] and (ä)-[ɑ].

(ȯ)-[ɒ] This sound is located midway between the (ä)-[ɑ] and the (ô)-[ɔ].

(řr)-[řr] This is a one tap trilled *r*. It is produced somewhat like the (d)-[d], with the tongue raised lightly to the gum ridge, and blocking the air slightly before releasing it.

(t̪)-[t̪] This is the dentalized (t)-[t]. The two sounds are produced in the same manner, except that the tongue is placed against the upper teeth, rather than on the gum ridge.

(d̪)-[d̪] This is the dentalized version of the (d)-[d].

(β)-[β] This sound is produced by pushing voiced air between the lightly closed lips and then moving them apart. It replaces *b* and *v* in Spanish and Japanese.

(ɸ)-[ɸ] This sound is made by pushing voiceless air through the lightly closed lips. It replaces (f)-[f] in Japanese.

Practice Paragraphs

Each of the dialect and accent sections contain a practice paragraph. The practice selection, *Evening Classes*, is from Appendix A and contains all of the sounds of American English presented in the same order as in the articulation chapters. When presented, the paragraph is in the dialect or accent of the specific section, both in American Heritage diacritics and the IPA.

Read and record the practice paragraph in each of the dialect and accent sections several times. Then try some of the shorter pieces in Chapter 11 using each dialect. Compare it with the Standard American section in Appendix A. Record your voice often to develop your skill in using these dialects.

STANDARD AMERICAN TO EASTERN AMERICAN

Consonant Sounds		Vowel Sounds	
(p)-[p]	no change	(ē)-[i]	no change
(b)-[b]	no change	(ĭ)-[ɪ]	no change
(t)-[t]	no change	(ā)-[e]	no change
(d)-[d]	no change	(ĕ)-[ɛ]	no change
(k)-[k]	no change	(ă)-[æ]	becomes (ȧ)-[a]. This sound is
(g)-[g]	no change		midway between the phonemes (ă)-[æ]
(f)-[f]	no change		and (ä)-[ɑ]. It is produced with the
(v)-[v]	no change		center of the tongue low in the center
(th)-[θ]	no change		of the mouth and with the lips
(*th*)-[ð]	no change		unrounded. Note that the symbol (ȧ) is
(s)-[s]	no change		not in the American Heritage
(z)-[z]	no change		Dictionary. It is used here to identify
(sh)-[ʃ]	no change		this particular phoneme. *Hat* becomes
(zh)-[ʒ]	no change		(hȧt)-[hat]. *Plant* becomes (plȧnt)-
(h)-[h]	no change		[plant].
(ch)-[tʃ]	no change	(ä)-[ɑ]	no change
(j)-[dʒ]	no change	(ô)-[ɔ]	becomes (ȯ)-[ɒ]. This sound is midway
(hw)-[ʍ]	no change		between the phonemes (ä)-[ɑ] and (ô)-
(w)-[w]	no change		[ɔ]. The back of the tongue is raised
(y)-[j]	no change		higher than for (ä)-[ɑ], but not as high
(r)-[r]	see discussion in		as for the (ô)-[ɔ]. The lips are slightly
	Special Considerations		rounded. The symbol (ȯ) is also not in
(l)-[l]	see discussion in		the AHD. *Bought* becomes (bȯt)-[bɒt].
	Special Considerations		*Talk* becomes (tȯk)-[tɒk].
(m)-[m]	no change	(ō)-[o]	no change
(n)-[n]	no change	(o͝o)-[ʊ]	no change
(ng)-[ŋ]	no change	(o͞o)-[u]	no change
		(ûr)-[ɝ]	becomes (û)-[ɜ]. *Church* becomes
			(chûch)-[tʃɜtʃ]. *Sir* becomes (sû)-[sɜ].
		(ər)-[ɚ]	becomes (ə)-[ə]. *Sister* becomes
			(sĭs'tə)-[ˋsɪstə]. *Ladder* becomes
			(lă'də)-[ˋlædə].
		(ŭ)-[ʌ]	no change
		(ə)-[ə]	no change

Diphthong Sounds

(ā)-[eɪ]	no change
(ī)-[aɪ]	no change
(ō)-[oʊ]	no change
(ou)-[aʊ]	no change
(oi)-[ɔɪ]	no change

Special Considerations

Eastern American English is the primary dialect of much of the Northeastern part of the country. Like Southern American, it has many local variants, such as New England American and Brooklynese. The characteristics listed here are those of the educated Easterner and differ principally in the low front and back vowels and the phoneme (r)-[r]. The (r)-[r] in Eastern is very similar to that of Southern American.

(îr)-[ɪr] becomes (ĭə)-[ɪə]. *Nearly* becomes (nĭə'lĭ)-['nɪəlɪ]. *Here* becomes (hĭə)-[hɪə].

(âr)-[ɛr] becomes (ĕə)-[ɛə]. *Careful* becomes (kĕə'fəl)-[`kɛrfəl]. *Chair* becomes (chĕə)-[tʃɛə].

(är)-[ɑr] becomes (äə)-[ɑə]. *Artist* becomes (äə'tĭst)-[`ɑətɪst]. *Car* becomes (käə)-[kɑə].

(ôr)-[ɔr] becomes (óə)-[ɒə]. *Short* becomes (shó'ət)-[`ʃɒət]. *More* becomes (móə)-[mɒə].

(o͞or)-[ʊr] becomes (o͞oə)-[ʊə]. *Surely* becomes (sho͞oə'lĭ)-[`ʃʊəlɪ]. *Your* becomes (yo͞oə)-[jʊə].

(īr)-[aɪr] becomes (īə)-[aɪə]. *Tired* becomes (tīəd)-[taɪəd]. *Fire* becomes (fīə)-[faɪə].

(our)-[aʊr] becomes (ouə)-[aʊə]. *Hours* becomes (ouəz)-[aʊəz]. *Power* becomes (pou'ə)-[`paʊə].

When the *r* appears between two vowels, it is more often pronounced as (r)-[r], for example: *Mary* becomes (mĕ'rĭ)-[`mɛrɪ].

Practice Paragraph

(ēv'nĭng klä'sĭz)

(ēch ēv'nĭng, ĭn'tərĕstĭng lĕ'sənz ånd klä'sĭz äə hĕld ăt *th*ĭs kŏ'lĭj. prŏbəblĭ ŏl əv *th*ĕm äə good, bŭt ə fyo͞o äə sû'tənlĭ səprī'zĭng. sŭm klä'sĭz, əv kŏəs, äə jŭst fĕə, bŭt ōn'lĭ wŭn ðə to͞o äə rē'lĭ wĭəd.

*th*ēz dāz, wē fīnd ĕjəkā'shənəl ĭnjoi'mənt wi*th*out' gō'ĭnɡ fäə frŭm hōm. *th*ə pē'pəl ho͞o bĭgĭn' tə stŭ'dĭ kăn gō ŏn, ånd håv grōth. *th*ō *th*ə sŭbjĕkts sŭm chōoz äə fo͞o'lĭsh, mōst äə yo͞o'zho͞oəli häəd ånd chä'lĭnjĭng. hwĕn sto͞o'dənts håv wûkt fŏə ə kŭ'pəl əv yĭəz rĭlĭ'jəslĭ, mĕ'nĭ nōtĭs *th*at *th*ĕə stŭ'dĭ ĭz sä'tĭsfīĭng).

[`ivnɪŋ `klæsɪz]

[itʃ `ivnɪŋ, `ɪntərɛstɪŋ `lɛsənz and `klasɪz ɑə hɛld at ðɪs `kɒ'lɪdʒ. `prɒbəblɪ ɒl əv ðɛm ɑə gʊd, bʌt ə fju ɑə `sɜtənlɪ sə`praɪzɪŋ. sʌm `kla 'sɪz, əv kɒəs ɑə jʌst fɛə, bʌt `onlɪ wʌn ɒə tu ɑə `rɪlɪ wɪəd.

ðiz dez, wi faɪnd ɛdʒə`keʃənəl ɪn`jɔɪmənt wɪðaʊt' `gɔɪŋ fɑə frʌm hoʊm. ðə `pipəl hu brɪ`gɪn tə `stʌdɪ kan go ɒn, fɪnɪʃ and hav groθ. thoʊ ðə `sʌbjɛkts sʌm chuz ɑə `fulɪʃ, moʊst ɑə `yuzhuəli hɑəd and `tʃalɪndʒɪŋ. ʍɛn `studənts hav wɜkt fɒəə`kʌpəl əv yɪəz rɪ`lɪjəslɪ, mɪnɪ noʊtɪs ðat ðɛə `stʌdɪ ɪz `satɪsfaɪɪŋ.]

Consonant Sounds

(p)-[p]	no change
(b)-[b]	no change
(t)-[t]	no change
(d)-[d]	in *nds* and *ndl* clusters is omitted. *Hands* becomes (hănz)-[hænz]. *Candle* becomes (kă´nəl)-[`kænəl].
(k)-[k]	no change
(g)-[g]	no change
(f)-[f]	no change
(v)-[v]	no change
(th)-[θ]	no change
(*th*)-[ð]	no change
(s)-[s]	no change
(z)-[z]	no change
(sh)-[ʃ]	no change
(zh)-[ʒ]	no change
(h)-[h]	no change
(ch)-[tʃ]	no change
(j)-[dʒ]	no change
(hw)-[ʍ]	no change
(w)-[w]	no change
(y)-[j]	no change
(r)-[r]	see discussion in special considerations
(l)-[l]	becomes (ə)-[ə] following (ĭ)-[ɪ], (ĕ)-[ɛ] and (ă)-[æ] before consonant. *Film* becomes (fĭəm)-[fɪəm]; *help* becomes (hĕəp)-[hɛəp].
(m)-[m]	no change
(n)-[n]	no change
(ng)-[ŋ]	Final *ng* becomes (n)-[n] especially in participles. *Talking* becomes (tŏk´ĭn)-[`tɔkɪn]. *Singing* becomes (sing'in)-['sɪŋɪn]. *Ngth* becomes (nth)-[nθ]. *Length* becomes (lĭnth)-[lɪnθ]. *Strength* becomes (strĭnth)-[strɪnθ].

Vowel Sounds

(ē)-[i]	becomes (ēə)-[iə] before *l*. *Feel* becomes (fēəl)-[fiəl]. *Meal* becomes (mēəl)-[miəl].
(ĭ)-[ɪ]	becomes (ĭə)-[ɪə] in stressed words. *Give* becomes (gĭəv)-[gɪəv]. *Big* becomes (biəg)-[bɪəg]. Becomes (ĕ)-[ɛ] before *ng* in one syllable words. *Ring* becomes (rĕng)-[rɛŋ]. *Thing* becomes (thĕng)-[θɛŋ].
(ā)-[e]	no change
(ĕ)-[ɛ]	becomes (ĕə)-[ɛə] is stressed words. *Check* becomes (chĕək)-[tʃɛək]. *Best* becomes (bĕast)-[bɛəst]. Becomes (ĭ)-[ɪ] before nasals. *Member* becomes (mĭm'bə)-[`mɪmbə]. *Send* becomes (sind)-[sɪnd].
(ă)-[æ]	becomes (ăĭ)-[æɪ]. *Laugh* becomes (lăĭf)-[læɪf]. *Sad* becomes (săĭd)-[sæɪd].
(ä, ŏ)-[ɑ]	no change
(ô)-[ɔ]	becomes (ôō)-[ɔo]. *Wrong* becomes (rôông)-[rɔoŋ]. *Saw* becomes (sôō)-[sɔo].
(ō)-[o]	becomes (ŭōō)-[ʌʊ]. *Coat* becomes (kŭōōt)-[kʌʊt]. *Home* becomes (hŭōōm)-[hʌʊm].
(ōō)-[ʊ]	becomes (ōōə)-[ʊə]. *Book* becomes (bōōək)-[bʊək]. *Should* becomes (shōōəd)-[ʃʊəd].
(ōō)-[u]	no change
(ûr)-[ɝ]	becomes (û)-[ɜ]. *Church* becomes (chûch)-[tʃɜtʃ]. *Sir* becomes (sû)-[sɜ].
(ər)-[ɚ]	becomes (ə)-[ə]. *Sister* becomes (sĭs'tə)-[`sɪstə]. *Ladder* becomes (lăĭ'də)-[`læɪdə].
(ŭ)-[ʌ]	becomes (ĕ)-[ɛ] before affricates. *Judge* becomes (jĕj)-[dʒɛdʒ]. *Such* becomes (sĕch)-[sɛtʃ].
(ə)-[ə]	no change

Diphthong Sounds

(ā)-[eɪ]	no change
(ī)-[aɪ]	becomes (äĭ)-[a:ɪ]. *Night* becomes (näĭt)-[na:ɪt]. *Buy* becomes (bäĭ)-[ba:ɪ].
(ō)-[oʊ]	becomes (ûōō)-[ʌʊ]. See (ō)-[o] above.
(ou)-[aʊ]	no change
(oi)-[ɔɪ]	becomes (ôĭ)-[ɔ:ɪ]. *Oil* becomes (ôĭl)-[ɔ:ɪl]. *Join* becomes (jôĭn)-[dʒɔ:ɪn].

Special Considerations

There is no single Southern Dialect. Rather, there are many dialects which have their origin in the southern states. The soft drawl of Atlanta, Georgia, is quite different from the New Orleans pattern. The educated Virginian sounds worlds apart from the *hillbilly* of the Great Smoky Mountains.

The characteristics presented here are representative of Southern American speech in general. It would be nearly impossible to list all of the possibilities. They will suffice to suggest the flavor of the South, which is often all the actor wishes to do.

The (r)-[r].   One important consideration is the use of the sound (r)-[r]. On the listing above it is indicated that there is no change. This is true in the initial position in words and in the medial position when an *r* follows a consonant. For example, there is no change in the production of (r)-[r] in the word *railroad* (rāl'rŭōōd)-[ˈreɪlrʌud]. When the *r* follows a vowel, either in the medial position before consonants, or in the final position, its pronunciation is considerably altered from that of Standard American English. Note the following:

> (îr)-[ɪr] becomes (ĭə)-[ɪə]. *Nearly* becomes (nĭə'lĭ)-[ˈnɪəlɪ]. *Here* becomes (hĭə)-[hɪə].

> (âr)-[ɛr] becomes (ĕə)-[ɛə]. *Careful* becomes (kĕə'fəl)-[ˈkɛəfəl]. *Chair* becomes (chĕə)-[tʃɛə].

> (är)-[ɑr] becomes (äə)-[ɑə]. *Artist* becomes (äə'tĭst)-[ˈɑətɪst]. *Car* becomes (käə)-[kɑə].

> (ôr)-[ɔr] becomes (ôə)-[ɔə]. *Short* becomes (shô'ət)-[ˈʃɔət]. *More* becomes (môə)-[mɔə].

> (ōōr)-[ʊr] becomes (ōōə)-[ʊə]. *Surely* becomes (shōōə'li)-[ˈʃʊəlɪ]. *Your* becomes (yōōə)-[jʊə].

> (īr)-[aɪr] becomes (īə)[aɪə]. *Tired* becomes (tīəd)-[taɪəd]. *Fire* becomes (fīə)-[faɪə].

> (our)-[aʊr] becomes (ouə)-[aʊə]. *Hours* becomes (ouəz)-[aʊəz]. *Power* becomes (pou'ə)-[ˈpaʊə].

When the *r* appears between two vowels, it is more often pronounced as (r)-[r], for example: *Mary* becomes (mĕə'ri)-[ˈmɛərɪ]. The vowel before the *r* may be diphthongized, but the *r* is produced normally.

Practice Paragraph

(ēv'nĭn klăĭ'siz)

(ēch ēv'nĭn, ĭən'trĭstĭn lĕə'sənz ăind klăĭ'sĭz äə heəld ăt *th*ĭəs kä'lĭj. präb'li ôōl əv *th*ěəm äə gōōəd, bŭt ə fyōō äə sû'tənlĭ səpräĭ'zĭn. sûm klăĭ'sĭz, əv kôəs äə jěst fĕə, bŭt ŭōōn'lĭ wŭn ôə tōō äə rē'əlĭ wĭəd.

*th*ēz dāz, wē fäĭnd ĭjəkā'shənəl ĭnjôi'mĭnt wĭ*th*out' gŭōō'ĭn fäə frŭm hŭōōm. pē'pəl hōō bĭgĭən´ tə stŭ'dĭ kăĭn gŭōō ôōn fĭən'ĭsh ăĭnd hăĭv grŭōōth. *th*ŭōō *th*ə sŭb'jĭkts sŭm chōōz äə fōō'lĭsh, mŭōōst äə yōō'zhōōəlĭ häəd ăĭnd chăĭ'lĭnjĭn. hwĭn stōō'dənts hăĭv wûkt fôə ə kŭ'pəl əv yĭəz rĭlĭə'jəslĭ, mĭ'nĭ nūōō'tĭs *th*ăĭt *th*eə stŭ'dĭ ĭz săĭ'tĭsfäĭn).

[ˋivnɪn ˋklæɪsəz]

[itʃ ˋivnɪn, ˋɪəntrɪstɪn ˊlɛəsənz ænd ˋklæisiz ɑə hɛəld æɪt ðɪəs ˋkɑˈlɪj. ˋprɑblɪ ɔol əv ðɛəm ɑə guəd, bʌt fju ɑə ˋsɜtənlɪ səˋpraɪzɪn. sʌm ˋklæɪ ˈsɪz, əv kɔəs ɑə jɛst fɛə, bʌt ˋʌunl wʌn ɔə tu ɑə ˋriəli wɪəd.

ðiz deɪz, we faɪnd ɪjəˋkeɪʃənəl ɪnˋjɔːɪmɪnt wɪðaut' ˋgʌuɪn fɑə frʌm hʌum. ðə ˋpipəl hu bɪ ˋgɪən tə ˋstʌdɪ kæɪn gʌu ɔon, 'fɪənʃ æɪnd hæɪv grʌuθ. ðo ðə ˋsʌbjɪkts sʌm chuz ɑə ˋfulɪʃ, mʌust ɑə ˋyuzhuəli hɑəd æɪnd ˋtʃæɪlɪndʒɪn. ʍɛn ˋstudənts hæɪv wɜkt fəɪ ə ˋkʌpəl əv yɪəz rɪˋlɪəjəslɪ, ˋmɪnɪ nʌutɪs ðæɪt ðɛə ˋstʌdɪ ɪz ˋsæɪtɪsfɑːɪn.]

STANDARD AMERICAN TO BRITISH ENGLISH

Consonant Sounds	
(p)-[p]	no change
(b)-[b]	no change
(t)-[t]	no change
(d)-[d]	no change
(k)-[k]	no change
(g)-[g]	no change
(f)-[f]	no change
(v)-[v]	no change
(th)-[θ]	no change
(*th*)-[ð]	no change
(s)-[s]	no change
(z)-[z]	no change
(sh)-[ʃ]	frequently becomes (s)-[s] when spelled with *c*, *s* or *ss*. *Issue* becomes (ĭs'yo͞o)-[`ɪsju]. *Pincers* becomes (pĭn'səz)-[`pɪnsəz].
(zh)-[ʒ]	no change
(h)-[h]	no change
(ch)-[tʃ]	no change
(j)-[dʒ]	no change
(hw)-[ʍ]	no change
(w)-[w]	no change
(y)-[j]	no change
(r)-[r]	see discussion in special considerations
(l)-[l]	no change
(m)-[m]	no change
(n)-[n]	no change
(ng)-[ŋ]	no change

Vowel Sounds

(ē)-[i]	becomes (i)-[ɪ] in the final position when spelled: *y*, *ly* and *lly*. This ending (i)-[ɪ] is produced with more stress than its counterpart (ē)-[i] of Standard American. *Carry* becomes (kâ'rĭ´)-[`kɛ`rɪ]. *Finally* becomes (fī'nəlĭ)-[faɪnəlɪ].
(ĭ)-[ɪ]	See the note in Special Considerations.
(ā)-[e]	no change
(ĕ)-[ɛ]	no change
(ă)-[æ]	frequently becomes (ä)-[ɑ], especially before *f*, *nc*, *nt*, *ss* and *th*. *Bath* becomes (bäth)-[bɑθ]. *Rather* becomes (räthə)-[`rɑðə]. See also the note in Special Considerations.
(ä)-[ɑ]	no change
(ô)-[ɔ]	becomes (ô:)-[ɔ:]. The sound is similar to (ô)-[ɔ], but with the lips more rounded and the jaw lowered. *Tall* becomes (tô:l)-[tɔ:l]. *Autumn* becomes (ô:təm)-[ɔ:təm]. Note that the symbol (ô:) is not in the AHD.
(ō)-[o]	becomes (əōō)-[əʊ]. *Only* becomes (əōōn'lĭ)-[`ʌʊnlɪ]. *Don't* becomes (dəōōnt)-[dəʊnt].
(o͞o)-[ʊ]	no change
(o͞o)-[u]	no change
ûr - [ɝ]	becomes (û)-[ɜ]. *Church* becomes (chûch)-[tʃɜtʃ]. *Sir* becomes (sû)-[sɜ].
(ər)-[ɚ]	becomes (ə)-[ə]. *Sister* becomes (sĭs'tə)-[`sɪstə]. *Ladder* becomes (lǎ'də)-[`lɑdə].
(ŭ)-[ʌ]	no change
ə - [ə]	no change

Diphthong Sounds

(ā)-[eɪ]	no change
(ī)-[aɪ]	no change
(ō)-[oʊ]	becomes (əōō)-[əʊ]. *Only* becomes (əōōn'lĭ)-[`əʊnlɪ]. *Don't* becomes (dəōōnt)-[dəʊnt].
(ou)-[aʊ]	no change
(oi)-[ɔɪ]	no change

Special Considerations

British English as presented here is the speech of the college-trained Londoner. It might also be called BBC English, the speech of the typical British Broadcasting Company announcer. It is often referred to as Standard English.

Because they are most closely related to it, one would expect that British English would have some similarity to Eastern and Southern American. This can be seen particularly in the approach each of these dialects has to the (r)-[r] phoneme.

The (r)-[r] Difference.   The (r)-[r] in British English is similar to that of Southern and Eastern American.

(îr)-[ɪr] becomes (ĭə)-[ɪə]. *Nearly* becomes (nĭə'lĭ)-[`nɪəlɪ]. *Here* becomes (hĭə)-[hɪə].

(âr)-[ɛr] becomes (ĕə)-[ɛə]. *Careful* becomes (kĕə'fəl)-[`kɛəfəl]. *Chair* becomes (chĕə)-[tʃɛə].

(är)-[ɑr] becomes (ää)-[ɑə]. *Artist* becomes (ää'tĭst)-[`ɑətɪst]. *Car* becomes (käə)-[kɑə].

(ôr)-[ɔr] becomes (ôə)-[ɔə]. *Short* becomes (shô'ət)-[`ʃɔət]. *More* becomes (môə)-[mɔə].

(oor)-[ʊr] becomes (ooə)-[ʊə]. *Surely* becomes (shooə'li)-[`ʃʊəlɪ]. *Your* becomes (yooə)-[jʊə].

(īr)-[aɪr] becomes (īə)[aɪə]. *Tired* becomes (tīəd)-[taɪəd]. *Fire* becomes (fīə)-[faɪə].

(our)-[aʊr] becomes (ouə)-[aʊə]. *Hours* becomes (ouəz)-[aʊəz]. *Power* becomes (pou'ə)-[`paʊə].

When the *r* appears between two vowels, it is produced as a one tap trill. The tongue tip touches the gum ridge in an action similar to the sound (d)-[d], only with faster movement and lighter contact. The most familiar example is the word *very*. It becomes (vĕ'rĭ)-[`vɛɾɪ]. (The symbol (ř) is used to represent the tongue action in this sound.) *Mary* becomes (mĕ'řĭ)-[`mɛɾɪ]. *Courage* becomes (kŭ'řĭj)-[`kʌɾɪdʒ].

When the *r* is in the final position and followed by a vowel, it will be pronounced as in Standard American. The sound is produced with less strength than the Standard American phoneme. *There are* becomes (thĕ'räə)-[`ðɛɾɑə]. *Here is* becomes (hĭ'rĭz)-[`hɪɾɪz].

The (ă)-[æ] Difference.   It is noted above that (ă)-[æ] becomes (ä)-[ɑ] in combination with certain other phonemes. Not all such words, however, receive the same treatment. *Ample, gas, hand, has, lamp, land* and *plastic* are all produced with the (ă)-[æ] sound. Some paired words are inconsistent. The *a* in *can't* and *aunt* is produced as (ä)-[ɑ], but in *can* and *ant*, it remains (ă)-[æ].

Unusual Pronunciations.   In addition to the changes above, British speakers pronounce a number of words in a totally unexpected manner. Note the following:
Clerk becomes (kläk)-[klɑk]. *Privacy* becomes (prī'vəsĭ)-[ˋprɪvəsɪ]. *Garage*
becomes (gă'räzh)-[ˋgærɑʒ]. *Schedule* becomes (shĕ'jəl)-[ʃɛdjəl].

Practice Paragraph

(ēv'nĭng klä'siz)
   (ēch ēv'nĭng, ĭn'tərĕsting lĕ'sənz ănd klä'sĭz ä hĕld at *th*ĭs kä'lĭj. prä'bəblĭ ô:l
əv *th*ĕm ä gōōd, bŭt ə fyōō ä sû'tənlĭ səprī'zĭng. sûm klä'sĭz, əv kôəs, ä jŭst fĕə,
bŭt əōōōn'lĭ wŭn ô: tōō ä rī'lĭ wĭəd.

   *th*ēz dāz, wē fīnd ĕjəkā'shənəl ĭnjoi'mənt wĭ*th*out' gəōōō'ĭng fä frŭm həōōōm.
*th*ə pē'pəl hōō bĭgĭn´ tə stŭ'dĭ kăn gəōōō ôn, fĭ'nĭsh ănd hăv grəōōōth. *th*ōōō *th*ə
sŭb'jĕkts sŭm chōōz ä fōō'lĭsh, məōōōst ä yōō'zhooəlĭ hääd ănd chä'lĭnjĭng. hwĕn
stōō'dənts hăv wûkt fôə ə kŭ'pəl əv yĭəz rīlĭ'jŭslĭ, mĕ'nĭ nəōōōtĭs *th*ăt *th*ĕə stŭ'dĭ
ĭz sä'tĭsfĭĭng).

[ˋivnɪŋ ˋklɑsɪz]
   [itʃ ˋivnɪŋ, ˋɪntərɛstɪŋ ˈlɛsənz ænd ˋklɑsɪz a hɛld at ðɪs ˋkɑlɪdʒ. ˋprabəblɪ
ɔ:l əv ðɛm ɑ gud, bʌt ə fju a ˋsɜtənlɪ səˋprɑɪzɪŋ. sʌm ˋklɑsɪz, əv kɔ:s a dʒʌst
fɛə, bʌt ˋəounlɪ wʌn ɔə tu ɑ ˋrɪlɪ wɪəd.

   ðiz dez, wi faɪnd ɛdʒəˋkeɪʃənəl ɪnˋjɔɪmənt wɪðaut' ˋgəouɪŋ fɑ frʌm həoum.
ðə ˋpipəl hu bɪˋgɪn tə ˋstʌdɪ kæn gəou ɔn, ˈfɪnɪʃ ænd hæv grəouθ. ðo ðə ˋsʌbjɛkts
sʌm chuz a ˋfulɪʃ, məoust a ˋyuzhuəlɪ had ænd ˋtʃɑlɛndʒɪŋ. ʌɛn ˋstudənts hæv
wɜkt fɔə ə ˋkʌpəl əv ˋyɪəz rɪˋlɪdʒəslɪ, mɛnɪ nəoutɪs ðæt ðɛə ˋstʌdɪ ɪz ˋsɑtɪsfɑɪŋ.]

STANDARD AMERICAN TO SPANISH

Consonant Sounds		Vowel Sounds	
(p)-[p]	no change	(ē)-[i]	no change
(b)-[b]	becomes (β)-[β]. There is no equivalent diacritic symbol for this sound. The phonetic symbol will suffice for both. The phoneme is made as if a (b)-[b] and (v)-[v] were combined. *Bed* becomes (βed)-[βɛd]. *Back* becomes (βäk)-[βɑk].	(ĭ)-[ɪ]	becomes (ē)-[i]. *In* becomes (ēn)-[in]. *Live* becomes (lēβ)-[liβ].
		(ā)-[e]	no change
		(ĕ)-[ɛ]	becomes (ä)-[e], especially in the medial position. *Pen* becomes (pän)-[pen]. *Test* becomes (tä̱st̯)-[t̯est̯]
(t)-[t]	becomes (t̯)-[t̯]. There is no American Heritage symbol for this sound. It is made with the tongue touching the upper front teeth, rather than the gum ridge. *Time* becomes (t̯īm)-[t̯aɪm]. *Later* becomes (lät̯'ĕr)-['let̯ɛr].	(ă)-[æ]	becomes (ä)-[ɑ]. *Apple* becomes (ä'pəl)-[`ɑpəl]. *Bath* becomes (bät̯)-[bɑt̯].
		(ä)-[ɑ]	no change
(d)-[d]	becomes (d̯)-[d̯]. There is no American Heritage symbol for this sound. It is made with the tongue touching the upper front teeth, rather than the gum ridge. *Day* becomes (d̯ā)-[d̯e]. *Under* becomes (än'd̯ĕr)-['ʌnd̯ɛr].	(ô)-[ɔ]	becomes (ō)-[o]. *Tall* becomes (t̯ōl)-[t̯ol]. *Bought* becomes (βôt̯)-[βot̯]. See also Special Considerations.
		(ō)-[o]	no change
(k)-[k]	no change	(o͞o)-[ʊ]	becomes (o͞o)-[u]. *Book* becomes (βo͞ok)-[βuk]. *Should* becomes (sho͞od̯)-[ʃud̯].
(g)-[g]	no change		
(f)-[f]	no change	(o͞o)-[u]	no change
(v)-[v]	becomes (β)-[β]. *Very* becomes (βĕ'řē)-['βɛři]. *Never* becomes (nĕ'βĕr)-[`nɛβɛr].	(ûr)-[ɝ]	changes dependent on spelling. *Bird* becomes (βird)-[βɪrd]. *Church* becomes (cho͞orch)-[tʃurtʃ]. *Were* becomes (wĕr)-[wɛr]. *Work* becomes (work)-[work].
(th)-[θ]	becomes (t̯)-[t̯]. This is the same substitution as for the (t)-[t] sound. *Think* becomes (t̯ēngk)-[t̯iŋk]. *Math* becomes (mät̯)-[mɑt̯].	(ər)-[ɚ]	changes dependent on spelling. The sound tends to be slightly stressed, as well. *Collar* becomes (kō'lär)-[`kolɑr]. *Sister* becomes (sēs'tär)-[`sɪst̯ɑr]. *Actor* becomes (äk'tōr)-[`ɑkt̯or]. *Surprise* becomes (so͞orprīs')-[sur`praɪs].
(th)-[ð]	becomes (d̯)-[d̯]. This is the same substitution as for the (d)-[d] sound. *There* becomes (d̯ĕr)-[d̯ɛr]. *Father* becomes (fä'd̯ĕr)-['fɑd̯ɛr].		
		(ŭ)-[ʌ]	no change
		ə - [ə]	no change
(s)-[s]	no change. See Special Considerations.		
(z)-[z]	becomes (s)-[s] when spelled with the letter *s*. *Easy* becomes (ē'sē)-[`isi]. *Was* becomes (wäs)-[wɑs].		
(sh)-[ʃ]	No change. See Special Considerations.		
(zh)-[ʒ]	no change		

Consonant Sounds (continued)

(h)-[h]	becomes (x)-[x]. This fricative sound is produced by raising the back of the tongue near the soft palate and squeezing air through the resulting narrow opening. *Hand* becomes (xän)-[xɑn]. *Behind* becomes (βixin')-[βi`xaɪn].
(ch)-[tʃ]	no change
(j)-[dʒ]	no change
(hw)-[ʌ]	no change
(w)-[w]	no change
(y)-[j]	no change
(r)-[r]	See discussion in Special Considerations.
(l)-[l]	no change
(m)-[m]	no change
(n)-[n]	no change
(ng)-[ŋ]	no change

Special Considerations

There is no one Spanish Accent. Rather, each country where Spanish is spoken has its own dialect of Spanish and therefore its own accent in English. The Spanish along the Mexican–United States Border, for example, is quite different from that of Argentina. The accent presented here, therefore, is representative of Spanish in general.

The (s)-[s] Difference. In blends with other consonants, the vowel (e)-[ɛ] may precede it. *School* becomes (ĕskōōl')-[ɛ`skul]. *Swim* becomes (eswēm)-[ɛ`swim].

The (sh)-[ʃ] Difference. In some dialects of Spanish, especially Mexican, this sound becomes (ch)-[tʃ]. *Shoes* becomes (chōōs)-[tʃus]. *Washing* becomes (wäch-ēng)-[watʃiŋ].

The (r)-[r] Difference. The (r)-[r] in the Spanish accent has several characteristics. When produced as a consonant, it is most often a one tap trill (somewhat like the sound (d)-[d]). It is represented here in both symbol systems as (ř)-[ř]. Following or preceding other consonants, the one tap trill is heard. *Train* becomes (ṭřān)-[ṭřen]. *Carpet* becomes (käř'pĕṭ)-[`karpɛṭ].

Between two vowels, however, a more lengthy trill is produced as the tongue flaps against the gum ridge. We symbolize that sound as (rr)-[rr]. *Career* becomes (kärrēr')-[kɑrrir']. *Terrible* becomes (ṭä'rrēbəl)-[`ṭerribəl].

The (ô)-[ɔ] Difference.   When spelled *au* or *ou* the (ô)-[ɔ] becomes (ou)-[aʊ]. *Auto* becomes (ou'tō)-[ˋaʊt̯o]. *Because* becomes (βēkous')-[βiˋkaʊs]. *Bought* becomes (βout̯)-[βaʊt̯].

Diphthong Soun

The diphthong sounds are produced in essentially the same manner as in Standard English, but are incompletely articulated. The (ī)-[aɪ] sound, for example, never quite reaches as close to (ē)-[i] as it does in English. The diphthongs appear to have been chopped off at the end.

Practice Paragra

(ēv'nēng klä'sĕs)

(ēch ēv'nēng, ēn'tərāstēng lā'sōns änd klä'sĕs ăř hāld ät d̯ēs kō'lāj. prō'βəβlē ōl ōf d̯äm ăř gōŏd̯, βut̯ ə fyōō ăř sĕr'tənlē sōōřpřī'sēng. som klä'sĕs, ōf kōōrs, ăř jōōst̯ fĕr, bŭt ōn'lē wŭn ōř t̯ōō ăř rē'lē wēřd̯.

d̯ēs d̯ās, wē fīn äd̯yōōkä'shənəl änjoi'mänt̯ wēt̯out̯' gō'ēng fäř fřom hōm. d̯ə pe'pəl hōō bēgēn´ t̯ə st̯ōō'd̯ē kăn gō ōn, fē'nēsh änd hăv grōt̯. d̯ō d̯ə sōōb'jĕkt̯s sōm chōōs ăř fōō'lēsh, mōst ăř yōō'zhooəlē härd̯ and chä'lənjēng. hwän st̯ōō'dänts häv wōřkt̯ fōř ə kōō'pəl ōv yērs rēlē'jōōslē, mā'nē nō't̯ēs d̯ät̯ d̯âr st̯ōō'd̯ē ēs sä't̯ēsfīēng).

[ˋivnɪŋ ˋklæsɪs]

[itʃ ˋivnɪŋ, ˋint̯ərest̯ɪŋ lesons ɑnd ˋklɑsɪs ăř held̯ at̯ d̯is ˋko'ledʒ. ˋproβəβli ol of d̯em ăř gud̯, bət̯ ə fju ăř ˋsĕřt̯ənli suřˋpřaɪsɪŋ. som ˋklɑsɪs, of kurs, ɑr just̯ fɛr, bət̯ onli wʌn oř t̯u ăř ˋřeli wiřd̯.

d̯is d̯es, wi faɪn edjuˋkeʃənəl inˋjɔɪmənt wit̯aʊt̯' ˋgoɪŋ fař from hom. d̯ə ˋpipəl hu biˋgin t̯ə ˋstud̯i kɑn go on, finiʃ and hɑv gřot̯. d̯o d̯ə ˋsubjɛkt̯s som tʃuz ăř ˋfuliʃ, most ăř ˋjuʒuəli hařd̯ and ˋtʃalendʒɪŋ. ʌen ˋstud̯ənt̯s hɑv wořkt̯ foř ə ˋkupəl of ˋyiřs řiˋlijusli, ˋmeni ˋnot̯is d̯at̯ d̯er ˋstud̯i is ˋsatisfaɪŋ.]

STANDARD AMERICAN TO FRENCH

Consonant Sounds	
(p)-[p]	no change
(b)-[b]	no change
(t)-[t]	no change
(d)-[d]	no change
(k)-[k]	no change
(g)-[g]	no change
(f)-[f]	no change
(v)-[v]	no change
(th)-[θ]	becomes (s)-[s]. *Think* becomes (sēngk)-[siŋk]. *Bath* becomes (bäs)-[bɑs].
(*th*)-[ð]	becomes (z)-[z]. *They* becomes (zā)-[ze]. *Breathe* becomes (brēz)-[briz].
(s)-[s]	no change
(z)-[z]	no change
(sh)-[ʃ]	no change
(zh)-[ʒ]	no change
(h)-[h]	becomes unpronounced. The sound is omitted in all positions.
(ch)-[tʃ]	becomes (sh)-[ʃ]. *Change* becomes (shānzh)-[ʃenʒ]. *Catch* becomes (käsh)-[kɑʃ].
(j)-[dʒ]	becomes (zh)-[ʒ]. *Job* becomes (zhäb)-[ʒɑb]. *Stage* becomes (stāzh)-[steʒ].
(hw)-[ʍ]	no change
(w)-[w]	no change
(y)-[j]	no change
(r)-[r]	becomes (ɼ)-[ɼ] a voiced, back of the tongue to soft palate fricative. Voiced air is squeezed between the back of the tongue and the soft palate whenever the letter *r* appears. *Rest* becomes (ɼĕst)-[ɼɛst]. *Tomorrow* becomes (tōmō'ɼō)-[to`moɼo].
(l)-[l]	no change
(m)-[m]	no change
(n)-[n]	no change
(ng)-[ŋ]	no change

Vowel Sounds	
(ē)-[i]	no change
(ĭ)-[ɪ]	becomes (ē)-[i]. *Itch* becomes (ēsh)-[iʃ]. *Little* becomes (lē'təl)-[`litəl]. Becomes (ē)-[ɛ̃] before *m* and *n*. This sound is produced by nasalizing the (e)-[ɛ]. *Immediate* becomes (ēmē'dēĕt)-[ɛ̃`midɪət]. *Since* becomes (sēs)-[sɛ̃s].
(ā)-[e]	becomes (ȧ)-[a] (as in the Eastern American substitution for (ă)-[æ]). *Place* becomes (plȧs)-[plas]. *Lady* becomes (lȧ'dē)-[`ladi].
(ĕ)-[ɛ]	no change
(ă)-[æ]	becomes (ä)-[ɑ̃] before *n*. The sound is produced by nasalizing the (ä)-[ɑ]. *Answer* becomes (äsĕr')-[ɑ̃`sɛr]. *Romance* becomes (rōmäs')-[ro`mɑ̃s].
(ä)-[ɑ]	no change
(ô)-[ɔ]	no change
(ō)-[o]	no change
(o͝o)-[ʊ]	no change
(o͞o)-[u]	no change
(ûr)-[ɝ]	is not a separate vowel. See (r)-[r] above.
(ər)-[ɚ]	becomes (ō:ɼ)-[o:r], and becomes stressed. The sound is produced making an (ar)-[ɑɼ] with the lips pursed. *Doctor* becomes (däktō:ɼ')-[dɑk`to:r]. *Better* becomes (bĕtō:r')-[bɛ`to:r].
(ŭ)-[ʌ]	no change
(ə)-[ə]	becomes (ō)-[ɔ] when followed by *nt*. This sound is the nasalized (ô)-[ɔ]. *Infant* becomes (ōfō)-[ɔfɔ̃]. *Judgment* becomes (zhŭzh'mō)-[ʒʌʒmɔ̃].

Diphthong Sounds

(ā)-[eɪ]	no change
(ī)-[aɪ]	no change
(ō)-[oʊ]	no change
(ou)-[aʊ]	no change
(oi)-[ɔɪ]	no change

Special Considerations

French stress patterns frequently differ from those expected in American English. For example, note the pronunciation *about*. English puts stress on the second syllable (əbout')-[ə`baʊt], but French has it on the first (à'bout)-[`abaʊt].

This stress difference causes a change in the production of the suffixes *-able, -ible, -tion* and *-sion*. Note the following:

(ĭbəl)-[`ıbəl] becomes (ēbəl)-[`ibəl]. *Impossible* becomes (ēpäsi'bəl)-[Ɛ̃pa-`sibəl]. *Horrible* becomes (ôri'bəl)-[ɔ`ribəl].

(ābəl)-[ebəl] and (ûbəl)-[ʌbəl] becomes (äbəl)-[abəl]. *Label* becomes (lä'bəl)-[`labəl]. *Capable* becomes (käpä'bəl)-[kep`abəl].

(shŭn)-[ʃʌn] becomes (sēyō)-[sijɔ̃]. *Attention* becomes (ətēsēyō')-[ətɛ̃si`jɔ̃]. *Mission* becomes (mē`sēyō)-[`misi`ɔ̃].

Practice Paragraph

(ēv'nēng klä'sēz)

(ēsh ēv'nēng, ē'tərĕstēng lĕ'sənz ād klä'sēz äꞃ ĕld ăt zēs kō'lēzh. prä'bəblē ōl ōv zĕm äꞃ good, bŭt ə fyoo̅ äꞃ sĕꞃ'tēle sĕꞃpꞃī'zēng. sōm klä'sēz, ōv kô:ꞃs, äꞃ joo̅st fĕꞃ, bŭt ōn'lē wôn ôꞃ too̅ äꞃ ꞃē'lē wĭꞃd.

zēz dāz, wē fīnd ĕjəkā'shənəl ēzhoimɔ̃' wēzout' gō'ēng fäꞃ fꞃōm ōm. zə pē'pəl oo̅ bēgēn' tə stoo̅'dĭ kän gō ōn, fē'nēsh ād äv grōs. zō zə soo̅b'jĕkts sōm shoo̅z äꞃ foo̅lēsh', mōst äꞃ yoo̅'zhooəlĭ äꞃd ād shä'lĕnzhĭng. hwĕn stoo̅'dĕs äv wôꞃkt fôꞃ ə koo̅'pəl ōv yĭꞃz rēlē'zhoo̅slē, mĕ'nē nōtēs' zät zĕꞃ stoo̅'dē ēz sä'tēsfĭēng).

[`ivnɪŋ `klasiz]

[ĭʃ `ivnɪŋ, `Ɛ̃tərɛstɪŋ `lɛsənz ād `klasiz aꞃ ɛld æt zis `ko'liʒ. `probəbli ol ōv zɛm aꞃ gʊd, bʌt ə fju aꞃ `sɛꞃtɛli `sɛꞃ`pꞃaɪzɪŋ. som `klasiz, ōv kɔ:ꞃs, aꞃ dʒʌst fɛꞃ, bʌt `onlɪ won ɔꞃ tu aꞃ `ꞃili wĭꞃd.

ziz dez, wi faɪnd ɛdʒə`keʃɔ̃nəl Ɛ̃`jɔɪmɔ̃ wizaʊt' `goɪŋ faꞃ fꞃom om. zə `pipəl u bɪ`gin tu `studi kæn go on, `finiʃ ād æv gros. zo zə `subjɛkts som shuz aꞃ `fuliʃ, most aꞃ `juzhəli aꞃd ād `ʃalɛ̃ʒɪŋ. ᴧɛn `studɛ̃s æv woꞃkt foꞃ ə `kupəl ov yĭꞃz ꞃ i`liʒəsli, `mɛni `notis zæt zɛr `studi iz `sætisfaɪɪŋ.]

STANDARD AMERICAN TO JAPANESE

Consonant Sounds	
(p)-[p]	no change
(b)-[b]	becomes (β)-[β]. *Boy* becomes (βoi)-[βɔɪ]. *About* becomes (aβout')-[əβaʊt].
(t)-[t]	No change. See Special Considerations.
(d)-[d]	no change
(k)-[k]	no change
(g)-[g]	no change
(f)-[f]	becomes (ɸ)-[ɸ]. This sound is produced like a voiceless (β)-[β]. Air is exhaled through the lightly closed lips. *Fun* becomes (ɸän)-[ɸɑn]. *Fifty* becomes (ɸēɸ'ti)-[`ɸiɸtɪ].
(v)-[v]	becomes (β)-[β]. *Voice* becomes (βois)-[βɔɪs]. *Never* becomes (nĕ'βä)-[`nɛβɑ].
(th)-[θ]	becomes (s)-[s]. *Think* becomes (sēnk)-[sink]. *Math* becomes (mäs)-[mɑs].
(*th*)-[ð]	becomes (z)-[z]. *That* becomes (zät)-[zɑt]. *Weather* becomes (wĕ'zä)-[`wɛzɑ].
(s)-[s]	No change. See Special Considerations.
(z)-[z]	no change
(sh)-[ʃ]	no change
(zh)-[ʒ]	no change
(h)-[h]	no change
(ch)-[tʃ]	no change
(j)-[dʒ]	no change
(hw)-[ʍ]	no change
(w)-[w]	no change
(y)-[j]	no change
(r)-[r]	becomes (ř)-[ř] in initial and medial positions. The sound is dropped when between a vowel and a consonant. *Right* becomes (řīt)-[řaɪt]. *Carry* becomes (kä'ři)-[`kařɪ]. *Work* becomes (wŭk)-[wʌk]. *Card* becomes (käd)-[kɑd]. See Special Considerations.

(continued)

Vowel Sounds	
(ē)-[i]	no change
(ĭ)-[ɪ]	becomes (ē)-[ɪ] in the medial position. *Give* becomes (gēβ)-[giβ]. *Sister* becomes (sēs'ta)-[`sistɑ].
(ā)-[e]	becomes (ĕ)-[ɛ]. *Able* becomes (ĕ'boo)-['ɛbu]. *Play* becomes (prĕ)-[přɛ].
(ĕ)-[ɛ]	no change
(ă)-[æ]	becomes (ä)-[ɑ]. *Apple* becomes (ä'poo)-[`ɑpu]. *Sad* becomes (säd)-[sɑd].
(ä)-[ɑ]	no change
(ô)-[ɔ]	no change
(ō)-[o]	no change
(oo)-[ʊ]	becomes (oo)-[u]. *Book* becomes (βook)-[βuk]. *Should* becomes (shood)-[ʃud].
(oo)-[u]	no change
(ûr)-[ɝ]	becomes (ä)-[ɑ]. *Church* becomes (chäch)-[tʃatʃ]. *Sir* becomes (sä)-[sɑ].
(ər)-[ɚ]	becomes (ä)-[ɑ]. *Sister* becomes (sēs'tä)-[`sistɑ]. *Ladder* becomes (řä'dä)-[`řɑdɑ].
(ŭ)-[ʌ]	no change
(ə)-[ə]	becomes (ä)-[ɑ]. *Upon* becomes (äpän')-[ɑ`pɑn]. *Sofa* becomes (sō'ɸä)-[`soɸɑ].

Diphthong Sounds

Although these sounds are made with approximately the same action as in English, they tend to be somewhat incomplete. The articulator movement is reduced. They sound a little short, although they are recognizable.

(ā)-[eɪ]	no change
(ī)-[aɪ]	no change
(ō)-[oʊ]	no change
(ou)-[aʊ]	no change
(oi)-[ɔɪ]	no change

Consonants (continued)

(l)- [l]   may become (ř)-[ř] in the initial and
            medial positions. *Long* becomes
            (řông)-[řɔŋ]. *Glass* becomes (gřäs)-
            [gřɑs]. In the final position, it
            becomes (o͞o)-[u] when followed by *e*.
            Table (tă'bo͞o)-[ˋtebu]. *People* becomes
            (pē'po͞o)-[ˋpipu]. When not followed
            by an *e*, the final *l* is often dropped.
            Ball becomes (ɸô)-[ɸɔ]. See Special
            Considerations.
(m)-[m]   no change
(n)-[n]   no change
(ng)-[ŋ]   no change

Special Considerations

Consecutive Consonants.   Unlike English, Japanese does not follow one consonant
with another. The word such as *stop*, for example, would be pronounced (sətä'p)-
[səˋtɑp]. *Completely* becomes (kaməpəřētə'řǐ)-[kɑməpəˋřitəři]. A vowel is inserted
between the two consecutive consonants.

The same situation exists when consecutive consonants occur between two
words. Note the following: *Nice day* becomes (nīs'ə dā)-[ˋnaɪsə de]. *Sleep well*
becomes (səřēp' awěl)-[ˋsəřip əwɔl].

Final Consonants.   Final consonants at the end of a phrase also receive the added
vowel. *A big dog* becomes (ə bēgə dôgə)-[ə bigədɔgə]. *Run home* becomes (rän'ə
hōm'ə)-[ˋrɑnə ˋhomə].

When (t)-[t] occurs in the final position, the sound (ō)-[o] is added, rather than
the (ə)-[ə]. *Sad* becomes (säd'ō)-[ˋsɑdō]. *My friend spoke* becomes (mī ɸřěn'dō
səpō'kə)-[maɪ ˋɸřendō səˋpokə].

When *t* and *d* are combined with other consonants in the final position, their
sounds are often dropped. *Rest* becomes (rě'sə)-[ˋrɛsə]. *Send* becomes (sě'nə)-
[ˋsɛnə].

Practice Paragraph

(ēβə'nēng kərä'sēzə)

(ēchə ēvə'nēng, i´nətəřĕsətēng lĕ'sənəz änd kəřa'sēz ä hĕř'ədo äto zēs kō'řäjə. přä'βəβəřē ô ōβ zĕm ä gōōd, bät ä yōō ä sä'tänəřē säpəřī'zēng. sŭm'ə kəřä'sēz, ōβ kôs, äɍ jäst'ə fĕ, bŭt ōn'əřē wän ô tōō ä řē'řē `wiřədō.

zēz dĕz, wē fīn ĕjəkä'shənōō ĭnəjoi'män wēzout' gō'ēng φä φəläm φōm. zä pē'pōō hōō bĭgēn' tä stä'dĭ kän'ə gō ôn, fī'nēsh änd häβ gəřōs. zō zä säb'əjĕkəs säm chōōz ä fōōřĕsh', mōsət ä yōō'zhoořĭ φäd änd chä'řĕnəjingə. hwĕnə sətōō 'dĭnsə φäβ wä'kət φô ä kä'pōō ōβ yĭzə řēřē 'jäsəře, mĕ'nē nōtēs'ə zätō zĕ sətä'dē ēz sä'tēsəfīēngə).

[`ivəniŋ kə`rasiz]

[itʃə `ivəniŋ, `inətəřɛsətiŋ `lɛsanəz andō kə`řasiz a `hɛřədo ato zis `kořadʒə. `pəřaβəβři ɔ oβ zɛm a `gudō, bʌt ä φju a `satənəři sə pəřaıziŋə. sam kə`řasiz, aβə kɔs, a dʒʌsə fɛ, bʌt `onəři wan ɔ tu a `řiři `wiřədo.

ziz dɛz, wi faın ɛdʒə`keʃənu ɛn`jɔımənə wi`zautō `goiŋə φa φřam homə. za `pipu hu bi`gin tu `stadi kan go ɔn, `finiʃə `ando haβə gəřos. zo za `saβədʒɛkəs sam chuz a `φuliʃə, mosto a `juzhuri `hado `ando `tʃařɛnədʒıŋə. ʍɛnə sə`tudənəs haβə `wakəto φɔ a `kapu aβ yız ři`řidʒəs ři, `mɛni `notisə zato zɛ sətadi iz `satisəφaıiŋə.]

From Other
Languages to English

For the student who comes to English from another language, there are some conditions to recognize and overcome. First, English is not always spelled the way it is sounded. Second, there are some sounds in English which are not in the first language. Also, some sounds are similar, but must be made in a slightly different way.

To help you recognize these new sounds and adjust to others, we have prepared the following sound analyses of selected languages, plus word pair practice material which focuses on the newly-needed physical adjustments to articulate English.

If you are in doubt about how to make a sound correctly, refer to the page describing that sound in the articulation chapters of the book.

MANDARIN CHINESE TO ENGLISH
(Yale Romanization System)

Consonant Sounds		Vowel Sounds	
p	as in pén	ē	as in nī
b	new sound, almost běn	ĭ	new sound
t	as in teng	ĕ	as in kěn
d	new sound	ă	as in da
k	as in kū	ä	as in ma
g	as in gù	ô	new sound
f	new sound	o͝o	new sound
v	new sound	o͞o	as in lu
th	new sound	ûr	new sound
ᵼħ	new sound	ŭ	as in Deng
s	as in sài		
z	new sound		

Consonant Sounds (continued)

sh	as in shū		
zh	new sound		*Diphthong Sounds*
h	as in hú		
ch	as in chū	ā	as in lèi
j	as in jř	ī	as in mài
hw	new sound	ou	as in māu
w	as in wèi	oi	new sound
y	as in yě	ō	as in âu
r	new sound		
l	as in lěng		
m	as in mén		
n	as in néng; put the tongue tip above teeth		
ng	as in máng		

Discussion

Unlike Chinese, pitch change does not change the meaning of an English word. English is clearer if you open your mouth more and extend the sounds more than in Chinese.

Word Pairs

(p-b)   [p-b]

peat	beat	dips	dibs	rip	rib
pit	bit				
pet	bet				
pat	bat	rapid	rabid	cap	cab
par	bar	cops	cobs	lop	lob
Paul	ball				
pull	bull				
plume	bloom	loops	lubes	loop	lube
purr	burr			Earp	herb
putt	but	pups	pubs	cup	cub
pace	base			ape	Abe
pie	by			tripe	tribe
poi	boy				
pout	bout				
pole	bowl	roping	robing	rope	robe

(t-d)   [t-d]

team	deem	liter	leader	beat	bead
till	dill	bitter	bidder	bit	bid
tell	dell	betting	bedding	bet	bed
tan	Dan	matter	madder	bat	bad
tot	dot	rots	rods	pot	pod
tall	Dahl	daughter	dauber		
tomb	doom	moots	moods	moot	mood
turn	Dern	hurts	herds	Bert	bird
ton	dun	butting	budding	cut	cud
tame	dame	eights	aids	late	laid
tie	dye	rights	rides	bite	bide
toil	Doyle			Voight	void
tout	doubt	pouter	powder	lout	loud
toll	dole	coating	coding	boat	bode

(l-r)   [l-r]

leap	reap	flee	free		
limb	rim	miller	mirror	dale	dare
lead	read	belly	berry	dell	dare
lamp	ramp	clash	crash		
lock	rock	clock	crock		
law	raw	claw	craw	wall	war
look	rook	pulling	purring	pull	poor
loom	room	clue	crew	duel	doer
lung	rung	clutch	crutch		
lace	race	belated	berated		
light	right	filing	firing	dial	dire
loyal	royal				
lout	rout	clown	crown	owl	hour
low	row	glow	grow	mole	more

(t-th)   [t-θ]

tree	three	eater	ether	heat	heath
trill	thrill	mitts	myths	wit	with
tread	thread	tents	tenths	debt	death
tank	thank	batless	bathless	mat	math
				swat	swath
taught	thought	forts	fourths	brought	broth

true	through	roots	Ruth's	toot	tooth
tug	thug			dirt	dirth
				fate	faith
tie	thigh	fates	faiths		
tow	throw				

(d-th)   [d-ð]

		breeds	breathes

seed   seethe

den	then		
Dan	than	ladder	lather
		fodder	father
		wordier	worthier
		udder	other
day	they		
die	thy	riding	writhing
dough	though	loads	loathes

(s-z)   [s-z]

seal	zeal	ceasing	seizing	peace	peas
sip	zip	gristle	grizzle	fierce	fears
				pence	pens
sag	zag			ass	as
Saar	Czar				
				sauce	saws
sue	zoo	looses	loses	deuce	dues
				hearse	hers
		buses	buzzes	bus	buzz
sane	Zane	lacy	lazy	face	faze
		prices	prizes	ice	eyes
sounds	zounds	dousing	dowsing	Boyce	boys
sewn	zone	doses	dozes	dose	doze

KOREAN TO ENGLISH

Because we are unable to provide the Korean characters needed for accurate pronunciation, we are not listing sample Korean words. However, there is practice material here for the new sounds.

Consonant Sounds		Vowel Sounds	
p		ē	
b		ĭ	new sound
t		ĕ	
d		ă	new sound
k		ä	
g		ô	new sound
f	new sound	o͞o	new sound
v	new sound	o͞o	
th	new sound	ûr	new sound
th̷	new sound	ŭ	
s			
z	new sound		
sh			
zh		*Diphthong Sounds*	
h			
ch		ā	
j		ī	
hw	new sound	ou	
w		oi	
y		ō	
r	new sound		
l	new sound		
m			
n			
ng			

Discussion

Although Korean is a distinct language with an ancient history, it has some characteristics of Chinese and has a similar grammar to Japanese. In Korean, only seven consonants (k, t, p, n, l, m, and ng) are pronounced at the end of a word or before a consonant, so you must concentrate on completing these and other consonant sounds at the ends of English words. The Korean t, n, and l sounds are made by the tongue touching the teeth. In English, the tongue must touch the gum ridge for t, d, n, and l.

Word Pairs

(p-f)   [p-f]

peat	feet	leaps	leafs	leap	leaf
pit	fit	ripped	rift	rip	riff
pear	fair	leapt	left	tip	tiff
pan	fan	napper	raffer	lap	laugh
par	far				
pall	fall				
pull	full				
pool	fool			poof	roof
pearl	furl				
pun	fun	cups	cuffs		
pace	face				
pie	fie				
poi	foy				
Powell	foul				
pole	foal			lope	loaf

(b-v)   [b-v]

beep	veep	Eben	even
bicker	vicar		
berry	very	ebber	ever
bat	vat		

boom	voom

bale	vale	cable	caver		
buy	vie				
Boyd	void				
bough	vow				
boat	vote	lobes	loaves	robe	rove

(l-r)   [l-r]

leap	reap	flee	free		
limb	rim	miller	mirror	bill	been
lead	read	belly	berry	dale	dare
lamp	ramp	clash	crash		
lock	rock	clock	crock		
law	raw	claw	craw	wall	war

look	rook	pulling	purring	pull	poor
loom	room	clue	crew	duel	doer

lung	rung	clutch	crutch		
lace	race	belated	berated		
light	right	filing	firing	dial	dire
loyal	royal				
lout	rout	clown	crown	owl	hour
low	row	glow	grow	mole	more

Word Pairs

(t-th)   [t-θ]

tree	three	eater	ether	heat	heath
trill	thrill	mitts	myths	wit	with
tread	thread	tents	tenths	debt	death
tank	thank	batless	bathless	mat	math
				swat	swath
taught	thought	forts	fourths	brought	broth
true	through	roots	Ruth's	toot	tooth
				dirt	dirth
tug	thug				
				fate	faith
tie	thigh	fates	faiths		
tow	throw				

(d-th)   [d-ð]

		breeds	breathes	seed	seethe
den	then				
Dan	than	ladder	lather		
		fodder	father		
		wordier	worthier		
		udder	other		
day	they				
die	thy	riding	writhing		
dough	though	loads	loathes		

(s-z)   [s-z]

seal	zeal	ceasing	seizing	peace	peas
sip	zip	gristle	grizzle	fierce	fears
				pence	pens
sag	zag			ass	as
Saar	Czar				
				sauce	saws
sue	zoo	looses	loses	deuce	dues
				hearse	hers
		buses	buzzes	bus	buzz
sane	Zane	lacy	lazy	face	faze
		prices	prizes	ice	eyes
sounds	zounds	dousing	dowsing	Boyce	boys
sewn	zone	doses	dozes	dose	doze

JAPANESE TO ENGLISH

Consonant Sounds		Vowel Sounds	
p	as in Nippon	ē	as in ii
b	as in bushi	ĭ	new sound
t	as in tori	ĕ	new sound
d	as in dai joobu	ă	as in kyaku
k	as in kichigai	ä	as in aki
g	as in gomenasai	ô	new sound
f	new sound, put lip under upper teeth	oo	new sound
v	new sound, put lip under upper teeth	o͞o	as in juu
th	new sound, put tongue under upper teeth	ûr	new sound
t̶h̶	new sound, put tongue under upper teeth	ŭ	new sound
s	as in soba		
z	as in doozo		
sh	as in shigoto		
zh	new sound		*Diphthong Sounds*
h	as in hai		
ch	as in ocha	ā	as in ei
j	as in ju	ī	as in nagai
hw	new sound	ou	as in ao
w	as in watashi	oi	as in oi
y	as in yama	ō	as in doozo, only longer
r	new sound		
l	new sound, touch the gum ridge		
m	as in miru		
n	as in namae		
ng	as in san		

Discussion

Some vowel and diphthong sounds need more time than in Japanese. There is no emphasis on syllables with ə.

Word Pairs

(p-f)   **[p-f]**

peat	feet	leaps	leafs	leap	leaf
pit	fit	ripped	rift	rip	riff
pear	fair	leapt	left	tip	tiff
pan	fan	napper	raffer	lap	laugh
par	far				
pall	fall				
pull	full				
pool	fool			poof	roof
pearl	furl				
pun	fun				
pace	face				
pie	fie				
poi	foy				
Powell	foul				
pole	foal			lope	loaf

(b-v)   **[b-v]**

beep	veep	Eben	even
bicker	vicar		
berry	very	ebber	ever
bat	vat		

boom	voom

bale	vale	cable	caver
buy	vie		
Boyd	void		
bough	vow		
boat	vote	lobes	loaves

(r-l) [r-l]

reap	leap	free	flee		
rim	limb	mirror	miller	beer	bill
read	lead	berry	belly	dare	dell
ramp	lamp	crash	clash		
rock	lock	crock	clock		
raw	law	craw	claw	war	wall
rook	look	purring	pulling	poor	pull
room	loom	crew	clue	doer	duel

rung	lung	crutch	clutch		
race	lace	berated	belated		
right	light	firing	filing	dire	dial
royal	loyal				
rout	lout	crown	down	hour	owl
row	low	grow	glow	more	mole

(t-th) [t-θ]

tree	three	eater	ether	heat	heath
trill	thrill	mitts	myths	wit	with
tread	thread	tents	tenths	debt	death
tank	thank	batless	bathless	mat	math
		swats	swaths	swat	swath
taught	thought	forts	fourths	brought	broth

true	through	roots	Ruth's	toot	tooth
				dirt	dirth
tug	thug				
		fates	faiths	fate	faith

tow	throw

(d-th) [d-ð]

breeds	breathes	seed	seethe

den	then		
Dan	than	ladder	lather
		fodder	father

		wordier	worthier		
		udder	other		
day	they				
die	thy	riding	writhing		
dough	though	loads	loathes		

(s-z)   **[s-z]**

seal	zeal	ceasing	seizing	peace	peas
sip	zip	gristle	grizzle	fierce	fears
				pence	pens
sag	zag			ass	as
Saar	Czar				
				sauce	saws
sue	zoo	looses	loses	deuce	dues
				hearse	hers
		buses	buzzes	bus	buzz
sane	Zane	lacy	lazy	face	faze
		prices	prizes	ice	eyes
sounds	zounds	dousing	dowsing	Boyce	boys
sewn	zone	doses	dozes	dose	doze

SPANISH TO ENGLISH

Consonant Sounds		_Vowel Sounds_	
p	as in para, explode air out	ē	as in kilo
b	as in boca, the lips are together	ĭ	new sound
t	as in tarde, the tongue must touch the gum ridge	ĕ	as in esta
d	as in donde, the tongue must touch the gum ridge	ă	new sound
k	as in kilo	ä	as in papa
g	as in gustar	ô	new sound
f	as in falta	o͞o	new sound
v	as in Valencia, the lower lip touches the upper teeth	o͞o	as in usted
th	new sound, do not vibrate the vocal folds	ûr	new sound
t͟h	as in nada, the tongue touches the teeth	ŭ	new sound
s	as in sabado		
z	as in los dios		
sh	new sound		
zh	new sound		

Consonant Sounds (continued)

h	as in mujer		
ch	as in leche	*Diphthong Sounds*	
j	new sound		
hw	as in Juan	ā	new sound
w	as in guante	ī	as in hay
y	as in yo	ou	as in aula
r	as in pero, without the tongue flapping	oi	as in hoy
l	as in libro, be sure the tongue touches the gum ridge	ō	new sound
m	as in mano		
n	as in noche, sound it stronger		
ng	as in manga, without the g sound		

Discussion

Both English and Spanish have the same Latin base. In English the consonants are more strongly stated than in Spanish. Spanish has some diphthongs (two part sounds) but not the ā and ō diphthongs. Practice extending these sounds. The ə sound is very important in English. Be sure you do not stress this sound in a word.

Word Pairs

(p—b)   **[p—b]**

peat	beat	dips	dibs	rip	rib
pit	bit				
pet	bet				
pat	bat	rapid	rabid	cap	cab
par	bar	cops	cobs	lop	lob
Paul	ball				
pull	bull				
plume	bloom	loops	lubes	loop	lube
purr	burr			Earp	herb
putt	but	pups	pubs	cup	cub
pace	base			ape	Abe
pie	by			tripe	tribe
poi	boy				
pout	bout				
pole	bowl	roping	robing	rope	robe

(b-v)   [b-v]

beat	veep	Eben	even
bicker	vicar		
berry	very	ebber	ever
bat	vat		

| boom | voom |

bale	vale	cable	caver
buy	vie		
Boyd	void		
bough	vow		
boat	vote	lobes	loaves	robe	rove

(sh-ch)   [ʃ-tʃ]

sheet	cheat	leashes	leaches	quiche	Keach
ship	chip	wishing	witching	dish	ditch
share	chair				
shad	Chad	masher	matcher	cash	catch
shop	chop	washer	watcher	wash	watch

| shuck | Chuck | bushes | Butches | bush | Butch |
| shoe | chew | | | | |

| shuck | Chuck | | | mush | much |
| Shane | chain | | | | |

| shore | chore | kosher | coacher |

(t-th)   [t-θ]

tree	three	eater	ether	heat	heath
trill	thrill	mitts	myths	wit	with
tread	thread	tents	tenths	debt	death
tank	thank	batless	bathless	mat	math
				swat	swath
taught	thought	forts	fourths	brought	broth

true	through	roots	Ruth's	toot	tooth
				dirt	dirth
tug	thug				
				fate	faith
tie	thigh	fates	faiths		
tow	throw				

(d-th)   [d-ð]

		breeds	breathes	seed	seethe
den	then				
Dan	than	ladder	lather		
		fodder	father		
		wordier	worthier		
		udder	other		
day	they				
die	thy	riding	writhing		
dough	though	loads	loathes		

(s-sh)   [s-ʃ]

see	she	leases	leashes	lease	leash
sip	ship			Swiss	shish
said	shed	messed	meshed		
sack	shack	massed	mashed	mess	mesh
sock	shock			crass	crash
sort	short				
		pussy	pushy		
sue	shoe				
sun	shun			muss	mush
say	shay				
sigh	shy				
sour	shower				
so	show				

TAGALOG TO ENGLISH

Consonant Sounds			*Vowel Sounds*	
p	as in palengke		ē	as in ese
b	as in bahay		ĭ	new sound
t	as in tatlo		ĕ	new sound
d	as in daga		ă	as in banana
k	as in kamote		ä	as in tatay
g	as in gabi		ô	new sound
f	new sound		o͞o	new sound
v	new sound		o͞o	as in ube
th	new sound		ûr	new sound
th	new sound		ŭ	new sound
s	as in sabo			
z	as in Luzon			
sh	as in siyam			
zh	new sound		*Diphthong Sounds*	
h	as in halika			
ch	new sound		ā	new sound
j	as in jeep		ī	new sound
hw	new sound		ou	as in Mindanao
w	as in walet		oi	new sound
y	as in yoyo		ō	as in pito, only longer
r	as in rabit			
l	as in laba			
m	as in mani			
n	as in nanay			
ng	as in nga nga			

Discussion

Since Tagalog has a Spanish base, you may need to make some of the same changes as in Spanish. See the previous section, Spanish to English, for some additional instruction.

Word Pairs

(p-f)   **[p-f]**

peat	feet	leaps	leafs	leap	leaf
pit	fit	ripped	rift	rip	riff
pear	fair	leapt	left	tip	tiff
pan	fan	napper	raffer	lap	laugh

par	far				
pall	fall				
pull	full				
pool	fool			poof	roof
pearl	furl				
pun	fun	cups	cuffs		
pace	face				
pie	fie				
poi	foy				
Powell	foul				
pole	foal			lope	loaf

(b-v)   [b-v]

beat	veep	Eben	even		
bicker	vicar				
berry	very	ebber	ever		
bat	vat				
boom	voom				
bale	vale	cable	caver		
buy	vie				
Boyd	void				
bough	vow				
boat	vote	lobes	loaves	robe	rove

(s-z)   [s-z]

seal	zeal	ceasing	seizing	peace	peas
sip	zip	gristle	grizzle	fierce	fears
				pence	pens
sag	zag			ass	as
Saar	Czar				
				sauce	saws
sue	zoo	looses	loses	deuce	dues
				hearse	hers
		buses	buzzes	bus	buzz
sane	Zane	lacy	lazy	face	faze
		prices	prizes	ice	eyes
sounds	zounds	dousing	dowsing	Boyce	boys
sewn	zone	doses	dozes	dose	doze

(t-th)   [t-θ]

tree	three	eater	ether	heat	heath
trill	thrill	mitts	myths	wit	with
tread	thread	tents	tenths	debt	death
tank	thank	batless	bathless	mat	math
				swat	swath
taught	thought	forts	fourths	brought	broth
true	through	roots	Ruth's	toot	tooth
				dirt	dirth
tug	thug			fate	faith
tie	thigh	fates	faiths		
tow	throw				

(d-th)   [d-ð]

		breeds	breathes	seed	seethe
den	then				
Dan	than	ladder	lather		
		fodder	father		
		wordier	worthier		
		udder	other		
day	they				
die	thy	riding	writhing		
dough	though	loads	loathes		

(s-sh)   [s-ʃ]

see	she	leases	leashes	lease	leash
sip	ship			Swiss	shish
said	shed	messed	meshed		
sack	shack	massed	mashed	mess	mesh
sock	shock			crass	crash
sort	short				
		pussy	pushy		
sue	shoe				

sun	shun		muss	mush
say	shay			
sigh	shy			
sour	shower			
so	show			

VIETNAMESE TO ENGLISH

Consonant Sounds		*Vowel Sounds*	
p	as in ep	ē	as in dī
b	as in bo	ĭ	as in ít
t	as in tìm	ĕ	as in bĕ
d	as in di	ă	as in ba
k	as in kho	ä	new sound
g	as in gā	ô	new sound
f	as in phai	o͞o	new sound
v	as in voi	o͞o	as in du
th	new sound	ûr	new sound
th		ŭ	as in do
s	as in soi		
z	new sound		
sh	new sound		
zh	new sound	*Diphthong Sounds*	
h	as in ho		
ch	new sound	ā	as in lay
j	as in chet	ī	as in quay
hw	new sound	ou	as in ao
w	new sound	oi	as in nôi
y	new sound	ō	as in hô
r	as in rôi		
l	as in lông		
m	as in minh		
n	as in nam		
ng	as in nga		

Discussion

Modern Vietnamese is a separate language which was influenced by Chinese during the one-thousand year rule by China. Since it is a monosyllabic tone language, you will need to practice the English diphthong sounds and the polysyllabic words of English. About half of the English vowel sounds are not in Vietnamese, and many consonants are not exploded or aspirated as much as they need to be in English.

Word Pairs

(t-th)   [t-θ]

tree	three	eater	ether	heat	heath
trill	thrill	mitts	myths	wit	with
tread	thread	tents	tenths	debt	death
tank	thank	batless	bathless	mat	math
				swat	swath
taught	thought	forts	fourths	brought	broth
true	through	roots	Ruth's	toot	tooth
				dirt	dirth
tug	thug				
				fate	faith
tie	thigh	fates	faiths		
tow	throw				

(d-th)   [d-ð]

breeds	breathes	seed	seethe

den	then		
Dan	than	ladder	lather
		fodder	father

		wordier	worthier
		udder	other
day	they		
die	thy	riding	writhing

dough	though	loads	loathes

(s-z)   [s-z]

seal	zeal	ceasing	seizing	peace	peas
sip	zip	gristle	grizzle	fierce	fears
				pence	pens
sag	zag			ass	as
Saar	Czar				

				sauce	saws
sue	zoo	looses	loses	deuce	dues
				hearse	hers
		buses	buzzes	bus	buzz
sane	Zane	lacy	lazy	face	faze
		prices	prizes	ice	eyes
sounds	zounds	dousing	dowsing	Boyce	boys
sewn	zone	doses	dozes	dose	doze

(sh-sh)   [s-ʃ]

see	she	leases	leashes	lease	leash
sip	ship			Swiss	shish
said	shed	messed	meshed		
sack	shack	massed	mashed	mess	mesh
sock	shock			crass	crash
sort	short				
		pussy	pushy		
sue	shoe				
sun	shun			muss	mush
say	shay				
sigh	shy				
sour	shower				
so	show				

(sh-zh)   [ʃ—ʒ]

leasher	leisure	leash	liege
Asher	azure		
Aleutian	allusion		
person	Persian		
glacier	glazier		

(s-zh)   [s-ʒ]

      leaser   leisure   lease   liege

      person   Persian

      glacier   glazier

APPENDIX E

Consonant Blends

In Chapter 8, practice material is provided for the various consonants in Standard American English. In most cases, the key words contain the target sound followed by a vowel. Many English words, however, contain combinations of consonants, or *blends*. In the word *scratch*, for example, the consonants *s, k,* and *r* are blended together in a single syllable and appear almost to be a single new sound.

Following are examples of each of the consonant blends in Standard American English. Practice them by saying the words alone and then by making up sentences containing them.

bl [bl]

black   unbleached
blades   unblemished
blood   unblessed
blow   unblotted
blue   unblown

br [br]

brain   debrief
branch   highbrow
breath   unbroken
bridge   unbrushed
brown   upbraid

bz [bz]

                              cabs
                              grabs
                              robes
                              rubs
                              stubs

dr [dr]

drain	address
drawer	adrenalin
dress	adrift
drink	adroit
drop	hundred

dth [dθ]

breadth
width

dz [dz]

aids
beads
kids
leads
weds

fl [fl]

flag	aflame
flame	afflict
flight	afloat
floor	affluent
flower	influence

fr [fr]

frame	affricate
free	afraid
friend	Africa
from	afright
front	befriend

fs [fs]

beliefs
cliffs
loafs
safes
spoofs

ft [ft]

after	deft
gifts	left
hefty	lift
laughter	miffed
loafed	soft

fth [fθ]

fifth

gl [gl]

glass	angling
gleam	aglow
glove	burglar
glow	English
glue	ugly

gr [gr]

grain	agree
grass	begrudge
great	ingrate
green	ingrown
group	regret

gz [gz]

exaggerate	bags
examine	eggs
example	frogs
exhausted	legs
exhort	logs

kl [kl]

clean	acclaim
clear	declare
clock	exclaim
cloth	incline
cloud	include

kr [kr]

crime   ascribe
crook   concrete
cruel   decry
crush   describe
cry   encroach

ks [ks]

    axes   complex
    boxer   leaks
    coaxing   picks
    taxes   tucks
    waxing   wicks

kt [kt]

    actor   backed
    connector   detect
    doctor   looked
    insects   sect
    respecting   talked

kw [kw]

queen   aqua
quick   aquaint
quiet   equal
quite   equip
quote   frequent

lb [lb]

    album   bulb
    bilberry   DeKalb
    bulbous
    elbow
    filbert

lch [ltʃ]

    belched   belch
    filching   filch
    gulches   gulch
    mulched   mulch
    pilchard   pilch

ld [ld]

building	bald
cauldron	called
children	cold
mildly	fooled
wilderness	mild

lf [lf]

belfry	elf
elfin	golf
sailfish	pelf
selfish	self
wilful	shelf

lj [ldʒ]

algae	bilge
bilges	bulge
bulging	divulge
divulged	indulge
indulges	

lk [lk]

bulky	bilk
hulking	bulk
pulchritude	ilk
sulking	milk
vulcanize	silk

lm [lm]

almanac	elm
almighty	film
almost	
elms	
filmy	

lp [lp]

alps	alp
gulping	help
helping	kelp
palpitate	scalp
scalper	whelp

ls [ls]

balsam	else
dulcimer	false
elsewhere	impulse
falsify	pulse
impulsive	

lt [lt]

falter	built
faulty	felt
jilted	halt
realtor	melt
wilted	salt

lth [lθ]

filthy	filth
healthy	health
stealthy	stealth
	wealth

lv [lv]

elves	delve
pelvis	dissolve
revolver	shelve
shelving	solve
solvent	

lz [lz]

	bills
	calls
	falls
	sells
	wills

mp [mp]

empire	bump
imply	damp
pumping	hump
stamps	jump
umpire	limp

mz [mz]

crimson	comes
damsel	farms
flimsy	homes
	names
	poems

nch [ntʃ]

bunches	bench
crunchy	bunch
inches	inch
lunches	paunch
raunchy	pinch

nd [nd]

bending	and
fender	command
kindergarten	mind
kindly	planned
window	sand

ngk [ŋk]

handkerchief	ink
monkey	link
sinker	pink
thinking	rink
uncle	sank

ngth [ŋθ]

lengthen	length
strengthen	strength

nj [ndʒ]

conjugate	arrange
conjure	change
danger	hinge
engine	lunge
manger	orange

ns [ns]

announcement	balance
concert	chance
convincing	insurance
dancing	pounce
fancy	romance

nt [nt]

painted	ornament
planted	payment
printed	point
rents	present
tents	punishment

nth [nθ]

panther	tenth

nz [nz]

Anzio	bones
pansy	fines
panzer	lanes
	nouns
	sons

pl [pl]

place	applause
plant	apply
play	complete
please	explode
pleasure	simply

pr [pr]

present	approach
price	deprive
print	impress
probably	improve
produce	surprise

ps [ps]

lapsing	apes
sapsucker	keeps
	rips
	ropes
	tapes

pt [pt]

aptly	accept
coptic	except
helicopter	hoped
ineptly	ripped
optometrist	stopped

rb [rb]

disturbance	blurb
furbish	curb
gerbil	disturb
turbulent	herb
verbal	serb

rch [rtʃ]

churches	birch
merchant	church
searching	lurch
virtual	perch
virtue	search

rd [rd]

cards	bird
curdle	card
girdle	hard
hardly	jarred
hurdle	word

rf [rf]

barfish	kerf
barfly	scarf
curfew	surf
garfish	turf
starfish	wharf

rj [rdʒ]

allergic	merge
barges	purge
perjury	surge
sergeant	urge
urgent	verge

rk [rk]

barks	dark
marked	jerk
parking	park
turkey	shark
worker	work

rl [rl]

curly	furl
early	girl
hurled	hurl
parlay	pearl
rarely	whirl

rm [rm]

alarmed	arm
charming	farm
farmer	form
harmful	warm
warming	worm

rn [rn]

concerning	burn
darning	fern
discernment	horn
learning	mourn
morning	turn

rp [rp]

chirping	harp
harpoon	sharp
serpent	tarp
sharpen	twirp
slurping	warp

rs [rs]

far̲ces	fier̲ce
hear̲ses	for̲ce
nur̲ses	hor̲se
pur̲ses	spar̲se
wor̲st	ver̲se

rt [rt]

assor̲ted	hear̲t
bar̲ter	par̲t
cour̲tship	quar̲t
par̲ty	smar̲t
shor̲ter	star̲t

rth [rθ]

bir̲thright	dir̲th
ear̲thly	for̲th
ear̲thy	gir̲th
for̲thright	hear̲th
wor̲thwhile	mir̲th

r*th* [rð]

far̲ther
far̲thing
fur̲ther
wor̲thy

rv [rv]

deser̲ved	cur̲ve
fer̲vor	ner̲ve
ner̲vous	ser̲ve
pur̲vey	swer̲ve
ser̲vant	ver̲ve

rz [rz]

mar̲zipan	career̲s
Tar̲zan	car̲s
	ear̲s
	mirror̲s
	stair̲s

shr [ʃr]

shred
shrewd
shrill
shrink
shrub

enshrine
enshroud
unshred
unshriven
unshrunken

sk [sk]

scale
scam
school
skin
sky

ascot
disco
escape
gasket
mesquite

ask
disc
desk
risk
task

skr [skr]

scram
scratch
scream
script
scrod

ascribe
describe
discrete
muskrat
rescratch

sl [sl]

slant
sleep
slip
slope
slow

aslant
asleep
dislike
unsling
whistler

sm [sm]

small
smart
smell
smile
smooth

sn [sn]

snail
snake
sneeze
snip
snow

sp [sp]

space	despicable	asp
special	display	clasp
speed	expense	crisp
spoon	expire	lisp
spy	inspire	rasp

spr [spr]

sprawl	offspring
spray	osprey
sprightly	respray
spring	unsprightly
sprout	unsprouted

st [st]

stage	astound	first
stamp	custom	last
star	distance	list
steel	disturb	released
still	instead	waist

str [str]

straight	astronaut
street	construct
stretch	destroy
strong	distribute
structure	instruct

tr [tr]

trade	attribute
transport	contrite
tree	country
trick	metric
trouble	sentry

ts [ts]

		coats
		dates
		meets
		nuts
		rights

tw [tw]

tweed   between
twenty   betwixt
twin   entwine
twirl   untwined
twist   untwist

thr [θr]

thrash   bathroom
thread   enthrone
throat   forthright
throng   heartthrob
through   Northridge

ths [θs]

                                            baths
                                            breaths
                                            faiths
                                            myths
                                            oaths

*th*z [ðz]

                                            bathes
                                            breathes
                                            smoothes
                                            tithes
                                            wreathes

sts [sts]

                                            insists
                                            lasts
                                            rests
                                            tests
                                            vests

sw [sw]

sweater   assuage
sweet   Aswan
swim   dissuade
swing   persuade
swallow   unsweetened

*th*d [ðd]

bathed
breathed
smoothed
tithed
wreathed

vd [vd]

curved
halved
loved
proved
saved

vz [vz]

gloves
grooves
knives
raves
stoves

Letters and Sounds

As we have previously stated, English is not a phonetic language. Spelling sometimes bears little relation to pronunciation. The following pages, therefore, contain two lists to assist you in the pronunciation of American English. They are the following:

1. The Sounds of American English Spelling.
2. The Spelling of American English Sounds.

THE SOUNDS OF AMERICAN ENGLISH SPELLING

The left-hand column lists the letters and letter combinations used in American English spelling. The center column contains the sounds corresponding to each spelling, and the right-hand column provides examples of each.

Vowels and Diphthongs

Spelling	Sound	Example
a	ā [eɪ]	mate
	ă [æ]	mat
	ä [ɑ]	father
	ĕ [ɛ]	any
	ô [ɔ]	fall
	ə [ə]	about
a	ā [eɪ]	maelstrom
	ē [i]	Caesar
ai	ā [eɪ]	hail
	ă [æ]	plaid
	ĕ [ɛ]	said
	ī [aɪ]	aisle

Spelling	Sound	Example
ao	ā [eɪ]	gaol
au	ô [ɔ]	author
	ā [eɪ]	gauge
	ō [o]	chauffeur
aw	ô [ɔ]	law
ay	ā [eɪ]	day
	ē [i]	quay
	ĕ [ɛ]	says
aye	ī [aɪ]	aye
e	ä [ɑ]	sergeant
	ā [eɪ]	cafe
	ē [i]	me
	ĕ [ɛ]	met
	ə [ə]	emblem
	ĭ [ɪ]	pretty
ea	ā [eɪ]	break
	ä [ɑ]	hearth
	ē [i]	meat
	ĕ [ɛ]	head
	ûr [ɝ]	earth
eau	ō [oʊ]	bureau
	yōō [ju]	beauty
ee	ā [eɪ]	negligee
	ē [i]	keen
	ĭ [ɪ]	been
ei	ā [eɪ]	eight
	ē [i]	ceiling
	ĕ [ɛ]	heifer
	ī [aɪ]	height
	ĭ [ɪ]	surfeit
eo	ē [i]	people
	ĕ [ɛ]	leopard
eou	ŭ [ʌ]	righteous
eu	oo [ʊ]	amateur
	ōō [u]	rheumatism
	yōō [ju]	feud

Spelling	Sound	Example
ew	ō [oʊ]	sew
	o͞o [u]	grew
	yo͞o [ju]	few
ey	ā [eɪ]	prey
	ē [i]	key
	ī [aɪ]	geyser
i	ē [i]	machine
	ī [aɪ]	mile
	ĭ [ɪ]	mill
	ə [ə]	cabinet
	ûr [ɝ]	firm
ia	yə [jə]	dahlia
ie	ē [i]	believe
	ĕ [ɛ]	friend
	ī [aɪ]	flies
	ĭ [ɪ]	sieve
ieu	o͞o [u]	lieutenant
iew	yo͞o [ju]	view
io	ə [ə]	attention
	yə [jə]	opinion
iou	ə [ə]	delicious
o	ĭ [ɪ]	women
	ō [oʊ]	old
	ŏ [a]	not
	ō [o]	obey
	ə [ə]	occur
	ô [ɔ]	lost
	o͞o [u]	do
	o͞o [ʊ]	wolf
	ûr [ɝ]	world
oa	ō [o]	boat
oe	ē [i]	subpoena
	ō [oʊ]	foe
	o͞o [u]	shoe
	ŭ [ʌ]	does
oi	oi [ɔɪ]	toil
	wī [waɪ]	choir

Spelling	Sound	Example
oo	ō [oʊ]	Roosevelt
	ōō [u]	food
	o͝o [ʊ]	good
	ŭ [ʌ]	flood
ou	ô [ɔ]	ought
	ōō [u]	you
	o͝o [ʊ]	could
	ou [aʊ]	loud
	ŭ [ʌ]	trouble
	ûr [ɝ]	journal
oy	oi [ɔɪ]	toy
u	ĭ [ɪ]	busy
	o͝o [ʊ]	put
	yōō [ju]	use
	ŭ [ʌ]	us
	ûr [ɝ]	burn
ua	ă [æ]	guarantee
	ä [ɑ]	guard
	wä [wɑ]	guava
ue	ē [i]	Portuguese
	ĕ [ɛ]	guest
	ōō [u]	blue
	wā [weɪ]	suede
ueue	yōō [ju]	queue
ui	ă [æ]	guimpe
	ī [aɪ]	guide
	ĭ [ɪ]	guild
	ōō [u]	fruit
	wē [wi]	suite
	yōō [ju]	suit
uy	ī [aɪ]	buy
y	ə [ə]	martyr
	ī [aɪ]	hydrogen
	ĭ [ɪ]	hymn
	y [j]	yell
ye	ī [aɪ]	dye

Consonants

Spelling	Sound	Example
b	b [b]	rob, Bob
bt	t [t]	debt
c	k [k]	card
	s [s]	deceit
cc	k [k]	account
ce	sh [ʃ]	ocean
ch	ch [tʃ]	church
	sh [ʃ]	chivalry
	k [k]	echo
cht	t [t]	yacht
ci	sh [ʃ]	delicious
ct	t [t]	indict
cz	z [z]	czar
d	d [d]	did
	t [t]	walked
dd	d [d]	add
dg	j [dʒ]	edge
di	j [dʒ]	soldier
dn	n [n]	Wednesday
f	f [f]	far
	v [v]	of
ff	f [f]	puff
g	g [g]	get
	j [dʒ]	gentlemen
	zh [ʒ]	mirage
gg	g [g]	laggard
gh	f [f]	cough
	g [g]	ghost
	p [p]	hiccough
ght	t [t]	eight

Spelling	Sound	Example
gm	m [m]	diaphragm
gn	n [n]	design
gu	g [g]	guarantee
	gw [gw]	guava
gw	gw [gw]	Gwendolyn
h	h [h]	home
j	j [dʒ]	jerk
	y [j]	hallelujah
	zh [ʒ]	bijou
k	k [k]	kind
kn	n [n]	knee
l	l [l]	lamb, eel
m	m [m]	moon
mn	m [m]	hymn
	n [n]	mnemonic
n	n [n]	nine
nc	ngk [ŋk]	uncle
ndk	ngk [ŋk]	handkerchief
ng	ng [ŋ]	bring
nk	ngk [ŋk]	ink
nx	ngksh [ŋkʃ]	anxious
p	p [p]	pale
pb	b [b]	cupboard
ph	f [f]	Philadelphia
	v [v]	Stephen
pn	n [n]	pneumonia
ps	s [s]	psalm
pt	t [t]	receipt
qu	k [k]	coquette
	kw [kw]	queer

Spelling	**Sound**	**Example**
que	k [k]	unique
r	r [r]	red
rr	r [r]	herring
s	s [s]	soon
	sh [ʃ]	sure
	z [z]	easy, these
sc	s [s]	scene
sch	s [s]	schism
	sk [sk]	school
se	sh [ʃ]	nauseous
sl	l [l]	Carlisle
sne	n [n]	demesne
ss	s [s]	confess
ssi	sh [ʃ]	confession
t	t [t]	tone
th	th [θ]	thin
	th [ð]	then
ti	sh [ʃ]	patient
v	v [v]	very
w	w [w]	were
wh	h [h]	who
	hw [ʍ]	where
x	gz [gz]	examine
	ks [ks]	wax
	z [z]	xylophone
xi	ksh [kʃ]	anxious
y	y [j]	yet
z	z [z]	zeal
	zh [ʒ]	azure

THE SPELLING OF AMERICAN ENGLISH SOUNDS

This list presents each sound in American English speech and indicates the various ways they might be spelled. The left-hand column lists the sounds, the center column the spellings, and the right-hand column an example for each.

Vowels and Diphthongs

Sound	Spelling	Example
ā [e, eɪ]	*ai*	daisy
	ao	gaol
	au	gauge
	ay	may
	aye	Faye
	ea	break
	ei	veil
	ey	they
ă [æ]	*a*	ask, abhor
ä [ɑ]	*a*	father
	ah	bah
	e	sergeant
	ea	hearth
ē [i]	*ae*	Caesar
	ay	quay
	e	me
	ea	meat
	ee	see
	ei	ceiling
	eo	people
	ey	key
	ie	believe
	oe	Croesus
ĕ [ɛ]	*a*	any, care,
	ai	said, air
	ay	says
	e	met, there
	ea	bread, bear
	ei	heifer, their
	eo	leopard
	ie	friend
	ue	guess

Spelling	Sound	Example
ī [aɪ]	*ai*	aisle
	ei	height
	ey	geyser
	eye	eye
	i	bite
	ie	flies
	oi	choir
	uy	buy
	y	by
	ye	bye
ĭ [ɪ]	*e*	English, pretty
	ee	been
	ei	surfeit
	ey	honey
	i	ill
	ie	sieve
	o	women
	u	busy
	ui	build
	y	hymn
ō [o, oʊ]	*au*	chauffeur
	eau	bureau
	eo	yeoman
	o	old
	oa	boat
	oo	Van Loon
	ou	though
	ow	low
	owe	owe
ŏ [a]	*a*	want
	o	hot
ô [ɔ]	*a*	fall
	ah	Utah
	al	talk
	au	taut
	augh	daughter
	aw	awful
	o	order
	ough	ought

Sound	Spelling	Example
o͞o [u]	*eu*	rheumatism
	ew	grew
	ioux	Sioux
	o	do
	oe	shoe
	oo	noon
	ough	through
	ue	blue
	ui	fruit
	wo	two
o͝o [ʊ]	*o*	woman
	oo	wood
	ou	could
	u	full
yo͞o [ju]	*eau*	beauty
	eu	feud
	ew	few
	ieu	lieutenant
	iew	view
	ou	you
	u	duty
	ue	sue
	ui	suit
ŭ [ʌ]	*o*	come
	oe	does
	oo	flood
	ou	double
	u	cup
ə [ə]	*a*	about
	e	item
	eou	righteous
	i	edible
	io	attention
	iou	gracious
	o	gallop
	u	circus
	ue	conquer
	y	martyr

Consonants

Sound	Spelling	Example
b [b]	*b*	bribe
	bb	bubble
ch [tʃ]	*ch*	child
	t	nature
	tch	watch
	te	righteous
d [d]	*d*	did
	dd	meddle
f [f]	*f*	for
	ff	muff
	ft	often
	gh	laugh
	ph	phrase
g [g]	*g*	go
	gg	egg
	gh	ghost
gz [gz]	*x*	example
h [h]	*h*	hear
	wh	whole
hw [ʍ]	*wh*	when
j [dʒ]	*dge*	judge, edge
	di	soldier
	g	gem
	j	joke
k [k]	*c*	come
	cc	account
	ch	echo
	ck	mock
	cq	acquire
	q	queer
	que	unique
ks [ks]	*x*	exercise
l [l]	*l*	let
	ll	Nellie

Sound	Spelling	Example
m [m]	*m*	my
	mb	dumb
	mm	dummy
	mn	hymn
n [n]	*gn*	gnome
	kn	knot
	mn	Mnemosyne
	pn	pneumatic
	sn	demesne
ng [ŋ]	*n*	anxious
	nch	anchor
	ng	long
	nk	ink
	nqu	conquer
p [p]	*gh*	hiccough
	p	pay
	pp	tripping
r [r]	*r*	ray, bar
	rr	berry
	wr	write
s [s]	*c*	ceiling
	ps	pseudo
	s	so
	sc	science
	sch	schism
	ss	miss
ks [ks]	*x*	box
	z	quartz
sh [ʃ]	*ce*	ocean
	ch	chaperon
	ci	judicial
	sci	conscience
	sh	shall
	ssi	confession
	ti	patience
	xi	anxious

Sound	Spelling	Example
t [t]	*bt*	debt
	cht	yacht
	d	walked
	phth	phthisic
	pt	receipt
	th	thyme
	t	to
	tt	sitting
th [ð]	*th*	their
th [θ]	*th*	thin
v [v]	*v*	valve
	f	of
w [w]	*u*	queen, suede
wä [wɑ]	*oi*	reservoir
y [j]	*eu*	feudal
	i	million
ny [nj]	*gn*	vignette
	n	manana
yo͞o [ju]	*u*	due
z [z]	*s*	busy
	sc	discern
	x	xylophone
	z	zouave
	zz	buzz
zh [ʒ]	*ge*	mirage
	j	bijou
	s	measure
	si	division
	z	azure

Glossary of Speech Terms

Abdominal breathing: Respiration characterized by controlled movement of the abdominal muscles.

Abdominal wall: The sheath of muscles interlaced across the lower front torso that contract to control exhalation.

Accent: (1) Principal stress given to syllables. It is symbolized by a ´ following the syllable that receives the stress in the AHD diacritics and by a ' before the syllable in the IPA. (2) Distinctive utterances produced in one language by a native speaker of another.

Affricate: Consonant produced by the combination of a stop-plosive and a fricative into a single sound, namely, ch [tʃ] and j [dʒ].

Alveolar ridge: The gum ridge behind the upper front teeth.

Articulation: Modification of the airflow by the lips, teeth, tongue, palate, and soft palate.

Aspiration: Release of a stop-plosive with an audible puff of air.

Back vowel: Vowel sound produced with the back of the tongue raised toward the palate, namely, ä [ɑ], ŏ [ɒ], ô [ɔ], ō [o], o͞o [ʊ], and o͞o [u].

Bilabial consonant: Consonant produced by contact between the lips that blocks or diverts the breath flow, namely, p [p], b [b], hw [ʍ], w [w], and m [m].

Breathiness: The vocal dimension that characterizes the passage of excessive through the vocal folds during phonation.

Breve: A marking (˘) placed over a vowel letter to form a diacritic symbol.

Central vowel: Vowel sound produced with the central or middle portion of the tongue raised toward the palate, namely, ŭ [ʌ], ə [ə], ûr [ɜ·], and ər [ɚ·].

Circumflex: A marking (ˆ) placed over a vowel letter to form a diacritic symbol.

Clavicular breathing: Respiration characterized by movement of the shoulders and the upper thorax.

Cognates: Pairs of sounds, articulated in the same place and in the same manner, of which one is voiceless and the other is voiced; for example, t [t] is the voiceless cognate of d [d].

Consonant: Speech sound produced by partial or complete obstruction of the airflow as it passes through the mouth or nose.

Dentalization: Misarticulation of tongue-to-gum-ridge consonants in which the tip of the tongue is placed against the upper teeth.

Diacritic symbols: Symbols used by dictionaries to represent speech sounds, which are formed from the ordinary letters of the alphabet combined with special markings.

Dialect: A geographic, socioeconomic, or ethnocultural variety of a spoken language.

Diaphragm: The dome-shaped muscle that separates the chest and the abdomen and that is used during respiration.

Diction: The degree of clarity of articulation and pronunciation.

Diphthong: Glide involving two vowels within a syllable, spoken with a single breath, namely, ā [eɪ], ī [aɪ], oi [ɔɪ], ou [aʊ], and ō [oʊ].

Duration: The amount of time it takes to say a word.

Exhalation: Expulsion of air from the lungs. Exhaled air is used to vibrate the vocal folds for speech.

Fading: Loss of power during speaking or reading aloud. It frequently occurs at the end of a sense unit.

Fricative: Consonant produced with the vocal passage narrowed to restrict outgoing air, so that audible friction is created, namely, f [f], v [v], th [θ], *th* [ð], s [s], z [z], sh [ʃ], zh [ʒ], and h [h].

Front vowel: Vowel sound produced with the front or the blade of the tongue, namely, ē [i] ĭ [ɪ], ā [e], ĕ [ɛ], and ă [æ].

Fundamental frequency: In phonation, the actual vibration of the vocal folds, measured in the number of vibrations per second.

Glide: Consonant produced by a change in the position of the articulators during its utterance, namely, hw [ʍ], w [w], y [j], and r [r].

Glottal stop: A clicking sound caused by rapid closure of the vocal folds, incorrectly substituted for a stop-plosive.

Glottis: The open space between the vocal folds.

Habitual pitch: The average pitch level of a person's vocalization.

Hard palate: The bony, front portion of the roof of the mouth, which separates the oral and nasal cavities.

Inflection: Downward and upward, pitch changes that occur within a single syllable or word.

Intercostal muscles: The muscles between the ribs, which assist in lowering and raising the rib cage and which are important in the respiration process.

International Phonetic Alphabet (IPA):   A set of symbols that can be used to represent the distinctive sounds (phonemes) of any language.

Kinesthetic perception: "Muscle sense," one's perception of how the muscular action of the body feels.

Larynx: The voice box, which contains the vocal folds, located in the neck.

Lateral lisp: The sound s [s] formed if the tongue tip is pressed against the upper teeth ridge, which allows air to be emitted over the sides of the tongue.

Lateral: Consonant produced by contact between the tongue tip and the gum ridge, so that vocalized breath is emitted at the sides of the tongue, namely, l [l].

Lip-teeth consonant: Consonant produced by contact between the lower lip and the teeth, namely, f [f] and v [v].

Lisp: Any distortion of the s [s] or z [z] sounds.

Lungs: Two large, elastic, spongy, cone-shaped, saclike organs in the thorax.

Macron: A marking (ˉ) placed over a vowel to form a diacritic symbol.

Mid vowel: Vowel sounds made with the center of the tongue raised to the center of the palate, namely, ŭ [ʌ], ûr [ɝ], ə [ə], ər [ɚ], ĕ [ɛ], and ô [ɔ].

Monotone: Lack of variation in pitch in speaking or reading aloud.

Nasal cavity: The air passage in the head directly above the roof of the mouth from the velum to the nose.

Nasal emission: Passage through the nasal cavity of plosive and fricative speech sounds that should be emitted through the mouth.

Nasality: The voice quality resulting from excessive nasal resonance in nonnasal sounds.

Nasal: Consonant produced with strong nasal resonance, namely, in American English, m [m], n [n], and ng [ŋ].

Optimal pitch: The pitch level at which the voice is most efficient, producing the required volume with the least expenditure of energy. It is normally found in the lower half of the pitch range.

Oral cavity: The air passage lying between the lips and the throat; the interior space of the mouth.

Oral resonance: Amplification and reinforcement of the voice in the mouth.

Palatal sounds: Speech sounds produced by the proximity of the middle or the back of the tongue and the palate.

Pause: The period silence between words and phrases.

Pharynx: The throat cavity from the nasal cavity to the larynx.

Phonation: Production of vocal tones when the breath stream passes between the lightly closed vocal folds, causing them to vibrate.

Phonetic alphabet: See **International Phonetic Alphabet**.

Phonetics: The study of speech sounds.

Pitch: A measure of how high or how low a speaker's voice is, determined by the frequency of its vibrations.

Plosive: See **Stop-plosive**.

Pronunciation: The way in which we say words; the utterance of words.

Rate: The number of words per minute in connected speech.

Resonation: Selective amplification and reinforcement of vocal tones by means of reverberation of sound in the oral, nasal, and throat cavities during phonation.

Resonators: The three body cavities that amplify and reinforce vocal tones, namely, the throat, the mouth, the nasal cavity.

Respiration: The process of breathing, which sustains life and is used in the production of speech.

Soft palate: The velum; the muscle tissue extending back from the hard palate toward the throat. When raised, it blocks air from passing into the nasal cavity; when lowered, as for nasal sounds, it allows air to pass through the nasal cavity.

Step shifts: Changes in pitch between words in phrases and sentences.

Stop-plosive: Consonant produced by completely closing off the breath stream, building up the pressure, and then suddenly releasing (exploding) the breath, namely, p [p], b [b], t [t], d [d], k [k], and g [g].

Thorax: The chest.
Trachea: The windpipe, the tube running between the bronchial tubes and the larynx.

Umlaut: A marking (̈) placed over a vowel letter to form a diacritic symbol.
Uvula: The pendulous, fleshy lobe at the end of the soft palate.

Velum: The soft palate.
Viscera: The soft organs of the body in the abdominal cavity.
Vocal folds: The two small strips of connective tissue (also called the *vocal bands* or *vocal cords*) located in the larynx. In phonation, air pressure causes them to vibrate.
Voice box: See **Larynx**.
Voiced sounds: Sound produced with a noticeable vibration of the vocal folds. All vowels are voiced sounds.
Vowel: A relatively uninterrupted flow of sound.

Windpipe: See **Trachea**.

Bibliography

Akin, Johnnye. 1958. *And So We Speak: Voice and Articulation*. Englewood Cliffs, N.J.: Prentice-Hall.

Anderson, Virgil A. 1977. *Training the Speaking Voice*. 3rd ed. New York: Oxford University Press.

Beckett, R. 1968. Pitch perturbation as a function of subjective vocal constriction. *Folia Phoniatrica*. 21:416–425.

Brodnitz, Friedrich S. 1987. *Keeping Your Voice Healthy*. San Diego: College Hill Press.

Capp, Glenn R., and Capp, Richard G. 1986. *Basic Oral Communication*. 4th ed. Englewood Cliffs, N.J.: Prentice-Hall.

Carrell, James A. 1968. *Disorders of Articulation*. Englewood Cliffs, N.J.: Prentice-Hall.

Ecroyd, Donald H., et al. 1966. *Voice and Articulation: A Handbook*. Glenview, Ill.: Scott, Foresman and Co.

Eisenson, Jon. 1939. *The Psychology of Speech*. New York: F.S. Crofts and Co.

———. 1979. *Voice and Diction: A Program for Improvement*. 4th ed. New York: Macmillan Publishing Co.

Fairbanks, Grant. 1960. *Voice and Articulation Drill Book*. New York: Harper & Row.

Fisher, Hilda B. 1975. *Improving Voice and Articulation*. 2nd ed. Boston: Houghton-Mifflin Co.

Gordon, Morton J. 1974. *Speech Improvement*. Englewood Cliffs, N.J.: Prentice-Hall.

Gray, Giles W., and Wise, Claude M. 1959. *The Bases of Speech*. New York: Harper & Row.

Greene, Margaret C. L. 1980. *The Voice and Its Disorders*. 4th ed. Philadelphia: J. B. Lippincott Co.

Hahn, Elise; Lomas, Charles W.; Hargis, Donald E.; and Vandraegen, Daniel. 1957. *Basic Voice Training for Speech*. 2nd ed. New York: McGraw-Hill Book Co.

Hanley, Theodore D., and Thurman, Wayne L. 1970. *Developing Vocal Skills*. 2nd ed. New York: Holt, Rinehart and Winston.

Jacobson, Edmund. 1978. *You Must Relax*. 5th ed. New York: McGraw-Hill Book Co.

Jesperson, Otto. 1889. *Articulation of Speech Sounds*. Marburg in Hessen, Germany: N.G. Elmert Verlag.

Joyner, J. B. 1968. Air flow rates as a function of vocal constriction in adult males. Unpublished Ph.D. dissertation, University of Southern California.

Judson, Lyman S., and Weaver, Andrew T. 1965. *Voice Science*. New York: Appleton-Century-Crofts.

Kantner, Claude E., and West, Robert. 1960. *Phonetics*. Rev. ed. New York: Harper & Row.

Kenyon, John S. 1958. *American Pronunciation*. 10th ed. Ann Arbor, Mich.: George Wahr Publishing Co.

Kenyon, John S., and Knott, Thomas A. 1953. *A Pronouncing Dictionary of American English*. 2nd ed. Springfield, Mass.: G. and C. Merriam Co.

King, Robert G., and DiMichael, Eleanor M. 1966. *Articulation and Voice*. New York: Macmillan Publishing Co.

Luter, James G., Jr. 1977. Pulsated voice as a function of vocal constriction in adult males. Unpublished Ph.D. dissertation, University of Southern California.

Mayer, Lyle V. 1987. *Fundamentals of Voice and Diction*. 8th ed. Dubuque, Iowa: William C. Brown.

McDonald, Eugene T. 1964. *Articulation Testing and Treatment: A Sensory Motor Approach*. Pittsburgh: Stanwix House.

Mencken, H. L. 1936. *The American Language*. New York: Alfred A. Knopf.

Moncur, John P., and Karr, Harrison M. 1972. 2nd ed. *Developing Your Speaking Voice*. New York: Harper & Row.

Murphy, Albert T. 1964. *Functional Voice Disorders*. Englewood Cliffs, N.J.: Prentice-Hall.

Murray, Elwood. 1937. *The Speech Personality*. New York: J. B. Lippincott Co.

Paget, Sir Richard A. 1930. *Human Speech*. Reprint 1976. New York: AMS Press.

Perkins, William H. 1971. Vocal function: Assessment and therapy. In *Handbook of Speech Pathology and Audiology,* ed. by L. E. Travis. New York: Appleton-Century-Crofts.

————. 1977. *Speech Pathology, An Applied Behavioral Science*. 2nd ed. St. Louis: C. V. Mosby Co.

Travis, Lee Edward, ed. 1971. *Handbook of Speech Pathology*. 2nd ed. New York: Appleton-Century-Crofts.

Van Riper, Charles. 1978. *Speech Correction*. 6th ed. Englewood Cliffs, N.J.: Prentice-Hall.

Van Riper, Charles, and Irwin, John V. 1958. *Voice and Articulation*. Englewood Cliffs, N.J.: Prentice-Hall.

Van Wye, B. C. 1936. The efficient voice in speech. *Quarterly Journal of Speech*. 22:642–648.

Index